YALE STUDIES IN THE HISTORY OF MUSIC, 5

William G. Waite, Editor

THE LANGUAGE OF THE

CLASSICAL FRENCH ORGAN

A Musical Tradition Before 1800

by Fenner Douglass

New Haven and London, Yale University Press, 1969

Published with assistance from the foundation
established in memory of Henry Weldon Barnes
of the Class of 1882, Yale College, and the Friends
of Music at Yale.
Library of Congress catalog card number: 72–81415
Designed by John O. C. McCrillis,
set in Baskerville type,
and printed in the United States of America by
Colonial Press, Inc., Clinton, Massachusetts.
Distributed in Great Britain, Europe, Asia, and
Africa by Yale University Press Ltd., London; in
Canada by McGill-Queen's University Press, Montreal; and
in Mexico by Centro Interamericano de Libros
Académicos, Mexico City.

Preface

The finest moments in classical French organ music are those in which the instrument and the music are fused inseparably together —when musical textures are perfectly molded to the indigenous characteristics of specified combinations of stops. This uniquely developed relationship, as it was exemplified in seventeenth- and eighteenth-century France, has provided the motivation for this book.

The French composers and theoreticians were generous with their advice to performers about interpreting the music of this period. Many of them wrote detailed instructions concerning the combinations of stops that complemented certain musical textures, and this volume will draw heavily from such informative sources. But I have felt it important that the reader view these instructions from the perspective of those instruments the composers knew and for which their music was written. For this reason much information about the development of the organ, as well as advice and instructions from the organ builders themselves, is given. Indeed, understanding of the "language" of the organ must necessarily accompany interpretation of the music.

This book will therefore appear to be as much a history of the instrument as an explanation of instructions for registrations. Wherever possible, personal judgment has been withheld and the facts have been presented without ambiguity, in order not to blur the precise and comprehensive legacy we have received from a time when standards of musical composition and instrument-making seem, by comparison, blissfully stable.

Organs of our time, particularly in the English-speaking countries, bear practically no resemblance to the French instruments of the late seventeenth century. Yet these are the very organs which we now attempt to understand. So fleeting have been the tastes of twentieth-century organ building, and so ephemeral the fashions of each succeeding decade, that we are left with instruments having no firm commitment to any particular trend of history. The organist hoping to interpret the music of the French classical period will be helped by the clear and well-punctuated guidance stemming from the best authorities of all—the men who composed the music. But the application of this information to present-day organs must ultimately be left to the good taste of the interpreter.

It will not be enough merely to understand the composers' language for registration. Only by the experience of listening to and playing instruments which have survived from earlier centuries can the inflections of that language and the key to translating it for practical use be discovered. These organs are the tonal link that keeps us in contact with the composers. One may enter the Church of Saint-Gervais in Paris, where a member of the Couperin family presided at the organ for almost two centuries, and still hear an organ built in the classical French tradition. In many musical textures one even hears the exact pipes that sounded for the great François Couperin when, still in his early twenties, he composed the two renowned organ masses. It is on such occasions— at Saint-Gervais or in Poitiers Cathedral or at Saint-Maximin— that the testimony of the early masters on registration makes immediate sense. And it is the obligation of everyone who is touched by the beauty of early French organ music to exert some influence toward the preservation of a diminishing number of old instruments, whose intrinsic value to future generations cannot be measured.

Where composers have given the keys to ornamentation in their prefaces, I have included that information along with their remarks on registration. Likewise, comments on the interpretation of pieces are carefully preserved in their original form in Appendix C.

Numerous inconsistencies in spelling will be found throughout the book, since I have tried in all cases to give spellings according to a faithful reading of the original texts. A great volume of foreign words appear, many of which are names of stops commonly transferred to English. I have chosen for the sake of simplicity to eliminate the use of italics for such terms, but to use capitals except when they are specifically ruled out in a quoted passage.

The generosity and encouragement of M. A. Vente of the University of Utrecht was of great help in formulating the first sections of this book. I am also deeply indebted to Professor Paul Roudié of Bordeaux for transcriptions of early manuscripts, to Professor Arlinei of Utrecht for translating the Antegnati text, and to Professor Arthur Terry of Belfast for translations from the Catalan. All other translations are my own responsibility. Generous assistance and advice was offered by Professors Paul Arnold, David Boe, and Benn Gibson at Oberlin. Most of all, I am grateful to Oberlin College for providing the time and financial assistance which made this work possible. Publication was assisted by a generous grant from the Friends of Music at Yale.

Oberlin, Ohio   F.D.
December 1967

Contents

ILLUSTRATIONS   following page 84

TABLES

Charts

Introduction

The organ, more than any other musical instrument, has assimilated numerous changes and experiments. Even at the point of its purest development, at a time when its musical potential attracted the interest of almost every important composer, a number of distinct national styles had evolved. Thus, when we study the instrument of the Baroque era in Italy, France, England, or northern Europe, we are confronted with a complicated pattern of mutual influence, parallel activity, independent achievement, and persistent national characteristics.

It is not surprising to discover that from time to time organ builders and composers handed down directions about the use of the instruments which absorbed their interest. The earliest observations on registration are almost as old as the oldest known keyboard music.[1] They make known a good deal about the handling of music on instruments which were designed under conditions quite different from those guiding most building today. Stylistic differences have been surprisingly wide in many localities and epochs, but never more so than the contrast between the contemporary American types of organ based superficially on neoclassic north European influence and the organs being played in France during the last years of the seventeenth century. It is particularly for this reason that organists of the last half of the twentieth century, who are intrigued by the subtle beauty of the French music from the *grand siècle*, are fortunate to have inherited a fully codified set of registration instructions—perhaps the most thoroughgoing of any epoch. Viewed against the details of the

---

1. Contact between organ builder and organist has always been close. In fact, through the centuries many builders have been organ players as well. The Antegnati family of Brescia, the Netherlanders Mors, Slegel, and Hagerbeer, Cormier of Toulouse, Filleul of Chartres, and Pieters of Delft were all organist-builders; Bach, the player-consultant, enjoyed frequent advisory contact with the builders Hildebrandt and Silbermann. Titelouze was the promoter of the builder Carlier. And more recently the bonds between Cavaillé-Coll and a number of organist-composers are well known.

instruments to which they applied, these instructions provide us with a valuable key to the interpretation of a large body of French organ music which was all but forgotten, and generally misunderstood, for over a century.

Thanks to the exhaustive research of France's Rokseth, Hardouin, and Dufourcq, Holland's Vente, Germany's Klotz, and many others, the facts of the organ's history over the past four or five hundred years now stand out boldly in association with the music of the great composers. No one can deny that Titelouze lived in quite a different tonal world from Scheidt, Couperin from Bach, and both Frenchmen from that of the great Romantic, Franck.

But, it can be argued, there is no such thing as an untouched, unrestored organ from the seventeenth or eighteenth century.[2] Even if there were, we are told, it is quite likely that there is a difference between what was pleasing and beautiful to seventeenth-century ears and what is most attractive now, in the twentieth. Indeed, what a musician, artist, or architect considers his finest work today he may himself reject tomorrow. Of what value can ancient documents be to a modern performer when they relate to the performance of music whose original function no longer exists?

Let the skeptic first discover what might be pleasing to his modern ears. Let him listen to the music of the French masters on the few instruments which can trace their lineage back for several centuries, regardless of their somewhat retouched state, their altered wind pressures or voicing, and their new pedal boards. Let him hear Couperin at Saint-Gervais, Frescobaldi at Brescia, and Bach at Zwolle. If he is still not susceptible to the particular marvel of each in its way, may his voice be forever muffled behind double swell shutters!

The old organs are our most important link with the great organ music of the past. While ancient instruments all have historical importance, those examples which survive from the most productive periods of composition are more than archeologically interesting. They contribute vividly to our understanding of the nature of

2. Cf. Norbert Dufourcq, "Où En Sommes-Nous," *L'Orgue*, No. 107 (1963), pp. 92–104.

the music itself. And it is only in relation to such instruments, however blemished, that we can inquire into the meaning of certain precepts of registration which have been handed down to us.

What is called the classical French tradition of registration relates to the handling of instruments built in a particular stylistic era, roughly between about 1650 and 1790. The extraordinary constancy of superficial design and specification in French organs over this long period was proof of the endurance of certain basic concepts governing organ building in the *grand siècle*. It might be said that this was a reflection of the order and ceremony of life at the court of Louis XIV.[3]

It is true that within the limits of the fundamental principles which guided the structural design of organs during this period, there were reasonably wide variations of tonal effect owing to differences of voicing and scaling techniques. Such differences were occasioned both by the evolution of the art and by the natural tendency among craftsmen to experiment with new thoughts in new situations. One should not assume that the finest organ builders of that time lacked the incentive to move within their wide powers of control over the sound of their instruments. Nor did their instruments fail to reflect changing musical taste. But a French organist could normally have expected to travel from place to place, always finding instruments which exhibited the same general plan of specification and design. Even the smallest organ was given its Plein Jeu, which is the first and essential ingredient of every organ of historic importance;[4] and the arrangements of other tonal groups followed in an orderly pattern which changed very little over the years.

These graciously proportioned instruments practically demanded a code of handling. In some places there were regulations affecting the organ music during the Mass, even describing the combinations of stops recommended for certain types of pieces.[5] But registration

---

3. See Wilfred Mellers, *François Couperin and the French Classical Tradition* (London, 1950), chap. 2: "Values and Standards in the Grand Siècle."

4. Cf. Ramon de Amezua, "Le Plein Jeu dans l'orgue moderne," *Bulletin of International Society of Organ Builders*, I, No. 1 (1961), 6–12.

5. For example, the *Règlement de 1630*, for the Cathédrale de Troyes, reprinted in E. Martinot, *Orgues et organistes des églises du diocèse de Troyes* (Troyes, 1941), pp. 47–51.

was important to the composers as well. Some of the commonest pieces came to be identified only by the name of the stop or combination of stops prescribed for their performance (Tierce en taille, Plein Jeu, and so on). As the composers felt the need for outlining a mannered style of registration, expressed in the shorthand system of titles, they also must have feared that foreigners would understand neither their instruments nor their music.[6] Thus a number took the extra trouble to go beyond the title system, recording the minute details of a tradition which was precise and rather inflexible. This is all the more remarkable when we observe that the tendency in the flourishing north European schools of organ composition was in the opposite direction.[7]

We have become accustomed to knowing next to nothing about the registration of Buxtehude's organ music and very little about Bach's. There is reason to think that they were both quite flexible in handling their instrument, though the acute student will detect frequent hints of intent here and there. As a result, some modern organists have come to confuse bizarreness in registration with musicianship. Perhaps when Bach wrote the great Prelude in B Minor—the superb structure of which makes his "Organo Pleno" indication superfluous—if he had called the piece "Mixtures" instead of "Prelude," we would not be hearing it today on 8′ and 2′ flutes, with the added receding effect of the swell for the contrapuntal episodes.

While a great architectural masterpiece of Bach may yet survive maltreatment in terms of registration, the effectiveness or charm of most French baroque organ music is almost totally lost out of its proper tonal context. Organ works of that period were born of the homophonic, Lullian opera style. Though some of the fugal pieces were conservative in texture, it was fashionable to imitate the opera techniques. Because the figurations, the voice texture, and the tessitura were best suited to the speech characteristics of certain kinds of pipes (as reeds vs. flutes) or to the particular richness of certain massive combinations (as Grand Jeu vs. Plein Jeu),

6. Cf. Jacques Boyvin, Preface to *Livre d'orgue* (1689), quoted in Appendix C.

7. Any strict code of registration in northwestern Europe during the 17th and 18th centuries would have been impossible to apply, due to sharp structural differences among organs.

the registrations became integrally connected with the music, and the composers left no doubt about it. Thus it cannot be too strongly stated that with respect to the French classical tradition of organ registration, we are dealing not only with the theory of manipulating stops (as was true up to the time of Mersenne) but also, and most particularly, with problems directly touching upon the music itself. A tradition of performance, rooted in the contribution of previous generations, in the pronounced change of musical style during the early seventeenth century, and in the requirements of the mass itself, served as a guide for the composers.[8]

8. French composers, concerned with writing music designed for special use in the mass (the priest and the organ alternating), were necessarily limited to short pieces with relatively unelaborate structure. See Introduction to *Five French Baroque Organ Masses*, ed. A. C. Howell (Lexington, Ky., 1961).

1. The French Organ in the Sixteenth Century

It is not too much to suggest that the refined taste of the classical French organ builders and composers was the consequence of a long maturing process, which had gone on since the beginning of the sixteenth century. In contrast to the relative stability of the classical period,[1] the Renaissance was an epoch of change and evolution in the history of organ building. It was an era of intense activity, in which mechanical and tonal improvements opened up new possibilities for design and color. The spacious churches in France and the Low Countries were often furnished with several organs, placed either in the west gallery or transept, or on the rood screen (orgue de jubé), or suspended on the walls of the nave. Late fifteenth- and early sixteenth-century France was invaded by Flemish craftsmen, who were providing much of the impetus for the astonishing developments that took place.

In the South of France there was prolonged infiltration of Italian influence throughout the Renaissance and baroque eras. Dufourcq mentions organs built by Italians in Carmes d'Aix (1448), Montpellier (1504), and Vaucluse (1506).[2] A number of organs in the southwest showed Italian attributes from the early sixteenth century, such as the instrument built by Arnaud de Guyssaurret for the Church of Saint-Seurin, Bordeaux (1514). There are eighteenth-century organs existing still today in southern France testifying to the continued Italian influence in the area of Provence.

1. The "classical" period in French organ building, during which a coherent system or procedure guided the work of all builders, is defined as roughly between 1650 and 1791 (death of F.-H. Clicquot).

2. Norbert Dufourcq, "Les Facteurs d'orgue étrangers en France du XIVᵉ au XVIIᵉ siècle," *La Revue Musicale*, No. 14 (1933), p. 185.

While Spanish influence could also be detected in southwestern France[3] in the Renaissance and Baroque eras, it was from the Low Countries[4] that the great impact on the main current of French organ development was felt, especially until the early seventeenth century. Organ builders from the Netherlands, active all over western Europe, were building instruments in England, Denmark, Italy, Spain, and especially in the neighboring countries—Germany[5] and France.[6]

With respect to exterior influences, then, organs in France during

3. Roussillon, whose chief city is Perpignan, was Spanish until the mid-17th century. The builder of the organ for Bayonne Cathedral in 1488, Maître Dominique de Castelbon, lived in Vitoria (Spain). See Pierre Sicard, *Les Orgues du diocèse de Bayonne, Lescar, Oloron* (Lyon, 1964).

4. In the period under discussion (ca. 1500–ca. 1600), the Netherlands, or Low Countries, comprised all of the present kingdoms of the Netherlands and Belgium, the Grand Duchy of Luxembourg, and French Flandre. In order to avoid confusion among the terms "Holland," "Dutch," and "Flemish," all references will be understood to cover the two important cultural subdivisions of 16th-century Netherlands, defined as follows: Southern Netherlands, or Southern Low Countries, include the southernmost portion of modern Netherlands—namely, the provinces of Noord Brabant and Limburg, plus Zeeus Vlanderen (Zeeland); all of modern Belgium; and French Flandre, Artois, and Cambrai. Northern Netherlands, or the Northern Low Countries, include the entire modern Netherlands, minus Noord Brabant, Limburg, and Zeeus Vlanderen.

The area of the Low Countries was under Spanish political domination until 1568, when the Northern Netherlands gained independence. In 1629 part of the Southern Netherlands was annexed by the north, creating what is now the border between Belgium and modern Netherlands. Although the earlier Spanish political domination was followed by Austrian rule, then French, before full independence was finally achieved in 1814–15, the cultural life of the Netherlands, divided between the north and south as described above, was not significantly influenced by either the Spaniards or the Austrians.

5. Dufourcq, *La Revue Musicale*, No. 14, p. 189: "Cet orgue flamand semble à la base des instruments allemands, italiens, français, espagnols, et anglais." For information on Netherlandish influence in German organ building, see Maarten A. Vente, *Die brabanter Orgel, zur Geschichte der Orgelkunst in Belgien und Holland im Zeitalter der Gotik und der Renaissance* (Amsterdam, 1958), chap. 14; Ernst Flade, "Hermann Raphael Rottenstein-Pock, ein niederländischer Orgelbauer des 16 Jahrh. in Zwickau i. S.," *Zeitschrift für Musikwissenschaft*, *15* (Leipzig, 1932), 1–24; T. Fedke, "Der niederländische Orgelbau in 16 Jahrh. und seine Bedeutung für Sweelincks Instrumentalmusik," *Musik und Kirche*, *26* (1956), 60–67; Hans Klotz, "Niederländischer Orgelbaumeister am Trier Dom," *Die Musikforschung*, 2 (1949), 36–49.

6. Vente lists twenty Netherlandish organ builders who worked in French churches during the 16th and 17th centuries, in "Influence des flamands sur les français en matière de construction d'orgues," *L'Orgue*, *48* (1948), 78–83.

the sixteenth century may be classed in two general groups—
namely, those in the northern part of the country, which submitted
to numerous innovations from the Netherlands, and those in the
south, which had a tendency to be influenced by the highly refined
Italian style of organ building.[7] In the early years of the sixteenth
century there was already a marked difference between these two
types. In Italy it appears that a relatively stable approach to
specification had taken root, which persisted at least until the early
seventeenth century.[8] There are still several excellently preserved
instruments in Bologna and Brescia which reflect the structural
and tonal attributes of Italian organs as far back as the sixteenth
century. As to the northern countries, on the other hand, the
sixteenth century was a period of rapid change and inventive activity. The Netherlanders not only led the world in discovery but
they built some of the most elaborately equipped organs of any
era. Small wonder that the French owe to the builders from the
Low Countries the development of the Grand Orgue itself. Even
the classical French Cornet was used in the Netherlands before its
introduction to France.

Such was the exuberant production of the sixteenth-century
builders, whose innovations were enriching the organ's tonal resources with each passing generation, that they sometimes included,
with the contractual documents, lists of stop combinations for the
use of the organists. These registrations not only show the growing
interest in tonal variety which was stimulated some years earlier
by the invention of the key channel chest, but they reveal the
predilection of Renaissance organ builders with registration as a

7. It is likely that up until about 1500, in southern France, most organs were not
markedly different from those built in the previous century. An instrument built by
Maître Dominique de Castelbon, a Spaniard, for the Cathedral of Bayonne, in 1488,
was stopless, and contained only Principal pipes (text reprinted in Sicard, p. 17).
The introduction of instruments based on Italian models around 1500 was probably
revolutionizing standards hitherto accepted in southern France.

8. Cf. specifications of two Italian-style organs constructed in southern France over
a 100-year period: (1) Church of Saint-Eloi, Bordeaux, see Table 3, E: Principal 6',
Octave, Fifteenth, Nineteenth, Twenty-second, Simballes, Flute Octave, Flute (2 2/3'),
Flute (2'); (2) Couvent des Frères Mineurs, Vaucluse, 1626 (contract reprinted in
N. Dufourcq, *Documents inédits relatifs à l'orgue français, 1* [2 vols. Paris, 1934–35],
183–84. Doc. 259): Monstre, Octave, Fifteenth, Nineteenth, Twenty-second, Simballes,
Grosse flutte, Octave, lead (flute), Twelfth, lead (flute), Fifteenth, lead, "en flutte."

means to musical expression. In *Die brabanter Orgel* Vente has collected many sources on registration from the Low Countries and western Germany which give an excellent impression of continuity, together with the fragmentary information so far discovered in France and Italy.[9] If, as has already been demonstrated, organ building in northern France and the southern Netherlands was practically identical in this period, then the Netherlandish instructions for the use of the instrument must apply equally to all organs of the same style in France. And if organists actually made use of all the combinations recommended by the designers of the instruments, we can safely conclude that there was even more variety and invention in the Renaissance style of organ playing than there is today. As the instrument was slowly channeled into a state of classical equilibrium, its use became more and more stereotyped. At least this was the case in France.

While some tonal variety was possible on organs of the Gothic period, it was not until the second half of the fifteenth century that stops, in the modern sense, were even in limited use. Yet most of the large cathedrals of western Europe and many smaller churches had organs of impressive dimensions and design, whose architectural beauty can still be judged from paintings, drawings, and a number of surviving examples of case work. The largest instruments of the fifteenth century were as large as most organs of the seventeenth and eighteenth centuries in terms of the number of pipes they contained. Strasbourg Cathedral in 1489 housed an organ with 2,136 pipes;[10] Amiens, in 1429, 2,500 pipes;[11] and the Grand Orgue at Reims, in 1487, by the builder Hestre (from the southern Netherlands), 2,000 pipes.[12] These immense instruments were divided into three or four separately encased sections, by far the most significant of which was the Grand Orgue, housed in the main case. On either side of the main case were erected matching towers, each with about two to five or more very long pipes (speak-

9. See Table 10 for a chronological list of these sources.
10. Norbert Dufourcq, *Esquisse d'une histoire de l'orgue en France du XIIIe au XVIIIe siècle* (Paris, 1935), p. 145.
11. Ibid., p. 76.
12. Vente, *Die brabanter Orgel*, p. 14.

ing on the basis of 12′, 24′, or 32′ pitch), called Trompes or Bordunen. The smaller case for the Positif à dos, or Rückpositiv, was placed forward of the main case on the gallery rail. In addition to the tonal resources already mentioned, which served for purposes that would be considered serious today, organs of the fifteenth and sixteenth centuries were always provided with a number of extra mechanical devices. Thus a large organ built around 1500 would most likely have been equipped with (1) a Grand Orgue; (2) a Positif à dos, or Cheyère; (3) Trompes, or Bordunen; and (4) extra contrivances.

1. A Grand Orgue, that stopless giant containing up to about 2,000 pipes or more, was called Blockwerk (also staend principael) in the Low Countries and Germany, and the chest for it was the Blocklade. The French words Fourniture, Principal, and Plein Jeu at that time meant the same thing. An enormous mixture, the Blockwerk started in the bass with five or more pipes per key, two of which (one open, one stopped) spoke the fundamental pitch— 6′, 8′, 12′, and so on, depending on the compass—and increased in number of ranks in the treble. At Chartres Cathedral, in 1481, two keys were added, each "furnished with a hundred and five pipes." [13] In the Grand Orgue of Amiens Cathedral (1549) an inventory of the organ gave the number of ranks for each key, pointing out that about a third of the pipes were not speaking.[14]

Holland's most ancient organ, which was built for the Nicolai Church in Utrecht, contains a Blockwerk dating from 1479 and 1547, the disposition of which is shown in Table 1, according to the reconstruction by Vente.[15]

The Blockwerk of Gothic and Renaissance organs is important today because of the role it played in the development of the classical types. During the long period of transition between the inflexible (though unquestionably full and brilliant) one-manual Blockwerk and the richly varied organs of the seventeenth century,

---

13. Portions of the text of the contract of 1481 were published in Charles Métais, "Les Orgues de la Cathédrale de Chartres," *Archives Historiques du Diocèse de Chartres*, *21* (1918), 6–7.

14. For this interesting text, as published by Durand in 1903, see Appendix A.

15. Vente, *Die brabanter Orgel*, p. 14.

TABLE 1. Reconstructed Disposition of Blockwerk in Nicolai Church, Utrecht

	F	d'	f'	f#'	g'	c#²	e²	a²
No. of ranks	VIII	XI	XII	XIII	XIV	XVI	XVII	XVII
	16	16	16	16	16	16	16	16
	8	8	8	8	8	8	8	8
					8	8	8	8
						8	8	8
				$5\frac{1}{3}$	$5\frac{1}{3}$	$5\frac{1}{3}$	$5\frac{1}{3}$	$5\frac{1}{3}$
							$5\frac{1}{3}$	$5\frac{1}{3}$
	4	4	4	4	4	4	4	4
		4	4	4	4	4	4	4
						4	4	4
Pitches	$2\frac{2}{3}$	$2\frac{2}{3}$	$2\frac{2}{3}$	$2\frac{2}{3}$	$2\frac{2}{3}$	$2\frac{2}{3}$	$2\frac{2}{3}$	$2\frac{2}{3}$
		$2\frac{2}{3}$	$2\frac{2}{3}$	$2\frac{2}{3}$	$2\frac{2}{3}$	$2\frac{2}{3}$	$2\frac{2}{3}$	$2\frac{2}{3}$
			$2\frac{2}{3}$	$2\frac{2}{3}$	$2\frac{2}{3}$	$2\frac{2}{3}$	$2\frac{2}{3}$	$2\frac{2}{3}$
	2	2	2	2	2	2	2	2
	2	2	2	2	2	2	2	2
		2	2	2	2	2	2	2
	$1\frac{1}{3}$	$1\frac{1}{3}$	$1\frac{1}{3}$	$1\frac{1}{3}$	$1\frac{1}{3}$	$1\frac{1}{3}$	$1\frac{1}{3}$	$1\frac{1}{3}$
	$1\frac{1}{3}$	$1\frac{1}{3}$	$1\frac{1}{3}$	$1\frac{1}{3}$	$1\frac{1}{3}$	$1\frac{1}{3}$	$1\frac{1}{3}$	$1\frac{1}{3}$

builders extended their imaginations in several directions. A second manual (Positif à dos) was added, and even a third division (sometimes without its own keyboard) made its appearance around 1500;[16] the pedals were developed, here for *cantus firmus*, there as a full bass division; and reeds came into general use, as well as many flute voices. But the large cathedral organs of northern Europe often retained their old Blockwerken, or Fournitures, and they were always the focal point in tonal design. This indivisible principal chorus persisted, while the instrument became enriched around it. The old Blockwerk of Notre Dame de Paris remained in use until 1600. So firmly situated was the idea of the prime importance of the principal chorus that it was nowhere forgotten or neglected, long after the old Blockwerk had been given up. Mixtures of today —our Fourniture, Plein Jeu, Cimbel, and Scharf—are all vestigial

16. M. A. Vente, *Bouwstoffen tot de geschiedenis van het nederlandse orgel in de 16ᵉ eeuw* (Amsterdam, 1942), p. 14.

remnants of those Gothic marvels. And the most important of all organ registrations, the Organo Pleno, or Plein Jeu combination, is also the oldest, since it has been passed down from the days when it was the only one.

The transition to the classical Plein Jeu from the ancient Fourniture without stops is clearly illustrated in the contract of 1542 for the rebuilding of the organ of Chartres Cathedral.[17] The reconstructed Grand Plein Jeu, based upon 16-foot pitch and reinforced with eight 32-foot Trompes in the pedals, consisted of five separate stops—namely, a single-rank 16-foot, a two-rank 8-foot, a three-rank 4-foot, a six-rank Fourniture (2′), and a three-rank cymbale.

2. A Positif à dos, or Cheyère, had a much smaller number of pipes, the case for which was always placed behind the player on the gallery rail. The tonal resources of the Positif were split up, even in the fifteenth century, first by using two chests, one of which controlled the fundamental pitch, the other the higher pitches. Because of the smaller size of the Positif chests, it was here that the first experiments with the key channel chest seem to have been carried on in northern Europe. Thus, aside from the possibility of changing manuals, some of the earliest instructions for registration changes refer to the Positif, equipped according to the latest fashion with single rank stops.

On those organs where the Grand Orgue was broken up into separate stops, however, there may have been a tendency for the Positif to remain relatively undeveloped, since the need for tonal variety was being satisfied on the Grand Orgue.[18] Such was apparently the case in the Positif à dos at the Church of Saint-Seurin, Bordeaux (1514), with only 4′ and 2′ pitches. Such a Positif resembled the more primitive *guide-chant* instruments, a quite independent Positif used only for accompaniment. Indeed, the impetus for the enrichment of the Positif à dos seems to have come from the Netherlands, where the most astonishing developments were taking place during the course of the sixteenth century.

17. Text of contract published in Métais, *Archives Historiques*, *21*, 14–16. (Arch. dép. d'Eure et Loire, G. 197, f. 519 v°). See Appendix A.

18. Pierre Hardouin, "La Composition des orgues qui pouvaient toucher les musiciens parisiens aux alentours de 1600," in *La Musique instrumentale de la Renaissance*, ed. Jean Jacquot (Paris, 1955), pp. 259–69.

3. The Trompes, or Bordunen, were divided equally in matching towers beside the Grand Orgue. These long pipes were played either from pedals, coupled to the Grand Orgue, in a way not unlike the pedal system of the Italian organs, or from manual keys called *clavier de teneure*. As early as 1432, in Troyes Cathedral, a pedal keyboard existed for playing Trompes.[19] In other organs, where the *clavier de teneure* controlled the Trompes, the manual key control was situated between the Grand Orgue and the Positif manuals to facilitate coupling the Grand Orgue to it. By the end of the sixteenth century all traces of the Trompes in French organs had disappeared [20] and a new conception of the use of pedals had been adopted. In the northern part of Holland, on the other hand, the Trompes (Bordunen) continued in occasional use, contributing to the development of the classical North German type of pedal organ. Vente reports that the ten Bordunen (20′) built in 1466 for the Bavo Church in Haarlem were incorporated in all renovations of that instrument until the eighteenth century.[21]

Trompes seem to have played no permanent role in the development of the French classical organ. Their disappearance toward the end of the sixteenth century may have been a result of the widespread damage to organs during the Wars of Religion; the predominant influence of Flemish organ builders in northern France, especially Normandy, which with Paris was the center of seventeenth-century organ development; the development of the *cantus firmus* pedal in Brabant; the awkwardness of the *clavier de teneure* for playing Trompes; and the rich development of the Grand Orgue, which had a tendency to discourage equal growth in other divisions.

4. As for the extra contrivances, mechanical gadgets operating on the wind of the organ were typical components of organs of the Renaissance. Some, such as the Tremulants and revolving stars (Étoiles, Zimbelstern), have survived up to the present day.

Pipes were the sound source for a number of such devices, such

19. ". . . fait un autre clavier à joer du pié pour faire contreteneure et plusieurs autres choses en icelles orgues"; quoted in Dufourcq, *Esquisse*, p. 167.
20. Ibid., p. 169.
21. Vente, *Die brabanter Orgel*, p. 12.

as the Rossignol (Nachtigall),[22] Harpes, and Canards. Mersenne described (1636) the Tambour as sounding two pipes of similar scale,[23] tuned apart to produce the beating effect of a drum. Probably no sizable instrument lacked one or several of the picturesque and delightful inventions ornamenting Renaissance organ cases. Angels blew trumpets; suns, moons, and stars revolved; and terrible masked faces gaped down on the faithful.[24] At Saint-Etienne, Troyes (1561), the Saint himself, on the case, moved, with two threatening figures on either side of him: "ung Saint Etienne se mouvant comme s'il etait en vie, et deux figures à ses côtés, tenant chacun une pierre en la main, comme s'ils voulaient le lapider." On the same organ case a nightingale flapped its wings.[25]

A seventeenth-century comment (1625) concerning the repair of the Grand Orgue in the Cathedral of Saint-André, Bordeaux, mentions two great human faces on the organ case, with large ogling eyes and long white beards, which moved by springs, amusing the people but "hindering" devotion.[26]

If large organs of the early sixteenth century in France and the Low Countries were apt to have the general attributes just described, smaller instruments reflected most promptly the extraordinary tonal vitality and inventiveness that characterized organ building in the Renaissance. From those years of continuous creative activity stem the first hints of a growing awareness of registra-

22. Cf. Dufourcq, *Documents inédits relatifs à l'orgue français, 1*, 183, Doc. 259: ". . . feront en oultre les tuyaulx convenables pour la constitution du chant d'un rossignol" (Vaucluse, Pradon, 1626).

23. Cf. ibid., p. 151, Doc. 230: "A Jehan Gautherot, mercyer, pour achat de deux peaulx de mouton emploiées à acoustrer le tambour et les souffletz" (Avallon, 1601).

24. Dufourcq, *Esquisse*, pp. 162–63 and 190–93. Also, see Yvonne Rokseth, *La Musique d'orgue au XVe siècle et au début du XVIe* (Paris, 1930), pp. 331 ff.

25. Dufourcq, *Esquisse*, p. 191.

26. The earlier existence of these mechanical masks was confirmed by a traveling Englishman a century earlier (1535), a certain Andrew Borde, whose "First Book of the Introduction of Knowledge" (1547) mentioned: "the principal town of Gascogne is Bordeaux; in Saint-André Cathedral is the most beautiful and the greatest organ in all Christianity: this organ contains several instruments and mechanisms, stars and heads of giants, which shake and cause the jaws to move, and the eyes, as fast as the organist 'plays' them" (reprinted by the Early English Text Society [London, 1870], p. 207). Excerpt taken from the *Chronique bordeloise de Gaufreteau, 2*, 142, as quoted by Paul Reyher in "Les Orgues de Saint-André au XVIe siècle," *La Revue Historique de Bordeaux et du Département de la Gironde, 2* (1909), 277.

tion per se. The spotty, incomplete knowledge of instruments and their use, especially in the early years of the century, leaves much over which the inquisitive may ponder, but suggests, too, that the organist-traveler from 1500 to 1550 would have found a strange assortment of instruments. He would certainly have been bewildered by the "modern" organs with their many independent registers and by the already distinct stylistic contrast between organs in the north or south of Europe. Yet it was for such instruments that the earliest keyboard music was created and the oldest instructions for registration recorded.

It has been mentioned that organ building in the north of France and the Netherlands followed parallel lines of development during most of the sixteenth century because of the great influence of Netherlandish craftsmen upon the French. This temporary identity of northern France with the style of the southern Netherlands leads us to a more complete understanding of the roots of French classical registration. And it helps to fill the void of derivative information that existed in France until the time of Mersenne.

On the contrary, however, there are some confusing facets to the story, which may never be satisfactorily explained. It is quite possible that future research will considerably alter what appears now to have been happening in the development of organs and their use during the early years of the sixteenth century. A quick glance at sixteenth-century organ information in France and the Netherlands leads to several conclusions:

1. Italian organ building undoubtedly influenced organ building in southern France, even more than has previously been noticed. The Italians were the first to develop the key channel chest, which provided the opportunity for selection of single ranks of pipes from the Ripieno (Organo Pleno, Plein Jeu). The slider chest was in use as early as 1480 (Cathedral of Orvieto), and the spring chest by 1507, in a six-stop instrument built for the church of Santa Maria, Monteortone.[27] This refinement of control over the tonal possibilities in Italian organs, which were all small, one-manual instruments, might have led to an early development of a language for

27. Padova, archivo di Stato, Notaio A. Scion, T. 2852, c. 59, mentioned in Maarten A. Vente, "Slider Chest or Spring Chest?" *Bulletin of International Society of Organ Builders*, 2, Nos. 1, 2 (1962), p. 9

registration. Such a language, except for the long-established term Ripieno, would certainly have been identified with the imitation of other popular musical instruments, as it was in southern France.

2. Paris in the sixteenth century, or at least until about 1580, was not the center of organ building in France. The great cathedrals had the grandest instruments.[28] But toward the end of the century, the focus of activity was turning in the direction of Paris, and it was there that the classical style of registration developed in the early seventeenth century.

3. While the Flemish builders exerted strong influence in northern France, there were quite independent processes of growth in northern Holland (Groningen) and northern Germany which did not seem to influence French building at all. The greatest differences were in the development of richly endowed independent manual divisions apart from the main one, and in the conception of the function of the pedal organ.

4. There is confusion about the meaning of some terms as employed at particular times: for instance, Cornet, Nasard, Flute, Bourdon, Cimbales, and Grand Jeu all meant one thing in the late seventeenth century but perhaps something different 150 years earlier. Fine distinctions of meaning applied also in different localities or for different builders.[29]

28. Hardouin, in *La Musique instrumentale*.
29. Vente, *Die brabanter Orgel*, pp. 157–58.

2. Toward Understanding the Language of the Jeux

It would be incorrect to say that before 1600 there was any real style of French registration, though several kinds of treatment may have developed for handling certain instruments or kinds of instruments. And very short is the supply of French organ music before Jean Titelouze's first publication, in 1623, of *Les Hymnes de l'église pour toucher sur l'orgue*.[1] Howell suggests that since only one copy of the celebrated Attaingnant publications (1531) has survived, possibly other examples of sixteenth-century French organ composition (masses) have been lost.[2] It is even more likely that organ contracts, lying unnoticed in departmental archives, contain information which could help us solve the riddles which abound in the sixteenth century.

From the list of sources given in Table 2, it will be noticed that there is a relatively small supply of information dealing directly with registration in France before 1636. Indeed, without the Bordeaux and Toulouse documents, which will be discussed here in detail, and one from Troyes, there is practically nothing. Therefore, for a source of aid to understanding French registration of the

1. For discussions of French organ music from 1500 to 1623, see Yvonne Rokseth, Introduction to *Deux Livres d'orgue parus chez Pierre Attaingnant en 1531* (Paris, 1925); also, Rokseth, *La Musique d'orgue*, chaps. 4–7; and Norbert Dufourcq, *La Musique d'orgue français de Jehan Titelouze à Jehan Alain* (Paris, 1949), pp. 1–29.

2. Howell, Introduction to *Five Baroque French Organ Masses*.

The likelihood that French organ composition was more productive than we realize is strengthened by other factors: first, we know that many churches in France were equipped with several handsome, richly ornamented organs; second, in the same period we have many highly developed organ compositions from Italy, Spain, and Germany; third, it is quite unlikely that the refined technique of Titelouze could have been achieved in a vacuum. Although much music on the organ must have been either transcribed from other compositions or improvised, the music of Titelouze is no more a manifestation of what the future might hold than a sign of the culmination of techniques already perfected.

TABLE 2. Chronological List of Major Sources on Registration Until 1636

Date	Location	Church	Author and Title
1504	's Hertogenbosch	St. Jan	Daniel van der Distelen
1505	Antwerp	OnzeLieveVrouw	D. van der Distelen
1505	Zwolle	St. Michael	Meester Johann _____
1510	Worms	St. Andreas	Anonymous
1510	Bordeaux	St.-Michel	Loys Gaudet
1511	Heidelberg		Arnold Schlick: *Spiegel der Orgelmacher und Organisten*
1514	Bordeaux	St.-Seurin	Arnaud de Guyssaurret
1522	Veurne	St.-Denis	Joris Buus
1531	Toulouse	St.-Etienne	Jacques Cormier
1538	Trier	Dom	Peter Briesger
1548	Bordeaux	Ste.-Eulalie	Jehan de Cyvrac
1551	Troyes	St.-Etienne	Francois Desoliviers
1563	Dresden	Schlosskirche	Herman Rodensteen
1572	Münster	Ueberwasserkirche	Jan Roose
1573	Bayreuth	Stadtkirche	Herman Rodensteen
1589	Antwerp	St. Jakob	Willem van Lare
1593			Girolamo Diruta: *Il transilvano*
1597	Bayreuth	Stadtkirche	Thimotheus Cumpenius
1601	St.-Valery-sur-Somme	St.-Martin	Isaac Huguet (?)
1608	Brescia		Costanzo Antegnati: *Arte organica*
1613	Barcelona	San Juan de las Abadesas	
ca. 1615	Freiburg (Schweiz)		
1616	Zoutleeuw	St. Leonhard	
1619	Wolfenbüttel		Michael Praetorius: *Syntagma musica*
1624	Lerida	Cathedral	Antonio Llorens
1624	Halle		Samuel Scheidt: *Tabulatura nova*
1636	Paris		Marin Mersenne: *Harmonie universelle*

seventeenth century, we have recourse to the southern Netherlands, where a good deal of work has already been done on early organ contracts. It was the builders of the instruments of the Low Countries, more than any others, who seem to have exerted the strongest influence upon the development of the French classical tradition.

A glance over the lists of registrations[3] shows that awareness of the possibilities for registration was developing along with each new refinement of the art of organ building. It was not until after the time of Mersenne (1636), however, that composers in France were writing music with specific tonal effects in mind. Even the advice of Titelouze and Scheidt served primarily as a guide to the manner in which their published scores might be managed at the instrument, in terms of using contrasting manuals, introducing the use of pedals, or showing the possibilities for playing a distinctive *cantus firmus*. The general lack of consistency in organ design during the sixteenth and early seventeenth centuries would have made it impossible for players to subscribe to inflexible rules; and prevailing styles of musical composition did not call for that kind of treatment. Not until 1650, when a new musical style had been accepted among organ composers in France, was a tradition firmly established for the handling of registration in specific musical textures. By that time, moreover, organ specifications had become remarkably stable over the land.

Looking back from the seventeenth century, one can distinguish in the registrations of the sixteenth century certain striking resemblances to combinations for which music was later written: in Van Lare's list for St. Jakob church in Antwerp (1589) there are early evidences of the Dessus de Cornet, the Dessus de Cromorne, and the Grand Jeu; in 1572 Roose's "Ordonantio" included a Dessus and a Basse de Trompette; Mersenne's lists (1636) reflect numerous combinations mentioned in earlier documents, both in France and the Netherlands; and the composition of the indispensable Plein Jeu, with its doubled fundamentals (stopped and open pipes), dates back to the organ's somewhat mysterious medieval past, when there were no stops at all. As the resources of the organ were increased, new tonal possibilities were introduced. Ensemble variety was provided through the development of new divisions within the tonal framework of the instrument, the compass of the keyboards was extended, and the pedals were used for independent voices. The story of registration, up until the time that the instrument became stabilized in design, is one facet of the record of the

---

3. See Appendix B.

instrument's history. As more is learned about the organ's history, the registrations recommended during the Renaissance period will relate more meaningfully to the music served by them.

The oldest known documents bearing specifically on registration so far discovered on French soil come from the southern region—that is, Bordeaux and Toulouse. Since considerably more is known now than was at hand when the generally accepted theories concerning sixteenth-century French organ registration were published,[4] it is appropriate that the instruments of Bordeaux and Toulouse, and the registrations listed for them, be examined from time to time. The documents whose interpretation has previously guided comment on this subject are the contract and expertise for the construction of an organ by Loys Gaudet (Gondet) for the Church of Saint-Michel, Bordeaux, 1510,[5] and "Instruction pour le jeu d'orgues," for the same date and church;[6] and the contract and related documents for the reconstruction of an organ by Jacques Cormier in the Church of Saint-Etienne, Toulouse, 1531.[7]

A possible interpretation of these important sources is supported by additional information contained in other Bordeaux contracts, the texts for which are given in Appendix A:

> Contract for the reconstruction of an organ by Arnaud Guyssaurret in the Church of Saint-Seurin, Bordeaux, 1514 [8]
> Contract for the construction of an organ by Jacques Loup in the Couvent des Frères Mineurs, Bordeaux, 1518 [9]

---

4. See esp. Rokseth, *La Musique d'orgue*, and Dufourcq, *Esquisse.*
The material that follows, published in the *Musical Quarterly* (*51*, No. 4 [Oct. 1965], 614–35), has been carefully reevaluated by the learned Pierre Hardouin in "Jeux d'orgues au XVIᵉ siècle," *Revue de Musicologie*, *52*, No. 2 (1966), 163–84.

5. Arch. dép. Gironde, G 2238, Nos. 47–51, 52. Reprinted in part in Dufourcq, *Documents inédits*, *1*, Docs. 140–42.

6. Arch. dép. Gironde, G 2238, Nos. 40, 41. Reprinted ibid., Doc. 143.

7. Arch. dép. Haute Garonne, 3 E 7067. Partially reprinted in J. Anglade, "Contribution à l'histoire de l'art méridional," *Annales du Midi, 1917–1918* (Toulouse), pp. 255–57. See also new transcription by P. Roudié in Appendix A.

8. Arch. dép. Gironde, G 1162, fᵒ 202 vᵒ. Reprinted in *Arch. Hist. de la Gironde, 52*, 57 (transcription by Cluzan).

9. Arch. dép. Gironde, 3 E 9456.

Contract for the construction of an organ by Bertrand Jehan
in the Church of Saint-Eloi, Bordeaux, 1529 [10]
Contracts for the construction of an organ by Olivier Hertault
(case) and Jean de Cyvrac (organ) in the Church of Sainte-
Eulalie, Bordeaux, 1548 [11]

Three sorts of information found in these sources are of special
interest—namely, the specifications of the organs, lists of possible
registrations, and the keys to those lists, given in terms of the specifications. In none of the documents known from this period in
France are all three kinds of information combined. This general
failing of contracts during the sixteenth century could not surprise
us today, for our own contracts neglect many of the most important
details of specification and design. Extremes of vagueness may
hinder a full and clear understanding of instruments from an early
period from which no correlative instruments have survived.[12] But
in some rare instances it is possible to piece together bits of detail
from a number of instruments related in time and location. Thus
it is remarkable to discover that contractual documents have survived which give valuable information about five early sixteenth-
century organs in Bordeaux alone, and still another of crucial
importance in Toulouse. From these and another important Bordeaux document [13] it is possible to correct a good deal of the confusion surrounding the early history of French organs.

In Table 3, pertinent information about specification and registrations is extracted from the six sources listed above. This information may be compared with the complete texts, given in
Appendix A.

10. Arch. dép. Gironde, 3 E 7143, f⁰ 129 r⁰–130 r⁰.
11. Arch. dép. Gironde, 3 E 6557, f⁰ 128 v⁰; 3 E 6557, f⁰ 129 v⁰.
12. For example, Loys Gaudet built an organ for the church of Sainte-Croix,
Oloron, in 1521. It was the same Master Loys who constructed the now-famous organ
of Saint-Michel in Bordeaux (1510). For the Oloron instrument, the contract stated
no details of specification whatever, but merely gave a comparison: ". . . a promis
et promect faire unes orgues de la grandeur sorte et manière de celles de l'église de
Saincte-Eulaye de Bordeaux et icelles mectre et pouser en l'église de Saincte-Croix
d'Oloron en Béarn" (Arch. dép. Gironde, 3 E 6650, f⁰ 221 r⁰. Transcription by Paul
Roudié).
13. See n. 6, this chapter.

TABLE 3. Specifications of Sixteenth-Century French Organs

Date, Place, Builder	Specification	Jeux	Key to jeux
A. 1510—Bordeaux Church of Saint-Michel Loys Gaudet (Gondet)	Principal 12′ (16′) Total of nine stops in grand orgue	1. Grant jeu 2. Jeu de papegay 3. Jeu de fleutes à 9 pertuys 4. Jeu de hauboys, or cornés 5. Jeu de cymbales 6. Jeu de fleutes d'alemans 7. Jeu de chantres	
	Positif à dos Deux anges sonnant les trompettes Saint Michel qui combattra le diable Estoilles Testes (masks)		
B. 1510—Bordeaux Church of Saint-Michel "Instruction pour le jeu de l'orgue"		1. Le grand jeu 2. Jeu de papegay 3. Les cornes 4. La fleute 5. Les cymbales 6. Les chantres 7. Les fleutes d'alement 8. La petite cimbale 9. Les gros cornetz 10. Le grand jeu doulx 11. Jeu de grans cornetz 12. Jeu des chantres	2–9 inclusive 1, 2 1, 5, 6 1 1, 2, 6, 9 1, 8 3, 8 1, 6 1, 2, 5, 6 1, 2, 3, 8, 9 1, 5, 6, 9 1, 2, 8

C. 1514—Bordeaux
Church of Saint-Seurin
Arnaud de Guyssaurret

1. Principal (16'), probably from F
2. Octave (8')
3. 15th (4')
4. 19th (2⅔')
5. 22nd (2')
6. 26th (1⅓')
7. 29th (1')
8. 36th (½'), or Flute 2'
9. Flute 6' (8')
10. Flute 3' (4')

1. Jocs de Papegueytz petitz
2. Jocs de Papegueytz grans
3. Plusieurs jocqs de Acquebutez
4. Jocz de cornetz
5. Jocs de grosses fleustes d'alemans
6. Petit jocs de chantres
7. Jocs de cymbales

"and many other jocs . . ."

D. 1518—Bordeaux
Couvent des Frères Mineurs
Jacques Loup

New chest and keyboard using old pipes,
probably from earlier Blockwerk

"Plus sera tenu ledit maistre de faire ung
jeu de fleutes de plomb d'allemant tout
neuf à la mode nouvelle avec sept tirans,
lesqueulx tirans se joueront en quinze ou
seze façons."

E. 1529—Bordeaux
Church of Saint Eloi
Bertrand Jehan

1. Principal 6' (8')
2. Octave (4')
3. 15th (2')
4. 19th (1⅓')
5. 22nd (1')
6. Simballes
7. Flute octave (4')
8. Flute (2⅔')—"pour faire
   les jeux de canars"
9. Flute 15th (2')—"qui sert
   d'ung petit jeu de flauioles de Poitou"

TABLE 3 (*Continued*)

Date, Place, Builder	Specification	Jeux
F. 1531—Toulouse Cathedral of Sainte-Etienne Jacques Cormier	According to contract: 1. Principal (8′) 2. Octave (4′) 3. 15th (2′) 4. 19th (1⅓′) 5. 22nd (1′) 6. Grosse flute (8′) 7. 12th flute (2⅔′) 8. 15th flute (2′) 9. Jeu de regales According to list bearing Cormier's signature: 1–6. same as above 7. Les cornes 8. La petite fleute 9. Les hautz bois	1. Le grand jeulx 2. Le jeulx de papegayl 3. Le jeulx des chantres 4. Le jeulx des fleustes dallemans 5. Le jeulx de pifres 6. Le jeulx sourt 7. Le jeulx de nazars petit 8. Le jeulx de nazars groulx 9. Le jeulx des cornes 10. Le jeulx des simballes 11. Le jeulx des fleustes 12. Le jeulx de petit carillons 13. Le jeulx de petites orgues 14. Le jeulx de petistes orgues en fleustes 　　et le sic de aliis 15. Le tabourin 16. Ung jeulx de regalles

G. 1548—Bordeaux
Church of Sainte-Eulalie
Jean de Cyvrac

Principal 12' (16')

Total of twelve stops, including régalles

Estoilles

". . . avecques les jeuz qui s'ensuyvent":

1. Le principal
2. Fleustre 6 pieds
3. Fleustre à neuf trous
4. Fleustre d'allemant
5. Flageotz
6. Doulssannes
7. Canards
8. Nazards gros
9. Moiens nazards
10. Petis nazards
11. Petis cornetz
12. Saqueboutes
13. Voix humaines
14. Musette
15. Petits phiffres
16. Gros cornetz
17. Papegaulx
18. Cymballes
19. Musette grande
20. Principal ou grand jeu fleustre

In three of the contracts the actual stop lists were given, unmistakably, along with mention of various numbers of jeux, bearing names characteristic of musical instruments, and other sounds (Papegay, Canards, Voix Humaines).[14] It will be seen that for these three organs it remains only to discover which stops were used for each jeu, but that for the other two contracts, which fail to give a specification, a meaningful interpretation of the jeux can be given only in terms of the other organs' specifications. Similarly, the "Instruction" of 1510 (Bordeaux, Saint-Michel) supplies a unique definition of the jeux in terms of the specification of the Saint-Michel organ of the same year. Had that specification been given in the contract, the problem of interpreting the numbers of the "Instruction" and deciphering the jeux for numerous other organs in that period would not be so troublesome today.

From the six contracts under discussion, from Bordeaux and Toulouse, it is immediately apparent that in the early sixteenth century a number of organ builders in southern France were erecting instruments bearing marked Italian characteristics. That is to say, the main section of the organ (Grant Jeu, Grand Orgue, Gros Corps de boucque) contained a more or less complete series of harmonics in single principal ranks, pitched from a 12′ or 6′ fundamental (comparable to our 16′ or 8′, but commencing on F). These ingredients of the Ripieno were supplemented by two or three flute voices.[15] When a Positif existed, it was modeled after no Italian prototype but rather resembled the small *guide-chant* instruments with 4′ and 2′ pitches. The Positif was placed in a separate case behind the player, on the gallery rail.[16]

---

14. There is confusion due to ambiguity in the word "jeu," which can be either a single register (stop) or a combination of several registers. This confusion might have been avoided, had Mersenne's (1636) finer division of jeux into jeux simples and jeux composés been universally applied a century earlier. Whereas Cormier's jeu de régales (Toulouse Cathedral, 1531) was clearly a single register, his subsequent listing of the "jeulx de l'orgue" in the same document referred to registrations.

15. The introduction of a reed voice in Toulouse, 1531, and Sainte-Eulalie, Bordeaux, 1548, was not typical of the usual Italian procedure.

16. Positifs mentioned in contracts for the churches of Saint-Michel and Saint-Seurin, Bordeaux, were actually Positifs-à-dos: for Saint-Michel, 1510, the contract stipulated: "la cheière de devant là où sera l'organiste, ou il y aura ung jeu d'orgue qui sera une chose singulière"; for Saint-Seurin, 1514, we read: "ung petit clavey et ung

For the interpretation of any sort of comment on registration, a stop list is needed. Unfortunately, this is missing from the most important of this series of documents—namely, those written for the Church of Saint-Michel, Bordeaux, 1510.[17] The key to the meaning of the unique "Instruction" for Saint-Michel's organ depends, therefore, upon a reconstruction of the missing specification. This can be done only in terms of the known specifications of other instruments in that geographical location during the same period and even then with debatable accuracy. A glance at the information supplied by other Bordeaux contracts and that of Toulouse, 1531, will provide the groundwork.

Saint-Seurin, Bordeaux, 1514

The contract of 1514 for Saint-Seurin, Bordeaux, gives the list of stops in order.[18] After listing ten stops of the Gros Corps de boucque, the new flexibility of this division is described: "[one] can multiply the 'jocqs' [jeux] of this organ in more than sixty different ways, such as jocs de papegueytz petitz et grans . . . plusieurs jocqs de Acquebutez [saqueboute], jocz de cornetz, jocs de grosses fleustes d'alemans, and petit jocs de chantres, jocs de cymbales, and several other jocs which will reveal themselves when the organ is completed; and everyone can judge for himself what is appropriate, and add new combinations of every sort, with beautiful effect."

The "jocs" (jeux) in this list of possibilities indicate combinations of stops—combinations which were already familiar to those for whom the document was written. "Acquebutez," "cornetz," "fleustes d'alemans," and "cymbales," all names of sixteenth-century musical instruments, called to mind specific tonal effects which would be made possible on the reconstructed Grand Orgue, which, one notes, would allow the player "more than sixty" possible variations of registration.

---

petit orgue qui sera darrey aquest qui sonnera lodeit orgue." Such was also the physical arrangement for the Rugwerk of the Netherlands and the Rückpositiv of Germany, which received rich development during the 16th century.

17. See Table 3, A and B.

18. See Table 3, C, and Appendix A.

The first item of business was "to remake . . . the chest, action, and wind conduits for the principau chest, according to the form and procedure presently in fashion." This seems to suggest that the old organ was a one-manual "principau" (or Fourniture = Block-werk). But in the next sentence we read that the Gros Corps de boucque, or Grand Orgue, would be furnished with eight pipes per key ("huict tuelz . . . per marches"), including the "prin-cipau," as well as the "Furniture," but not counting the flutes. Thus the old organ might have had a double chest, allowing the selection of a multi-rank "principau" and a "Furniture," which controlled the higher pitches. Whichever had been the case, the wording of the contract emphasizes repeatedly that the rebuilt organ would have a Grand Orgue with separate and independent stops, which would permit many registrations which had not been possible on the old instrument. The addition of a "petit clavey" and a "petit orgue" (Positif à dos) was not mentioned until after the discussion of registration possibilities on the Grand Orgue.

Couvent des Frères Mineurs, Bordeaux, 1518

Although this contract (see Appendix A) does not list the stops for the organ, valuable support for our argument is found in the remark: "the builder will further be held to the construction of a *jeu de fleutes de plomb d'allemant*, completely new according to the new fashion, with seven draw stops; these draw stops may be played in fifteen or sixteen different ways [combinations]." In other words, the reconstructed instrument was to include a new "jeu de fleutes d'allemant," of lead, which was defined specifically as a seven-stop group, capable of fifteen or sixteen practical combinations. The "new fashion" was, of course, the method of providing selective stops by using key channel chests, as opposed to the old-fashioned mixture organ. The "jeu de fleutes d'allement," as described here and in other sources under discussion, seems to indicate a general category for registration, rather than a specific, rigid combination of pitches within the flute family.

Church of Saint-Eloi, Bordeaux, 1529

Again we encounter an Italian-style specification. This contract leaves no doubt about the exact stops ("jeus") to be installed within the old casework, but the possibilities for colorful stop combinations are only suggested. It is likely that the second flute listed, between the 4' and 2' pitches, was a $2\frac{2}{3}'$, and that it was the chief ingredient for "les jeus de canars," just as in the seventeenth century the Tierce $1\frac{3}{5}'$ was the most important color in the Jeu de Tierce. The separate "quinziesme de flautes" serves for making up "ung petit jeu de flauioles de Poitou," a title for registration not found in the other documents.

Cathedral of Saint-Etienne, Toulouse, 1531

Because some details of this contract have been analyzed by Randier, Rokseth, Dufourcq, and others, it attains an importance second only to the documents for Saint-Michel, Bordeaux. Its historical significance has been further enhanced by the fact that 1531 was also the year of publication for the organ pieces edited by Attaingnant, in Paris, a matter which will be discussed later.[19]

The contractual documents leave little doubt that the instrument was to be reconstructed in the Italian style. The specification was similar to the others of the period, except for the introduction of a reed stop ("jeu de regales"). Of further importance are the two listings of the specification which have come down to us,[20] differing in nomenclature. The "XIIe de la fleute" is equated to "les cornes," [21] the "XVe de la fleute" to "la petite fleute," and "ung jeu de regales" to "les hautz bois." Here we find the ambiguous employment of descriptive words ("cornes," "petite fleute," "regales," and "hautz bois") for single stops, alongside the use of the same terms to indicate registrations.

Church of Sainte-Eulalie, Bordeaux, 1548

A list of twenty registrations ("jeuz") is given in a contract which is otherwise extremely vague. We know only that the instrument had twelve stops, based upon 12' pitch, and including a reed ("régalles"). But this is sufficient to avoid confusion which might result in mistaking the "jeuz" for a list of twenty stops in the organ.

19. See below, p. 40 ff.

20. See Appendix A.

21. Cf. Appendix B: C. Antegnati, *L'arte organica* (1608). The "cornetto" is identified particularly with the distinctive 2 2/3' pitch.

The instrument could very likely have been Italian in style, in which case the twelve stops might be reconstructed like this:

Principal 12' (16')
Octave 6' (8')
Fifteenth (4')
Nineteenth (2⅔')
Twenty-second (2')
Twenty-sixth (1⅓')
Twenty-ninth (1')
"Cymballes" or thirty-third (⅔')
Octave flute (8')
Flute fifteenth (4')
Flute twenty-second (2')
"Régalles"

If, indeed, the organ were built in that style, the expanded possibilities for variety would explain the elaborate list of registrations given in the contract.

I may now return to the main problem of providing a key to the "Instruction" of 1510 for the organ at the Church of Saint-Michel, Bordeaux. This "Instruction" was not a part of the contract but, rather, was intended to be used as an aid to the organ player, who would not otherwise be familiar with the ordinary combinations of stops for an instrument built in the "modern" style (i.e. with individual stops). Each combination, with its identifying name—such as Grand Jeu, Jeu de Papegay, Cornès, and so forth—was defined according to the numbering of the organ's nine stops. Thus the Jeu de Papegay could be heard by drawing numbers one and two, and so on. But today, since the organ no longer exists, we must turn to the surviving contract in search of a key to the numbering system of the "Instruction."

The contract itself [22] did not list nine stops but did mention that number of components for "l'orgue de fornitures" (Grand Orgue).[23] After an order to the builder, Gaudet, to construct "l'orgue de

22. See Dufourcq, *Documents inédits*, *1*, 77, Doc. 140.
23. The registrations that followed applied only to the Grand Orgue, as in the organ for Saint-Seurin, 1514.

fornitures" on the basis of a 12′ length, we read, "garny de neuf tuyaulx et neuf mitres." "Neuf tuyaulx" meant "nine ranks," [24] and "neuf mitres" apparently referred to the groupings of front pipes for the case. But the expected identification of the nine stops is missing. Instead, the text continues "pour la différance des sons [for variety of sounds]," followed by an enumeration of seven jeux:

> Grant jeu
> Jeu de papegay
> Jeu de fleutes à neuf pertuys
> Jeu de hauboys, aultrement nommez cornetz
> Jeu de cymballes
> Jeu de fleutes d'almans
> Jeu de chantres

Up to this time, various attempts at reconstructing the actual stop list of Saint-Michel's organ have been based upon the notion that the seven jeux (above) were names of seven of the instrument's nine stops. The assumption has been that the remaining two stops, to make up the required total of nine which we know existed in the organ, must have been inadvertently left out. Thus reconstructions of Saint-Michel's specification have hitherto been founded upon the names of the seven jeux plus two more, ordered from a vacuum to accommodate the numbering system of the "Instruction."

It was M. A. Vente, of Utrecht, who first noticed the possibility of basic fault in earlier readings of the Bordeaux documents.[25] Noticing the striking similarities between the contracts for Saint-Michel, 1510, and Saint-Seurin, four years later, he suspected that the seven jeux were names of registrations, while the real specification, unmentioned in the contract, was based on the same Italian approach to the Ripieno as the instrument at Saint-Seurin.

The first error originated, apparently, in Randier's early (1922) reconstruction of a specification for the Saint-Michel organ;[26] and it has been repeated again and again by Rokseth, Dufourcq,

---

24. Cf. wording for the Saint-Seurin contract, 1514: "garnyt de huiet tuelx."

25. Verbal communication with Maarten A. Vente, Utrecht, 1963.

26. F. Randier, "Les Orgues et les organistes de l'église primatiale Saint-André de Bordeaux, du XVᵉ siècle à nos jours," *Revue Historique de Bordeaux et de la Gironde, 14* (1921).

and others. It is probably also at the root of another regrettable mistake which has gained substance by reiteration—namely, the failure to recognize the real specification for the organ in Toulouse Cathedral, 1531.[27] In the latter instance the result has been a serious misunderstanding about the performance of sixteenth-century organ music—especially the works published in Attaingnant's celebrated collection of 1531.

A possible new interpretation of the contract for Saint-Michel, as it reflects in the "Instruction" for the same instrument, is founded upon: (1) a new reading of the actual contract of 1510; (2) the real specification of the Toulouse organ, according to the contract of 1531; (3) comparison of (1) and (2) with the facts given in the contracts for four other Bordeaux organs built before 1550 (C, D, E, and G, Table 3).

1. Portions of the text of the 1510 contract of Gaudet for Saint-Michel, Bordeaux, were published for the first time by Randier in 1921,[28] and a more complete transcription appeared in 1934, by Dufourcq.[29] A comparison of these two transcriptions with a photograph of the original contract reveals that in the sentence dealing with specification, the Randier transcription is more faithful to the text. Here are the two:

> [Dufourcq] . . . et premierement a promis le dit maistre Loys faire les dites orgues tous completz ainsi qu'il s'apartient, a la longeur de dotze pietz le greus tuyau, garny de neuf tuyaulx et neuf mitres. Pour la différence des sons, le Grant jeu . . .

> [Randier] Premièrement sera complet l'orgue de fornitures, ainsi s'apartient à la longueur de dotze piez le gros tuyau garny de neuf tuyaux et neuf mytres. Et pour la différence des sons le grant jeu . . . First, the "orgue de fornitures" will be perfected, as required, at the length of twelve feet for the largest pipe, equipped with nine ranks (tuyaux) and nine "mytres." [30] And for tonal variety, the Grant Jeu.

27. See Rokseth, *Deux Livres d'orgue*, p. XVI.
28. See n. 26, this chapter.
29. See Dufourcq, *Documents inédits*, *1*, 77, Doc. 140.
30. See above, p. 31.

Then follow the seven jeux listed above, which are not stop names but registrations.

The "orgue de fornitures" refers, without doubt, to the earlier nonselective "mixture organ," which was now about to be rebuilt with modern stops. The important instructions, for purposes of the contract, were that the "orgue de fornitures" would be based on a twelve-foot principal and completed as required with nine registers. Since the organ was to be rebuilt according to the "new fashion" recently introduced (from Italy?)—that is to say, in a layout which was already quite stylized—a complete listing of the stop names was not as interesting as the new and attractive tonal effects which would be possible with the new arrangement. The most typical registrations were then identified by names which had come into use, such as Grant Jeu, Flute d'allemand, and so on.

2. The organ of Toulouse Cathedral, 1531, built by J. Cormier. The registrations, or jeux, listed in the contract for the Cathedral of Saint-Etienne, Toulouse, 1531, cannot be mistaken for stops. Yet, in the introduction to Rokseth's superb edition of the Attaingnant *Deux Livres d'orgue, 1531*, these fifteen odd registrations were published as the actual specification. In order to correct this misreading, I give, in Appendix A, the pertinent portions of the original documents, which include two listings of the specification for that instrument. A strong stylistic connection between Toulouse's organ of 1531 and the series of Bordeaux instruments from the same period becomes immediately acceptable.

3. As I have noted,[31] the specifications of several instruments in the period under discussion showed Italian attributes. We know, also, that Italian organs throughout the sixteenth century showed remarkable stability as to tonal design. It is not surprising, then, to find that the known specifications for the churches of Saint-Seurin and Saint-Eloi, and for Saint-Etienne, Toulouse, are not only Italian in concept but very similar in detail.

The wording of the contracts leaves no doubt about the listings of jeux, or registrations. Indeed, it would be quite impossible to accept the twenty jeux given for the twelve-foot organ of Sainte-

31. See above, p. 26.

Eulalie, Bordeaux (1548), as stops.[32] Yet, this is at the root of earlier reconstructions of Saint-Michel's stop list.[33] Table 4 lists three modern reconstructions for that instrument's specification, given for reasons of comparison with the "Instruction."

TABLE 4. Bordeaux, Church of Saint-Michel, Builder: Loys Gaudet (1510)

Specification, as Reconstructed by:

Rokseth (1930)	*Dufourcq (1934)*	*Douglass-Vente (1964)*
1. Principal	1. Flute 12′	1. Prestant 16′ (from F)
2. Fourniture	2. Nasard & Quarte de	2. Octave 8′
3. Papegay (Quinte 4½′)	nasard (Papegay)	3. Fifteenth 4′
4. Fleutes à neuf pertuys	3. Flûte d'allemand	4. Nineteenth 2⅔′
5. Cornet	4. Flûte à neuf trous	5. Twenty-second 2′
6. Cymbale	5. Hautbois-Cornet	6. Twenty-sixth 1⅓′
7. Fleutes d'Almans	6. Cimballes	7. Twenty-ninth 1′
8. Chantres	7. Fourniture	8. Flute 8′
9. Petit nasard	8. Chantres	9. Flute 4′
	9. Petit nasard	

Instruction for Registration of the Organ (1510)

    a. Grand jeu: all stops excepting the first
    b. Jeu de papegay: 1, 2
    c. Les cornès: 1, 5, 6; jeu de grans cornaiez: 1, 5, 6, 9 (second version)
    d. La fleuste: 1 alone
    e. Les cimbales: 1, 2, 6, 9
    f. Les chantres: 1, 8; or 1, 2, 8 (second version)
    g. Les fleutes d'Alement: 3, 8
    h. La petite cimbale: 1, 6
    i. Les gros cornetz: 1, 2, 5, 6
    j. Le grand jeu doulx: 1, 2, 3, 8, 9

As an example of the confusion resulting from acceptance of the Rokseth-Dufourcq reconstructions, we cite four contrasting definitions of the Jeu de Papegay. These follow different systems of

32. This is shown clearly in the wording of the contract: "faire leurs orgues de douze piedz à douze tirans avecques les jeuz qui s'ensuyvent."

33. If the contract failed to give sufficient identification for its ranks of pipes, it did spell out exactly what extra devices the organ should have: two angels sounding trumpets, Saint Michel "in combat with the devil," and moving stars and heads.

numbering the stops, none of which is orderly or feasible, in terms of tonal structure.

Jeu de Papegay = Quinte $4\frac{1}{2}'$ (Rokseth)
Jeu de Papegay = Nasard and Quarte de nasard (Dufourcq)
Jeu de Papegay = Petit nasard or Larigot (Gravet)[34]
Jeu de Papegay = Foundations 8' and 4' (Hardouin)[35]

Using the typical Italian specification suggested above, the "Instruction" [36] would be solved in a manner quite unlike any previous comment. For this solution, see Table 5. Additional support for this key to the earliest French instruction for registration may be found in the following broad considerations.

1. Marked Italian attributes of instruments in the same area. That the organ of Saint-Michel very closely resembled the others described here is vastly more feasible than the notion that they were conceived in entirely different tonal worlds, as acceptance of the Rokseth-Dufourcq approach would suggest. Since it is known that Italian organ builders had already arrived at a remarkably stable approach to tonal schemes, it would be reasonable to suppose that the Bordeaux stop lists were practically identical.

2. Organ contracts not infrequently expressed the competitive spirit, which was one determinant in the extravagant development of the instrument during the sixteenth and seventeenth centuries. We may observe it within the contract for Saint-Michel's organ, already quoted above;[37] and it is quite possible that the ten stops of Saint-Seurin's organ were deliberately planned to be just one more than Saint-Michel's nine. We have noticed also that in 1521 the Church of Sainte-Croix, Oloron, ordered an organ to be built by the same Loys Gaudet, just like that of "Sainte-Eulaye"

34. N. Gravet, "L'Orgue et l'art de la registration en France, du XVIe au debut du XIXe siècle," *L'Orgue*, No. 100 (1961), pp. 202–57.

35. Hardouin, in *La Musique instrumentale*, pp. 259–69. It should be mentioned with emphasis that this view has more recently been revised by Mr. Hardouin in his painstaking study mentioned above, n. 4, this chapter.

36. See Table 3, B.

37. See Dufourcq, *Documents inédits, 1*, Doc. 140: "this master Loys [Gaudet] has promised to construct this organ just as well and beautifully as any organ to be found within thirty *lieux* around Bordeaux, in terms of size and plan."

Table 5. Key to "Instruction" According to New Reconstruction of Saint-Michel's Specification (1510)

	1 Principal 16'	2 Octave 8'	3 15th 4'	4 19th 2⅔'	5 22d 2'	6 26th 1⅓'	7 29th 1'	8 Flute 8'	9 Flute 4'
Grand jeu	X		X	X	X	X	X	X	X
Jeu de papegay	X	X	X						
Les cornès	X	X			X	X			
Jeu de grans cornaiez	X				X	X			X
La fleuste	X								
Les cimbales	X	X				X			X
Les chantres	X	(X)						X	
Les fleutes d'Alement			X					X	
La petite cimbale	X					X			
Les gros cornetz	X	X			X	X			
Le grand jeu doulx	X	X	X					X	X

(Eulalie), Bordeaux.[38] Other interesting indications of the competitive urge are found in the following contracts from France and the Netherlands:

> a. Contract of 1455, Oudekerk, Delft:[39] "a new 16' organ to be made . . . in the same manner and shape as the organ in St. Martin's Cathedral in Utrecht; better, and not worse."
>
> b. Contract of 1504, Notre-Dame des Tables, Montpellier:[40] "this organ to be made better beyond comparison than that of the Couvent des Cordeliers in Montpellier."
>
> c. Contract of 1542, St. Walburga Church, Oudenaarde:[41] "Let it be known that Meester Cornelis de Moer, organ builder living in the city of Antwerp and now being in this city of Oudenaarde, personally appeared before the elders of the city, and agrees to make . . . for the church wardens of the parochial church of St. Walburga in Oudenaarde an organ, under such conditions as follow: it must have a case made in exactly the same manner, with the same materials, and everything else of the same size, even the stops belonging to it, after the example of the large organ in St. Michiel's Church in the city of Ghent, not worse or smaller, but preferably bigger and better. And moreover the aforesaid Meester [Cornelis], by express promise and condition, must make and deliver one extra stop in this organ . . . than is now in the aforesaid organ of St. Michiel . . . and it is decided that if any stops presently in the organ at St. Michiel might be changed, then in such a case the same Mr. [Cornelis] must alter his design accordingly, as the church wardens with advice from the city elders would like to have it."
>
> d. Contract of 1551, Saint-Etienne, Troyes:[42] "equipped

---

38. See n. 12, this chapter.

39. Quoted in Vente, *Boustoffen tot de geschiedenis*, p. 112.

40. Quoted in J. Planté, "La Facture des orgues au XVIe siècle," *Bull. de la Comm. Hist. et Archéol. de la Mayenne*, Ser. 2, *1* (1888–89), 251.

41. Quoted in M. A. Vente, *Proeve van een repertorium van de archivalia betrekking hebbende nederlandse orgel en zijn makers tot omstreeks 1630* (Brussels, 1956), pp. 134–35.

42. Quoted in A. Gastoué, *L'Orgue en France, de l'antiquité au début de la periode classique* (Paris, 1921), p. 69.

with pipes as large as the Montre pipes in the organ at Sainte-Geneviève, Paris."

3. The language of the jeux. The similarity of terms used for registration (jeux) in the Bordeaux and Toulouse contracts proves that, at least for organs in southern France, there was already a simple system of combinations in use, based upon familiar names of musical instruments and so on. This nomenclature, as employed in Bordeaux, was not necessarily the exclusive property of organ builders in southern France who made instruments in the Italian-oriented style and listed jeux for them. It appeared also in the north, where the details of applying it on other sorts of instruments could not have corresponded exactly with definitions used in Bordeaux. In 1515 the builder Pierre de Estrada agreed to build an organ probably quite unlike the instruments of Bordeaux, for the Church of Saint-Vivien in Rouen. After promising to install a new "principal par devant" and second "principaulx de derriere," from old pipes, Estrada stated that he would "construct many diverse jeux as follows: the double principal all alone if one wishes, [or] with a jeu de haultboys, les cornetz, les flustes d'Allemaigne, les cimballes, les roussignolletz which will sing with the organ, les flaiolletz, with which the flustes d'Allemaigne will sing when simphronye is desired and a tabourin de Suisse, and all together at the wish of the player with another jeu de trompes clerons, and another de douchainnes." [43]

Exactly what the jeux meant for this organ cannot be clarified until more is learned about early sixteenth-century organs in the Rouen area. It is quite possible that only the "principal par devant" and the "principaulx de derriere" actually belonged to the specification of the organ, while the jeux were, once more, registrations which could be used along with the double Principal or for purposes of relief from it. We can be sure of two observations—namely, that the language of the jeux moved from organ to organ and from style to style, and that any continuity of meaning with respect to that language must have first depended upon stylistic continuity in the instrument. It was incorporated here and there in the nomenclature for single or compound stops throughout the sixteenth

43. See Dufourcq, *Documents inédits*, *1*, 40, Doc. 58.

century, and even into the jargon of classical French registration.

Still, the use of the language encountered in Bordeaux and Rouen persisted. The contract for the organ of Sainte-Chapelle (1560), built by François des Oliviers, seemed to make it clear that the jeux were represented at the console by separate stops:

> Item, fornira le sommier de dix registres sans emprunter en sorte que ce sont, a scavoir, la principalle de devant, l'octave de la principalle, les flustes à neufz troux, les flustes d'allement, les jeux de nazards, les cimballes, le jeu de douzaine, les fiffres, les haultboys et cornetz, la voix de trompette de guerre, lesquelles registres posera le plus près du clavier que faire de pourra pour les tirer sans bouger de sa place.[44]

But again, as with the organ of 1531 for Toulouse discussed below, errors have been repeated because of the misunderstanding of that word "jeu" when it refers to a combination of stops. Hardouin finally unearthed the actual text of the contract for another instrument built by François des Oliviers in 1551 for Saint-Etienne de Troyes.[45] The flowery language used to describe registrations possible on the new instrument has been erroneously accepted as the actual stop list since a partial reprint of the text was published by Prévost.[46] The pertinent portion of the contract is given as follows, according to the Hardouin transcription (1966):

> Se fera ung sommier grand et neuf pour poser 10 Registres sur lesquelz y aura 10 compaignies de tuyaulx, a chascune marche ung tuyeau et aucune doubles pour estre plus armonieux pour former le Plain Jeu d'orgues afin qu'ils soient oys par toute ladicte eglise, lesquels registres feront la diversité des jeulx quy s'ensuyvent et premièrement ung plain jeu bien armonieulx, ung jeu de flutes (d'allemens, ung jeu de navraz, ung jeu de flustes 8 comme dessus) a neuf trous, ung jeu de Haults boys avec la sacqueboutte et le cornet sonnent comme quattre joueurs quy est une chose excellante, ung jeu de Voix humaines contrefaictes comme quattre chanttres a voix

---

44. Ibid., p. 69, Doc. 118.

45. For the complete text of the contract, see Hardouin, *Rev. de Mus.*, 52, 180.

46. Mémoires de la Soc. de l'Aube, 1904. See A. Cellier and H. Bachelin, *L'Orgue, ses éléments, son histoire, son esthétique* (Paris, 1933), p. 76.

tramblant, ung jeu de cimballes, ung jeu de doubles flutes, ung de fiffres, ung jeu de doucines, ung jeu resemblant a la voix d'un faulcet, ung jeu de harpes, ung jeu de brodes chantanz comme pelerins quy vont a S. Jaques avec une voix tramblant, ung jeu de fiffre d'allement avec le tabourin sonnant comme en une bataille avec 3 aultres fiffres sonnans 3 diverses sons, ung jeu de musette sonnant comme ung berger estant aux champs.

It remains to unravel the confusion surrounding the performance of sixteenth-century French organ music. A coincidence of dates may be responsible for the prominence accorded to the organ of Saint-Etienne Cathedral, Toulouse, with respect to the registration of organ pieces published by Attaingnant in Paris in the same year.[47] In the introduction to Rokseth's elegant modern edition (1925) of these epochal pieces, the Toulouse instrument served as a model to illustrate the sorts of sounds available to an organist of the mid-sixteenth century.[48] The modern organist, equipped with the stop list of the Toulouse instrument, was to be guided in choosing registrations for the exquisite pieces of the Attaingnant collection.

Rokseth's version of the specification was taken from Anglade's transcription of excerpts from the original documents of 1531, as published in 1917 in the *Annales du Midi*.[49] Unfortunately, the reading of Anglade's excerpts and the photographs of the complete documents in question[50] prove that Rokseth was in error; and the alleged specification of the Toulouse instrument, reiterated by Dufourcq (1934), Sumner (1952),[51] and others, was not a stop list but a list of registrations. The organ was rebuilt with a new Grand Orgue in the Italian style, like those of Bordeaux, but for the addition of a reed stop.

The two documents in question are: an order for materials necessary for the rebuilding of the organ along with instructions

---

47. The Attaingnant publications of 1531 contain the only surviving French organ music of any importance during the entire 16th century.

48. Rokseth, Introduction to *Deux Livres d'orgue*, p. XVI.

49. See n. 7, this chapter.

50. See transcription of these documents by Paul Roudié, Appendix A.

51. W. L. Sumner, *The Organ* (London, 1952), p. 69.

about procedure (enlargement of case, provision of new keys, addition of a star, etc.); and the contract itself, which enumerates nine stops for the revised instrument or portion thereof. At the end of the first of these important documents will be observed a list of "jeulx" ("Sansuit les diferand des jeulx de l'orgue . . ."), or registrations, which have been identified mistakenly as the specification. Immediately below, added in a different hand, with the signature of the builder, Cormier, is the real list of the nine stops which were to be built in the instrument, comparing exactly with the list in the contractual document.

These portions of the two documents may be translated thus:[52]

[1] Here follow the different registrations for the organ, first of all

        Item le grand jeulx
        Item le jeulx de papegayl
        Item le jeulx des chantres
        Item le jeulx des fleustes d'allemans
        Item le jeulx de pifres
        Item le jeulx sourt
        Item le jeulx de nazars petite et groulx
        Item le jeulx des cornes
        Item le jeulx des simballes
        Item le jeulx des fleustes
        Item le jeulx de petit carillons
        Item le jeulx de petites orgues
        Item le jeulx de petites orgues en flaustes et sic de aliis
        Item le tabourin
        Item ung jeulx de regalles
        Three draw stops will be needed for the flute stops and the "soubres doziems" [Flute twelfth]
        [In a different hand:]
        le principal
        la octave
        la XV[e]
        la XIX[e]

52. For complete texts, see Appendix A.

> la XXIIe
> les nefs [?], la grosse fleute
> les cornes
> la petite fleute
> les hautz bois
>
>   Cormier [signed]

[2] Let it be known by all those here present that . . . the superintendents . . . in the metropolitan church of Sainct Estienne de Tholouse . . . have let the contract for reconstructing the organ in this church to *maistre* Jacques Cormier, master organist of Tours, and to make for this organ the stops which follow, namely, "le principal, la octave, le XVme, la XIXe, la XXIIe, la grosse fleute, la XIIe de la fleute, la XVe de la fleute, et ung jeu de regales," which make in all nine different stops, for the price and sum of one hundred and forty *livres tournois.*

We infer that the reconstruction of the instrument touched only the Grand Orgue, which was to be revised from an earlier indivisible fourniture (mixture organ) to a nine-stop division in the Italian style; that there was a Positif à dos, which offered some additional source of tonal variety ("le jeulx de petites orgues," "le jeulx de petites orgues en fleustes"); and that the fourteen possibilities given for registration could, in fact, be amplified beyond the standard combinations mentioned ("et sic de aliis").[53]

However, if we cannot accept the Rokseth-Dufourcq approach to registrations possible on the Toulouse instrument, what were the actual combinations of stops sketched out by the language of the "jeulx," which so closely resembled the names of registrations employed twenty years earlier in Bordeaux? The answer to this question, should it be discovered somewhere in the vast, unexplored resources of archival materials, would be interesting indeed, for it would provide an important link between the instrument and the music in a period fascinating from every point of view. Failing the evidence which could give us the key to the famous "Instruction" from Bordeaux, 1510, we have arrived (see Table 5) at a reconstructed specification for Saint-Michel's organ which

---

53. Cf. Saint-Seurin's "more than sixty ways" of combining its ten stops.

Table 6. A Solution to the Registrations for Saint-Etienne, Toulouse, 1531

Jeux	1 Principal 8'	2 Octave 4'	3 15th 2'	4 19th 1⅓'	5 22d 1'	6 Flute 8'	7 Flute 2⅔'	8 Flute 2'	9 Regal
Grand jeu	X	X	X	X	X	(X)			
Papegayl	X	X							
Chantres	X								
Fleustes d'allemans		X				X			
Pifres					X	X			
Sourt*	X					X			
Nazars petits		X				X	X		
Nazars grands		X	X	X		X	X		
Cornez	X					X	X	X	
Simballes	X	(X)		X					
Fleustes						X			
Petit carillon									
Petites orgues									
Petistes orgues en fleustes									
Tabourin		X							
Regalles						(X)			X

* Sourt = sourd = deaf, mute = doeff (old Dutch) = principal (soft in quality). Cf. Antegnati, *L'arte organica*, 1608: "The principal alone is very, very delicate, and I usually play on it at the Elevation of the Mass"; and N. Dufourcq, "Les orgues de Notre-Dame à Saint Omer au XVIme siècle," *Bull. de la Soc. Acad. Antiquaires de la Morinie*, Fas. 319, 77 (1948), 215–16: contract of 1515 for organ built by Charles Waghers of Hazebrouck: for the Positif, "ung sourt de six piez." In context, this "sourt" can mean only "principal."

gives a reasonable guess about what the "Instruction" actually meant. Likewise, we might reconstruct a new "Instruction" to apply to the known specification and registration list for Toulouse in 1531 (see Table 6). Such educated conjecture, though dubious on a number of counts, has been guided in part by comparison with several German, Italian, and Netherlandish sources on sixteenth-century organ registration.[54]

54. See Appendix B.

3. Registration in the Pre-Classical Period (1531–1636)

The Bordeaux and Toulouse instruments of the early sixteenth century, so closely related in structure, have provided verification of the existence of a codified style of registration, which was in use for three decades and more in southern France. But we are left with the realization that the application of this plan of registration, however interpreted, is hardly more suitable to the performance of the French pieces published in Paris by Attaingnant than to the music of the Venetian organ composers during the same years. Although organists in Bordeaux and Toulouse may well have played the anonymous pieces published by Attaingnant on the instruments under discussion, instruments like those in the south have not been found in Paris or in Rouen.

More likely would the owner of those pieces have chosen to play them, or other works of similar texture, upon an instrument in the new northern style. The Grand Orgue, built along such stylistic lines and very strongly influenced by the splendid innovations of the Netherlanders, would be given some single-rank registers, but the completion of the Plein Jeu would be accomplished by a rich development of mixtures, derived from the ancient Fourniture, or Blockwerk. Flute and reed voices may have been found in such an instrument, providing tonal colors which, in organized and balanced groups, were to be the bread and butter of instruments of the next century. While the eventual function of the Positif à dos had not yet been brought into focus, a large instrument in the north would very likely have included such a division. And there may have been a number of Trompes[1] set apart from the main case of the instrument and played either by pedals or a separate manual keyboard (*clavier de teneure*).

An instrument planned according to *les méthodes nouvelles* was

1. See Figure 2.

built from 1537 to 1540 by two organist-builders, Gratien de Cailly
and Symon le Vasseur, for the Church of Notre-Dame, Alençon.
Its elaborately carved casework still stands. Sharply contrasting
with the southern instruments which have been discussed, the
Alençon organ showed extraordinary development in the Grand
Orgue, with companion choruses of principals and flutes. A glance
at the stops built in this organ broadens our impression of the
tonal colors available to the performer of France's earliest known
organ compositions. The specification[2] is given in Table 7.

TABLE 7. The Organ in the Church of Notre-Dame, Alençon, 1537–40,
Built by Gratien de Cailly and Symon le Vasseur

Grand Orgue		*Positif à Dos*
16' Principal	These stops serve as the	8' Trompette
8' Principal*	principal du corps	Voix humaines
4' Principal	(plein jeu)	Harpes
VIII Fourniture		
Cymbale		
8' Stopped Flute (pour faire le nazard)		
4' Flute		
4' Flute		
2' Flute (pour servir au jeu du nazard)		
1⅓' Flute (pour le nazard)		
1' Flute (petit jeu de nazard)		
Tremblant		
Rossignol		

* The omission of the "jeu de six piedz destain" in the text of the contract as published by Despierres is probably an error, as the number of stops making up the
principal du corps is given three times. Also, earlier in the contract there is mention
of "des tuyaulx de six piedz." See Appendix A.

In the middle of the sixteenth century large numbers of France's
important organs must still have retained their late fifteenth-
century character—that is, their Blockwerk divisions, Trompes,
and so on. But more interesting are some of the advanced attributes
of the Alençon instrument, which help to clarify the evolution of

2. See Appendix A for the complete text of the contract, as published by Mme.
G. Despierres, in "Les Orgues de Notre-Dame d'Alençon," *Bull. de la Soc. Scient.
Flammarion Argentan*, No. 6 (1888), pp. 165–72.

the instrument during a period about which much remains to be discovered. Some of these considerations are as follows.

The Plein Jeu

The wording of the contract clearly differentiates between narrow-scale principal stops and wide-scale flute stops[3] on the Grand Orgue. With a retrospective glance toward the still familiar Fourniture (or Principal, or Blockwerk), the three principals of 12′, 6′, and 3′ (comparable to our 16′, 8′, and 4′, but commencing on F) were all of tin, "pour myeulx fournir a la fourniture." "La fourniture" refers to the total group of stops, five in number, which have replaced the indivisible, multi-rank Fourniture. The next two items, completing the "Principal du corps" (Plein Jeu) are "une fourniture," a single register controlling eight ranks, and "une cymballe," undoubtedly a higher pitched register with several additional ranks. Thus we observe that the Plein Jeu, as defined for this instrument, was made up only of the principals.[4] Organs in France and the Netherlands usually admitted the fundamental ranks of Bourdons to the Plein Jeu, while the north German tradition (including Groningen) did not.[5]

The compositions of the Fourniture and Cymbale were unfortunately not given. Dufourcq's suggestion that a Cymbale in this period might have contained Tierce pitches[6] is not plausible. More reasonable is the chance that Alençon's mixtures in 1537 contained only unisons and quintes, which were what remained after the 16′, 8′, and 4′ principals were drawn out of the old Fourniture. A comparison with Vente's reliable reconstruction of Utrecht's Blockwerk[7] from the Nicolai Church, 1479 and 1547, would even introduce the possibility that Alençon's eight-rank Fourniture could have contained $5\frac{1}{3}'$ pitches, which were definitely components of the seventeenth-century French 16′ Plein Jeu.[8]

---

3. I.e. the tin pipes (principals) and the lead pipes (flutes).

4. Cf. Dufourcq, *Documents inédits*, *1*, 169, Doc. 247. The "Plain jeu" for Rodez Cathedral (1627) was described as containing only principals.

5. Cf. Vente, *Proeve*, pp. 29 (Bruges, 1557), 189 (Trier, 1584); and M. Praetorius, *Syntagma musicum*, Wolfenbüttel, 1619.

6. See Dufourcq, *Esquisse*, p. 160.

7. See Table 1.

8. Cf. Jean Fellot, *L'Orgue classique français* (Sèvres, 1962), chap. 1.

Whatever the exact components of the mixtures may have been, the pattern had been set, after the model of the Netherlands, to enrich the single principal ranks with Fournitures and Cymbales. The mixtures of the Grand Orgue were there to stay.

The Composition of the Grand Orgue

If any single attribute could be named to differentiate French organs from those in the Netherlands in the sixteenth century, it would be the unique development of the Grand Orgue toward a position of conspicuous prominence. The Grand Orgue at Alençon was built at a time when the organ builders of the Netherlands were preoccupied with the invention of the Bovenwerk, an extra manual division which never gained general acceptance in France. On organs which were given a Bovenwerk, the Hoofdwerk (Grand Orgue) often was retained as a Blockwerk. This suggests that the invention of the Bovenwerk was motivated by the fact that it was cheaper, or more practical, to leave the plenum undisturbed and to introduce tonal variety by adding a new, third key channel chest. The Bovenwerk was placed above the Blockwerk and played from a separate manual or from the main manual. Its original components were flute ranks only. Eventually, of course, the Blockwerk was broken up, and the Bovenwerk was endowed with some principal colors and reeds, as a foil to the Rugwerk (Positif à dos).[9] Table 8 illustrates the rapid adoption in the Netherlands of the idea of a third manual division.[10]

Had the sixteenth-century French builders applied the principle of the Bovenwerk, for which there must have been ample precedent in their experience, the organ's future in France might have been

9. For more information on the development of the Bovenwerk, see Vente, *Bouwstoffen tot de geschiedenis*, pp. 21–23.

10. It should be mentioned that still another manual division had already made its appearance in organs of the Netherlands before 1500—namely, the Borstwerk, which was originally an adaptation of the portable Regal. Although its use in the 16th century diminished as the richer possibilities of the Rugwerk and Bovenwerk were realized, it was often used in place of a Rugwerk, perhaps for reasons of economy or space. In the 17th century the Borstwerk (Brustwerk) appeared often in large instruments with Rückpositif in northern Europe, and still in the late 18th century, after the Rückpositif had lost its appeal. While the Borstwerk was never incorporated into the classical plan of French organs, the popular Echo in French organs functioned in a limited sense as a substitute. Cf. Vente, *Bouwstoffen*, pp. 13–14, 18–19.

TABLE 8. Development of the Bovenwerk in the Netherlands

1. Abbey of Averbode, 1517 (Builder, Willem Boets van Heyst):

Rugwerk	Hoofdwerk	Bovenwerk
Prestant 4'	Prestant 8'	Fluitkoor 8'
Mixtuur	Mixtuur	
Cimbel	Cimbel	
Fluit 4' or 2'		
Trommen		

2. In 1530 the same organ was rebuilt, with an enlarged Bovenwerk:

Bourdon 16'
Holpijp 8'
Fluit 4'
Quint (fluit) $2\frac{2}{3}$'
Trompet 8'
Kromhoorn 4'
Regaal 4'

3. Lüneburg, 1551–52, Johannes Kirche (Builder, Hendrik Nijhoff, Amsterdam and 's Hertogenbosch):

Rugwerk		Hoofdwerk
Prestant 8	Quintadeen 8	Prestant 8
Octaaf 4	Roerfluit 4	Octaaf 4
Mixtuur	Sifflet $1\frac{1}{3}$	Mixtuur
Scherp	Ruispijp	Scherp
	Baarpijp 8	
	Regaal 8	
	Schalmei 4	

Bovenwerk		Pedaal
Prestant 4	Roerfluit 8	Nachthoorn 2
Superoctaaf 2	Fluit 4	Fluit 1
	Nasard $2\frac{2}{3}$	Trompet 8
	Gemshoorn 2	
	Cimbel	Manual compass: F-a''
	Trompet 8	Spring chests

very much altered. The fact that the Bovenwerk was eventually ignored encouraged disproportionate development of the Grand Orgue, which, in turn, tended to suppress the urge to subdivide the main case. By the seventeenth century the unsubdivided Grand

Buffet was an established, idiosyncratic feature of the French classical tradition.

The Composition of the Positif à Dos

The eventual musical function of the Positif à dos was not fully realized in sixteenth-century French organs, as it was in those of the Netherlands. Hardouin suggests that the idea of the Positif suffered as organ builders concentrated on breaking up the old Fournitures.[11] In some instruments, the earlier *guide-chant* instruments were joined to the main organs, so that a single player might manage both. Such was the case at Saint-Seurin, Bordeaux, 1514, and at Saint-Germain-l'Auxerrois, Paris, 1551.[12] In Alençon and Chartres[13] the Positif received only the reed stops, which perhaps proved more useful on a separate keyboard, used against the flute or principal ranks of the Grand Orgue. In the Netherlands, on the contrary, the Positif was given its own principal chorus; and in many instruments it was extravagantly equipped with a variety of stops—principals, flutes of wide and narrow scale, and reeds— while the Hoofdwerk remained a Blockwerk.

The Use of the Term "Nazard"

From the sixteenth to the eighteenth centuries the term "nazard" was used with considerable flexibility in France, the Netherlands, and Spain. One of its earliest appearances, in Toulouse (1531), has already been mentioned,[14] where "le jeulx de nasars petits et grans" indicated combinations of stops familiar enough to have remained undefined. In the Alençon contract of 1537, the text of which is given in Appendix A, "nazard" was used again not only for a specific registration or a category of combinations but also for a single stop. The phrases "pour faire le nazard" and "pour servir au jeu de nazard" must refer to a combination or a number

---

11. Hardouin, in *La Musique instrumentale*, p. 260.

12. From unpublished material kindly communicated by Pierre Hardouin, Paris.

13. An interesting parallel to Alençon's Positif (completed 1541) was provided in Chartres (1542), where the Positif contained "cornets à anches qui sera mis et posé en ung petit fust derrière le joyeur." See below, p. 56.

14. See above, p. 41.

of possible combinations within the group of flute stops enumerated. But a single stop is doubtless indicated by "petit jeu de nazard," which probably spoke a unison pitch, rather than the quint pitch with which nazards later became exclusively identified.[15]

The references to "nazard," listed below, picture it in its broader role of a combination of stops or as a compound stop:

> 1535, Chalon-sur-Saône:[16] une douzième et une quinzièsme de plomb faictez en fleuttes qu'il fera pour ung nasard quant l'on vouldra [a twelfth and fifteenth of lead made in the manner of flutes which will serve for a nasard when desired].

> 1557, Bruges, St. Donaas:[17] een scuflet ofte spilpype ludende een quinte, dewelcke ghespeelt zynde metten monsterdoove constitueren zal den ghemsenhoorne ende ghespeelt zynde metten bordoen zal constitueren den nasaer [a sifflet or spill-pype sounding a quint, which when played with the front principal will constitute the gemshoorne, and played with the bourdon will constitute the nasaer].

> 1559, Sarcelles:[18] ung jeu de petit nazar pour jouer avec les

15. That quint flute ranks were in use in the Netherlands before the word "nazard" was applied to those stops is shown by Vente in *Die brabanter Orgel* (pp. 156–58). In Averbode, in contracts of 1530 and 1562, wide scale quints were described as "large, strange quint" ("groote, vreemde quynte") and "groeve quinte"; other contracts used "quinte flutte." "Nazard" as a single stop designation started appearing around the middle of the 16th century:

    (a) 1545—Hasselt, St. Steven
    (b) 1551—Lüneburg, St. Johannes (Nijhoff, Brabant builder)
    (c) 1551—Amersfoort, St. Joris
    (d) 1554—Bergen op Zoom
    (e) 1555—Schwerin, Dom
    (f) 1556—Gouda, St. Jan (een nazet)
    (g) 1560—Hazebrouck, St. Eligius (een asare)
    (h) ca. 1560—Harderwijk, OLV Kerk (een asaet)

See Vente, *Bouwstoffen*, pp. 86 (a), 63 (b, d), 79 (c), 58 (e), 126 (f), 135 (h); *Proeve*, p. 85 (g).

16. Quoted in Planté, *Bull. de la Comm. Hist. et Archéolog. de la Mayenne*, 1, 255–56.

17. Vente, *Proeve*, p. 29.

18. Dufourcq, *Esquisse*, p. 157.

flûtes, pour faire ung jeu de cornet [a petit nazard to be played with flutes, in order to make a jeu de cornet].

1560, Dijon, Sainte-Chapelle:[19] les jeux de nazards.

1569, Bruges, St. Walburga:[20] quintefluute dewelcke met die hoolpype constitueert het Nazar en met de Doove den ghemsenhoorne [quinte flute which with the hohlpijp constitutes the Nazar and with the principal makes the gemshorn].

1580, Gisors, St. Gervais and St. Protais:[21] un nazard de deux tuyaux sur chaconne marche [a nazard with two pipes for each key].

1585, Arras, St. Vaast:[22] une grosse quinteflutte pour faire le nasart.

1586, Couvent des Augustins, Paris:[23] [the contract for the renovation of the organ mentioned that the old "nasard" had two ranks].

1590, Trier, Dom:[24] ein sesquialter, so man nennet vocem humanam oder nasaten.

1594, Fougères, St. Sulpice:[25] ungn jeu de nazart de plomb aussi estoffé, garny de sa quarte qui seront deux tuyaux sur chacune marche en cestuy jeu [a nazard of lead, also stopped, equipped with its quarte (2′), which will make two pipes per key for this stop].

1620, Amiens, Cathedral:[26] un nazart ouvert à deux tuiaux sur marche portant la quarte, quy sera faict de tiercain.

19. Dufourcq, *Documents inédits*, *1*, 69, Doc. 118.
20. Vente, *Proeve*, p. 41.
21. Dufourcq, *Documents inédits*, *1*, 124–25, Doc. 208.
22. Vente, *Die brabanter Orgel*, p. 121.
23. Dufourcq, *Documents inédits*, *1*, 142–44, Doc. 222.
24. Vente, *Proeve*, p. 191.
25. Dufourcq, *Documents inédits*, *1*, 56–57, Doc. 92.
26. From contract, October 13, 1620, as quoted in Georges Durand, *Les Orgues de la Cathédrale d'Amiens* (Paris, 1903), p. 19.

1621, Rouen, St. Vivien:[27] une petite fluste qui servira de nazard.

1627, Rodez Cathedral:[28] la doutzième de la monstre qui servira pour faire le nazard.

1629, Treguier Cathedral:[29] unne quinte flutte pour servir de nazart.

1632, Rouen, St. Godard:[30] une quinte fluste, pour servir de nazard.

1636, Mersenne, M., *Harmonie universelle:*[31]

a. "Nazard" registrations of Charles Raquette
   1. Bourdon 8, Nazard $2\frac{2}{3}$, Flute 4, Flute 1
   2. Bourdon 8, Nazard $2\frac{2}{3}$
   3. Bourdon 8, Nazard $2\frac{2}{3}$, Flute 1
   4. Nazard $2\frac{2}{3}$, Flute 4, Flute 1
b. Mersenne's "Nazard" registrations
   Grand Orgue
   1. Bourdon 16, Bourdon 8, Prestant 4, Nazard $5\frac{1}{3}$[32]
   2. Bourdon 8, Prestant 4, Doublette 2, Nazard $2\frac{2}{3}$
   3. Bourdon 16, Bourdon 8, Prestant 4, Doublette 2, Nazard $2\frac{2}{3}$, Larigot $1\frac{1}{3}$ ("very strong Nazard")
   Positif
   1. Bourdon 8, Prestant 4, Nazard $2\frac{2}{3}$, Tremulant
   2. Bourdon 8, Flajolet 1, Nazard $2\frac{2}{3}$, Tremulant
   3. Bourdon 8, Prestant 4, Doublette 2, Nazard $2\frac{2}{3}$, Petit Nazard $1\frac{1}{3}$ ("strong Nazard")

To the impressive count of Nazards recommended by Mersenne and Raquette in 1636 may be added the three "nasart" combina-

27. Dufourcq, *Documents inédits, 1*, 120–21, Doc. 203.
28. Ibid., *1*, 167–69, Doc. 247.
29. Ibid., *1*, 133–35, Doc. 215.
30. Ibid., *1*, 110–13, Doc. 187.
31. Marin Mersenne, *Harmonie universelle;* R. Chapman, trans., *The Books on Instruments* (The Hague, 1957), "Sixth Book of the Organ," Propositions III and XXXI.
32. Mersenne leaves us in doubt about the pitches of his "Nazards," a matter which is discussed later.

tions in the instructions for the organ in San Juan de las Abadesas Church, Barcelona,[33] 1613, and no fewer than eighteen more Spanish "nazarts" included in the numerous registrations listed for Lerida Cathedral in 1623.[34] Three of these were built on 4' and 2' pitches only. Vente reports that in Spain Nasardos (pl.) sometimes meant, too, a sort of bass Cornet, with $2\frac{2}{3}'$, 2', and $1\frac{3}{5}'$ pitches.[35]

The term Nazard (Nasat, Nasardos, Nasaer, Asaet, Asare, etc.) was so widely circulated in the early seventeenth century, and applied to such a variety of combinations, that we may safely conclude that hints concerning Nazards during the sixteenth century alluded to the existence of a whole family of registrations which were popular in France. By the 1530s, in those French instruments which followed the "modern" practice of separating the registers, flute ranks sounding unison and quint pitches were already appearing in organized groups on the Grand Orgue. The combinations possible among the components of the flute chorus, along with useful ranks of principals (particularly the 4'), were generally classed as "les jeux de nasards." And the most distinctive members of the sixteenth-century flute family (i.e. those sounding $2\frac{2}{3}'$, $1\frac{1}{3}'$, and even 2' and 1') were soon individually identified with the sounds of the registrations themselves. The separate Tierce, a latecomer in France,[36] arrived too late to be classed with the Nazards, for it had already been heard as the spiciest ingredient in the new Dessus de cornet (imported from the Netherlands around 1580). By the time of Mersenne (1636) the combinations called "Nazards" were many, but the stops bearing the same name were narrowed down to the quint ranks ($5\frac{1}{3}'$,[37] $2\frac{2}{3}'$, and $1\frac{1}{3}'$), which lent special character to the traditional Nazard combinations.

The use of the single-rank Nazard in French organs continued throughout the seventeenth and eighteenth centuries. But distinc-

33. F. Baldello, "Organos y organeros en Barcelona," *Anuario Musical*, *1* (1946), 225–27.

34. See Appendix B.

35. Vente, *Die brabanter Orgel*, p. 158.

36. Dufourcq, *Esquisse*, p. 264. One of the earliest known appearances of the separate, wide-scale Tierce was in Poitiers, 1611.

37. Ibid., p. 264: "Mersenne cite le Gros nasard 5 $\frac{1}{3}'$ à la douzième de la Montre de 16: nous ne l'avons trouvé dans aucun devis d'orgue à la même époque."

tive Nazard registrations apparently diminished in number, possibly because of the marked change in musical style around the middle of the seventeenth century. The Nazard tended to be identified with and most frequently employed as a companion to the ubiquitous Tierce. It was used without the Tierce for *Récits de Nazard*, as a thickening or stabilizing aid to a reed stop, for the accompaniment for a *Basse de Trompette*, or for one of the voices of a *Duo*, *Trio*, or *Quatuor*.

According to the limited knowledge we have today from organ contracts and related documents between about 1530 and 1580, it appears that no other organ in northern France had achieved a greater degree of flexibility and structural balance than the instrument of Alençon. In 1541 it was completed. In 1542 the great organ in Chartres Cathedral was scheduled for a major renovation, requiring disassembly and reconstruction according to a new structural plan, "dedans le viel fust." This important instrument was cautiously modern in concept. The wording of the contract suggests ways of combining registers, reminding us of the language employed in the south for instruments of quite a different style:[38]

> Contract for rebuilding the great organ of the Church of Chartres, Thursday, 16 November, 1542 . . . with Robert Filleul, organist . . . to make and to be perfected by the aforesaid Filleul the great organ of the church of Chartres according to the following, to wit, that it will be agreed to take down, demolish, and disassemble the chests and wind supply of the great organ, to rebuild it, to situate it within the old casework, to make and complete the front pipes ["la monstre de tuyaulx"] in conformity with the stops ["jeux"] which follow, that is a plain jeu 16' reinforced with a "double" of eight 32' pipes for the bass in the pedal, the keyboard commencing at fa, ut; and these will be the eight largest pipes of the organ which will be played in the pedal; the aforementioned plain jeu will be supplied with two pipes [ranks] of 8', three pipes of 4' on each key, and six others of 2' fourniture

38. The original text of the contract is given in Appendix A, as quoted in Métais, *Archives Historiques*, *21*, 14–16.

appropriate for this organ, and there will be twelve pipes for each key[39] without the cornets and cymbale ["sans le jeu des cornets et cymbale"].

Item . . . a double nazart with four pipes on each key, and to use this nazart ["pour faire ledit nazart," i.e. the practical registration] the two 8' pipes of the plain jeu will be drawn.

Item it will be possible to play the 16' alone and with the 32' pedal and other stops which follow. It will be possible to play the pedals with all the stops of the organ, and with the aforementioned jeu de cornets.[40]

Item the register ["jeu"] with two 8' pipes, from the plain jeu, can be played alone and with any of the other stops.

Item the register with three 4' pipes, from the plain jeu, can be played alone and with all the other stops with the exception of the aforementioned nazart and cymbale.

Item a fourniture stop with six pipes per key from the plain jeu which cannot be played alone without being associated with the preceding large stops ["groz jeuz"].

Item a cymbale stop with three pipes per key, which will be played with all the preceding stops, save for the aforementioned nazart.

Item a jeu de cornets à anches which will be placed in a small case behind the player of the organ, which can be played alone and with all the other stops, excepting the cymbales and fourniture of the organ. And this cornetz stop will have its own wind supply and chest.

Item a tremblant stop.

As the doubled and tripled ranks at 8' and 4' pitches, along with the eight 32' pedal Trompes, were certainly intended to provide sonority sufficient to fill the immense nave of Chartres Cathedral,

39. The 16' counts, of course, as the twelfth rank of the "plain jeu."
40. This would necessitate couplers from Positif-à-dos to Grand Orgue and Grand Orgue to Pedal.

we can recognize characteristic similarities to the instrument completed a year earlier in nearby Alençon. The identical structure for the Plein Jeu included principal pitches at 16′, 8′, and 4′, with Fourniture and Cymbale registers; there was a Positif-à-dos, equipped with reeds only ("jeu de cornetz à anches"). But Alençon's instrument, while lacking 32′ Trompes, was apparently given much greater flexibility in flute registers, an attribute which governed subsequent developments in the instrument.

The two smaller instruments described below were built along the same general lines—that is, with a subdivided Fourniture retaining the high pitches in compound stops, some contrasting flute voices, and perhaps a reed stop. The customary 6′ keyboard, starting with F, is translated at right to the modern 8′ system:

Baigneux, 1532 (Arch. Nat. H⁵ 3737²) communicated by P. Hardouin[41]

Le principal 6′	(8′) Principal
Ung jeu de fourniture 3′, III–IV–V	(4′) Fourniture III–V
Ung jeu de cymballes	Cymbale
Ung jeu de flustes de plomb 3′	(4′) Flute
Un autre jeu de flustes 1½′	(2′) Flute
Ung jeu aussy de plomb 2′	(2⅔′) Nasard
Ung ange tenant une trompette	Angel holding a Trumpet
Ung tabourin	Tabourin
Un jeu de petis oiseaulx	Rossignol

Sarcelles, 1559[42]

Parement (Montre) 6′	(8′) Principal
Principal 3′	(4′) Principal
Grosse flute à 9 trous	(8′ or 4′) Flute
(Doublette) 1½′	(2′) Doublette
Grosse cymbale ⅔′	(1′) Cymbale
Petite cymbale à reprise de double en	

41. For complete text, see Hardouin, *Rev. de Mus.*, 52, 182.

42. Published by F. Mazerolle in "Marchés passés pour la construction des orgues d'Ivry et de Sarcelles," *Correspondance historique et archéologique* (Ivry-sur-Seine, 1895), vol. 2.

double

Gross nazard 2'

Petit nazard ("pour faire un jeu de cornet")

Saqueboutte 3'

Tremblant, Rossignol, 2 Anges à Trompette, 2 Etoiles

Petite cymbale

$(2\frac{2}{3}')$ Nasard

$(1\frac{1}{3}')$ Larigot

$(4')$ Reed

There remained a basic difference of approach between instruments of the North and South of France. Organs in Baigneux, Alençon, and Sarcelles followed structural patterns quite commonly found in the Netherlands during the same period, though the French instruments were never as ambitiously laid out in terms of divisions. On the contrary, there is still evidence of persistent Italian influence in the organs of Bordeaux, at least until the middle of the sixteenth century. Even the penetration of strong thrusts of influence from the north, during the period around 1600, did not eliminate the tendency among some organ builders in the south of France to nod in the direction of Italy or Spain.

We have seen that the language of the jeux remained in use in Bordeaux at least until 1548 (Sainte-Eulalie). It is interesting that a small instrument, built there for a private individual in 1558, still retained the same basic structural characteristics which had been observed in organs of that city for a half century. The instrument built by Jehan Pistre, Bordeaux, in 1558, for Pierre de Labatut, a great merchant, had five stops:[43]

> le principal 3' en flustes
> octave du principal en flustes
> 15th du principal
> une régalle consonant au principal
> ung jeu tramblant

Though the confusing facets of the story of French organs in the period 1550–80[44] may remain with us until much more energy is

---

43. Arch. dép. Gironde, 3 E 11143, fº 233 rº—235 rº. Transcribed by P. Roudié, Bordeaux. For complete text, see Appendix A.

44. Cf. above, pp. 13, 17.

applied to the problem, a number of well-documented changes took place at the end of the century which channeled French organ building toward classical stability. A transition was accomplished with astonishing rapidity between organs of the Alençon-Chartres-Baigneux-Sarcelles type and the superbly specified instrument built in Gisors in 1580 by Nicolas Barbier. One wonders how an instrument with the fully developed structure generally associated with the French classical organ could have appeared so early, especially in the midst of the religious and political turmoil which resulted in the destruction of many organs. The specifications for the instrument in Gisors are given in Table 9.

TABLE 9. Gisors, Saint-Gervais et Saint-Protais, 1580, Builder: Nicolas Barbier*

Grand Orgue (48 keys)	*Pedal* (28 keys)
Monstre 16	Jeu de pédalles 8′ de grosse taille, fait
Jeu de 8′ de plomb	de bois de fente
Bourdon de 4′, sonnant 8′	Autre jeu de pédalles en sacque-bouttes,
Un jeu de 4′, nommé prestam	28 keys
Doublette 2′	
Fourniture IV–VI (added in supplement	
to contract)	*Positif*
Cimballe III	Jeu en bourdon 4′ sonnant 8′
	4′ de plomb
Les jeux nommés ci dessus serviront	Jeu de 2′ de plomb
pour le Plain Jeu	Petite quinte, le corps d'estain
	Cimballe II
Fluste 4′	Jeu de crosme horne [sic] 8′
Nazard de deux tuyaux sur chacune	
marche	
Sifflet 1′	
Quinte fluste faicte à biberon	
Jeu de cornet V, 25 keys (C sol fa ut)	
Trompette 8′	
Clairon 4′	
Régalle pour servir de voix humaine, 48	
keys	
Tremblant	

* Dufourcq, *Documents inédits*, *1*, 122–24, Doc. 206, 207.

The 1580s witnessed the introduction of a number of important changes in organs of the Paris-Rouen area, but it remains a mystery how they could have been all anticipated in one magnificent gesture, such as is expressed in the documents relating to the organ of Gisors. Essentially all the elements of the fully developed seventeenth-century classical French instrument were already in place in this instrument. With an eye on the numerous innovations introduced to Paris by the Flemish Langhedul family (from the 1580s), Vente suggests[45] that Barbier might have been a Netherlander. If, indeed, he had not been born north of the border (which was then considerably south of what it is today), he did assuredly leave evidence in the Gisors instrument that his inspiration stemmed to a large extent from the southern Netherlands school of organ building.

The innovations that the Langhedul family[46] introduced to Paris, which apparently had already been incorporated in the Gisors plan, included the following structural improvements and tonal inventions.[47]

> Consistent use of trumpet reeds, and especially the introduction of the Clairon 4'. The Cromorne 8' was used in Paris for the first time in the organ of Saint-Gervais, 1601.
>
> The use of systematically repeated ranks (reprises) in the Fourniture and Cymbale, an elementary facet of the classic Plein Jeu.
>
> The use of the Dessus de Cornet of five ranks, which reinforced the reeds in the treble and acted as a solo register. At Notre-Dame-de-Paris the "Cornet à boucquin" was erected on a separate chest.
>
> The use of a *cantus firmus* pedal, with 8' flute and reed stops.
>
> The full development of the resources of the Positif à dos. Though some Positif sections had been given several stops,

45. Vente, *Die brabanter Orgel*, p. 126.

46. Vente traces the origins of the Langheduls in Ypres, West Flanders (southern Netherlands) and gives convincing proof of the immense influence of the Langhedul-Carlier-Titelouze circle in establishing the French classical tradition of organ building. (See *Die brabanter Orgel*, pp. 124 ff.)

47. See Hardouin, *La Musique instrumentale*, pp. 261–63.

as in the Positif of François des Oliviers for Saint-Germain-l'Auxerrois (1551), the first complete division in Paris was that of Saint-Gervais (1601).

Compass of keyboards extended down to C, 45 to 48 notes. The result was the gradual disappearance of 6' and 12' stops.

Around 1600 Paris and Rouen were the centers of development in organ matters. The members of the Langhedul family whose influence was felt strongly in this development were Jan, who arrived in 1586 and worked on organs at the Couvent des Augustins, Saint-Jacques-la-Boucherie, and Saint-Eustache, and his son Matthijs, who built the new organ for Saint-Gervais in 1601, then made important changes in instruments at Saint-Lou, Saint-Eustache, Saint Jehan-en-Grête, and the Hôpital du Saint-Esprit. Meanwhile, another great organ builder of the Langhedul school, Crespin Carlier, was called to Rouen by Jean Titelouze. Titelouze, the organ expert and composer, teamed up with Carlier and Langhedul, the builders. Without the strong guidance of these individuals, the stylistic course of organ building and organ music in France would undoubtedly have been retarded. By the 1630s a new style of instrument, which had been outlined with unfathomable accuracy in Barbier's Gisors organ of 1580, had been accepted over most of the land. It was that kind of instrument which Mersenne described and for which he listed registrations in his *Harmonie universelle* (1636), the greatest theoretical contribution touching upon the French organ, up to the time of Dom Bedos (1766).

It is evident that the record of preferences for registration depended upon the organ's capability for tonal variety and upon the interior arrangements of its component parts. Thus the history of registrations on the organ, even when narrowed down to a particular style of building to which certain registrations apply, is tied up inextricably with the tonal structure. By the time of Mersenne's publication all the tonal ingredients of the French classical organ were in use, both in France and in the Netherlands. In the Netherlands organ building had already reached its apogee; in France the fulfillment of a national style, and the composition of music which would eventually perpetuate that style, had only just begun. It comes as no surprise that Mersenne's comments on registration for the organ have documented the most up-to-date thinking about combining organ stops at a moment which is quite crucial in terms of the literature, and summed up as well the practice of earlier years. The registrations from the *Harmonie universelle* are, then, transitional.

In order to establish continuity from the very early style of registration which we have discovered in southern France to the more sophisticated lists of Mersenne, it is necessary to search beyond France's borders, for there is a dearth of material available in France itself. Fortunately for that period, when organ building seems to have been most firmly guided by the inspiration of enterprising craftsmen from the Netherlands, an impressive series of lists for registration is available to us from the Netherlands. By combining this information with the sources already mentioned from France and the important sources from Italy and Spain before 1636, we can gain a chronological impression of the possibilities for combining stops, from the time that stops were invented. Passed down from generation to generation during what was perhaps the organ's most fascinating evolutionary period, we see the language of the jeux as it survived from an earlier century and was employed by Mersenne; we see the introduction of new combinations, as reflected in the manipulation of new sounds, and the early uses of many registrations which later were so popular that they inspired compositions. The language of the jeux, and the combinations to which they applied, were in the process of constant redefinition, according to the changes to which the organ submitted, until finally the instrument itself had become relatively stabilized. Mersenne's lists serve us best as guides to understanding the connection between sixteenth-century practice and the seventeenth-century registrations which were provided by several composers. And, of course, they are a valuable aid to the interpretation of the music of France's first great organ composer, Jean Titelouze.

Among the sources given in Table 2, some will be found in Appendix B. For the most part, the information stems from organ contracts. A few theoretical treatises supply information otherwise lacking. But in no case before 1650 (with the exception of Antegnati, 1608) did the author of a document on registration attempt to relate his advice to certain musical textures. While it is quite probable that these lists were seriously heeded in the sixteenth century, when the handling of stops was a relatively new idea to organ players, it is equally likely that an organist of that day felt at liberty to choose whatever combination seemed appropriate to the occasion and to the instrument at hand. He might have played the same composition one time on the Plein Jeu and another time on the flutes; on this organ with pedals, on that one without. An organist today should feel compelled to inform himself closely concerning the possibilities of registration in earlier times, but many an educated eyebrow would be raised in scorn if a twentieth-century player should employ the more bizarre registrations advised in these lists, while performing the music of Titelouze, Sweelinck, Scheidt, Frescobaldi, or Cabezon.

The reader should be warned that Mersenne's description of the organ, which includes the lists of registrations, should not be considered altogether authoritative with respect to the details of the instrument's history. More than thirty years ago Dufourcq met with problems as he wrote his comprehensive *Esquisse d'une histoire de l'orgue*.[48] Mersenne's remarks simply did not fit the picture in every detail, as it was revealed in the documents of the time.

A doubting glance at Mersenne's lists of combinations in the "Sixth Book of the Organ" reveals a number of impossible inconsistencies.[49] Indeed, Propositions III and XXXI disclose such an assortment of riddles that we are forced to distrust anything unusual that turns up in this work, such as the apparent existence of a Flute 16' in the Pèdale (Proposition XXXI, Table of Single Stops for the Grand Orgue).

An analysis of Mersenne's "Sixth Book of the Organ," or the portions dealing with registration, as given in Appendix C, should take into account the following discrepancies:

1. Conflicting descriptions of the Plein Jeu (Plain Jeu).
    a. Proposition III, paragraph 1: five stops are used to make

48. See n. 37, this chapter.
49. See translations of the text in Appendix C.

up the Plain Jeu, selected from the organ's twenty-two stops. [50]

b. Proposition III, paragraph 2: The Plain Jeu is made up of "seven or eight stops," which are then listed with nine names, which include the Tierce, not normally used for the Plein Jeu. [51]

c. Same paragraph: the next sentence lists seven letters for the Plain Jeu. This is the second definition of the Plain Jeu in a single paragraph, and omits both the Cymbale and the Tierce.

d. In the actual table of "Ieux composez" which accompanies the "Table des Ieux de l'orgue" in the original edition, the Plain Jeu comprises eight stops, still including the Tierce, but excluding the Cymbale. This is an unprecedented grouping for any period.

e. Proposition XXXI: the "Table des simples Ieux des grands Orgues" omits mention of a Montre 8'. Thus, in the table of "Ieux composez des precedens," the Plain Jeu lacks an open 8' stop. Furthermore, its seven ingredients omit the Bourdon 16' and the Tierce, while including all the mixtures once again.

f. Proposition XXXI: "Ieux meslez ou composez pour le Positif." Note the omission of the Bourdon 8' (B) from the Plain Jeu.

2. Problems and puzzles found in Proposition III, "Table des Ieux de l'orgue."

a. If B = Bourdon 8' stopped = speaking pitch 16',
then D = Bourdon 4' stopped = speaking pitch 8',
and M = Fluste 2' stopped, à *cheminée* = speaking pitch 4'.

b. If N and O actually represent identical pitches of 1', which seems unlikely, then there would be no 2' pitch in the family of flute stops. Then N could have been a stopped 1', speaking 2' pitch.

c. With respect to P, it goes without saying that the Cornet 1'

---

50. Note that the "Table of the Stops" following gives only twenty-one for the organ.
51. See below, p. 75, for other appearances of the Tierce in Plein Jeu in the 17th century.

was based on a stopped rank, though Mersenne fails to
mention it. Once again we encounter confusion between
speaking pitch and actual lengths of pipes. The Cornet
begins at 2′.

d. We find a similar snag in T. Comparison with Proposition
XXXI, "Table des simples Ieux des grands Orgues," T,
shows that the speaking pitch of the Cromorne was 8′, the
Cromorne having a half-length resonator. Mersenne leaves
the reader in doubt in Proposition III, by describing the
half-length Cromorne in the same way as the full-length
Cleron (R).

The "Table des Ieux de l'Orgue" may now be revised, so
that the pitch levels can be read correctly:

Mersenne		Revision to Actual Pitch	
A	Monstre 16′	A	Monstre 16′
B	Bourdon 8′ stopped, or 16′ open	B	Bourdon 16′
C	8′ open	C	Open 8′
D	Bourdon 4′ stopped	D	Bourdon 8′
E	Prestant 4′	E	Prestant 4′
F	Doublette	F	Doublette 2′
G	Fourniture 1′	G	Fourniture 1′
H	Cymbale $\frac{1}{4}$′	H	Cymbale $\frac{1}{4}$′
I	Flageollet $1\frac{1}{2}$′	I	Flageollet $1\frac{1}{3}$′
K	Tierce, the same	K	Tierce $1\frac{3}{5}$′
L	Nazart	L	Nazart $2\frac{2}{3}$′
M	Fluste 2′ stopped à cheminée	M	Fluste 4′
N	Fluste douce 1′	N	Fluste douce 2′
O	Flageollet 1′	O	Flageollet 1′
P	Cornet V 1′	P	Cornet V 2′
Q	Trompette 8′	Q	Trompette 8′
R	Cleron 4′	R	Cleron 4′
S	Voix Humaine	S	Voix Humaine 8′
T	Cromorne 4′	T	Cromorne 8′
V	Pédale d'anche 8′	V	Pédale d'anche 8′
X	Pédale de Fluste 8′	X	Pédale de Fluste 8′

3. Inconsistencies in Proposition III, "Ieux composez."

    a. The "Table des Ieux," as revised above, will yield some alterations among the "Ieux composez," specifically those combinations using D, M, N, P, and T. Since N and O no longer list the same pitch, the apparent identity of pitches between Nazard DLN and Flageollet DLO will be avoided.

    b. Among the "Ieux composez" one puzzles over the Gros Cornet DKL. The designation "Gros" seems to apply to pitch rather than to scale, as in Gros Bourdon, Grosse Cymbale, and Gros Cornet. Why, then, should the Bourdon 16′ be omitted from the first registration given under Gros Cornet? Could DKL be a misprint for BKL?

    c. Corresponding with Trompette et Cleron, three combinations are given: DEG, EG, and DEGR. Of these, none makes use of the Trompette, and the Cleron appears only once. Instead, we find the Fourniture (G) in them all, a most unreasonable choice. This is an obvious blunder, G having been printed for Q (Trompette).

    d. In order to realize both combinations for the pedal— Pédale de Fluste (DMX, DLX) and Pédale d'Anche (CDETV, CDEMB), a pedal coupler must be in action. This perhaps needs no mention. But there is no rationale for the second combination associated with Pédale d'Anche (CDEMB), which includes neither a pedal stop nor a reed voice of any sort.

4. Irregularities in Proposition XXXI, "Table des simples Ieux des grands Orgues."

    a. The omission of an open 8′ has already been mentioned because of the result in the Plein Jeu. But since there is no more important stop in the organ than the open 8′, the perplexing question arises: How many other combinations would have been altered had the Montre 8′ been given its proper place?

    b. After reading the explanatory language for B, C, D, E, and F, all of which is redundantly clear, we find Mersenne faltering again with "G." If this Nazard is about $5\frac{3}{4}′$ long and stopped, then its speaking pitch must be $10\frac{2}{3}′$. That is not "à la Douziesme de la Montre," but a twelfth from 32′.

It seems logical only that this Nazard was meant to be $2\frac{2}{3}'$ long, stopped, which would result in a speaking pitch of $5\frac{1}{3}'$.

c. The error in "G" is repeated for H. This "autre Nazard," being "at the octave of the preceding," should be described as $1\frac{1}{3}'$, stopped, with a speaking pitch of $2\frac{2}{3}'$. Such an explanation suits the subsequent definition of Q, which is correctly described as $1\frac{1}{3}'$ open.

d. In I, Mersenne says "La Fleute d'Allemand à quatre pieds, & est à cheminée," which suggests that its speaking pitch is $8'$. This would provide the instrument with two flutes of $8'$ and none of $4'$. We conclude that consistency in language would correct I to read, "La Fleute d'Allemand à deux pieds," speaking $4'$ pitch.

e. Another error appears in "O." The "other Cymbale" could not, by any process of logic, commence on $2'$ and $\frac{1}{3}'$. In order for this stop to make sense, the text should read: "L'autre Cymbale à deux tuyaux sur marche, dont le premier est en C sol de demi-pieds ouverts [the other Cymbale has two ranks per key, of which the first is on C sol, one half-foot open]." Only then could the "other Cymbale" continue the pattern of pitches already set up for the "grosse Cymbale" (N).

f. Finally, we arrive at the problems of pitch suggested in X and Z, the two pedal flutes. As Dufourcq pointed out many years ago, organs in northern France during this period are not known to have included pedal flute stops of the pitches described by Mersenne: "huict pieds bouchez" and "quatre pieds bouchez," which are translated to $16'$ and $8'$ speaking pitches. Once more, we are confronted with a difficult decision. Should the errors discovered in G, H, and I influence judgment in this instance, as well? If we can accept the notion that Mersenne repeated the same mistakes in X and Z, an assumption that is not totally unfounded in the light of the preceding discussion, then X and Z would read:

    X The Pédale is $4'$ stopped.

    Z The Fleute en Pédale is $2'$ stopped.

Lest Mersenne's contribution be underestimated or ignored, we should remember that some of the apparent inconsistencies between the registrations in Proposition III and Proposition XXXI may reflect differences in instruments of the early seventeenth century. The Table of the Stops and the "Ieux composez" given

TABLE 10. Specification of the Organ at Notre Dame de Paris (ca. 1630)

GRAND ORGUE, third manual, permanently coupled to the Boucquin

  16 Plein Jeu, VIII–XVIII

    BOUCQUIN, 47 keys

  16 Bourdon
   8 Bourdon
   4 Prestant
    Nazard
   II Doublette and Tierce (narrow)
    Dessus de Trompette et Clairon

    POSITIF, 48 keys

8 Montre	4 Flute à cheminée
8 Bourdon	II Nazard and Quarte
4 Prestant	Dessus de Cornet
2 Doublette	Trompette
Flageollet	Clairon
IV Fourniture	Voix Humaine
III Cimballe	
	Tremblant
No PEDAL	

in Proposition III were laid out by Charles Racquette, organist of Notre Dame de Paris, while those collected for Proposition XXXI outlined "the greatest number of combinations which are provided by the most excellent builders for the largest organs in Europe." The organ presided over by Racquette at Notre Dame was neither modern nor ordinary. It was odd.[52] A glance at Table 10, giving the specification of that instrument about 1630, shows that the ancient (but still stopless?) Fourniture was still functioning from the third manual, coupled permanently to the Boucquin (second manual, finished in 1620). Thus, in giving the stops for the Plein

52. From material kindly loaned by Mr. Pierre Hardouin.

Jeu, it is possible that Racquette drew the flutes and principals of the Boucquin with the Grand Orgue Fourniture. The narrow-scale stops from the Boucquin were the Prestant 4' and the Doublette-Tierce. This could help to explain the bizarre combination for the Plain Jeu, as given in Proposition III. Furthermore, the unusual list of stops for the Positif and Boucquin at Notre Dame may also account for some of the other extraordinary differences between the registrations given by Racquette and those in Proposition XXXI. In the former, for example, Racquette does not suggest the combination of Bourdon 16' with either the Voix Humaine or the Flageollet. These would have been impossible at Notre Dame. They appear in logical sequence, however, in Proposition XXXI, which specified the Grand Orgue with those stops, according to the thinking of the Carlier school. Was Racquette trying to base his advice upon his admiration for the latest developments, while reflecting at the same time his way of handling the hodgepodge at Notre Dame?

4. The Classical French Organ

To picture the established pattern of French organ building from about 1650 to 1790 as being fixed inflexibly within rigid concepts would be misleading. Still, fixed it was from several points of view. We can observe that there was general acceptance of, and apparent satisfaction with, the basic structural aspects of the instrument as it had evolved through the sixteenth century and into the post-Titelouze era.[1] This atmosphere of stability, to which Titelouze himself had made significant contributions, prevailed during the entire period of flowering in French organ composition. Without this, it is doubtful that composers would have been able to leave numerous detailed instructions on registration.

It has been mentioned earlier that adherence to the "classical" principles in terms of specification and other crucial considerations[2] did not hinder the natural artistic evolution of the French organ or its music through its most extended period of glory. Variations in scaling and voicing techniques, slight alterations in specification, and inevitable changes of musical taste resulted in a gradual tonal shift which is still heard in instruments surviving today. This shift was companion to changes in compositional textures. While it might be debated, on the one hand, whether or not the changes in the instrument after around 1730 were improvements, it cannot be disputed, on the other hand, that the quality of organ music after the early eighteenth century declined rapidly. These alterations in the instrument may have accommodated certain modulations in taste concerning musical texture. But the instrument did

1. Figures 11, 12, and 13, from Dom Bedos de Celles' *L'Art du facteur d'orgues, 1* (4 vols. Paris, 1766–70), give a clear impression of the internal layout of a French organ of the classical period.

2. Jean Fellot has described more clearly than any other French writer just what this classical French type was and how it differed from instruments of other eras. In the following paragraphs much is owed to his *L'Orgue classique français*, published in 1962, in the series "Musique de tous les temps."

not suffer internal decline, at least to the degree that the music did.

An organist's success in the eighteenth century sometimes depended upon his ability to improvise dramatic and exciting interludes in church concerts or in the "Concerts Spirituels" at the Tuileries. Daquin, Balbastre, and others gained special notice for a thundering portrayal of the Last Judgment, a piquant imitation of the warbling of birds, or a simulated roar of cannon. Hunting songs, fanfares, battles, and storms were the order of the day.[3] Daquin is reported to have played "more splendidly than ever; he thundered in the *Judex crederis*, which evoked such vivid excitement in the hearts of the audience that everyone turned pale." [4]

Even Dom Bedos, the scholarly, organ-building monk, nodded to the fashion of his day when he prescribed registrations for imitating "airs de fifre et de tabourin" and the singing of little birds. Nor was he unaware of the fact that organs no longer sounded as they had 75 years earlier, when he emphasized that his instructions differed in certain respects from those of "an organist named Mr. LeBègue . . . toward the beginning of this century." [5] Dom Bedos was concerning himself with those combinations "generally in use by the large majority of the best organists today" (i.e. 1770), rather than the late seventeenth-century organists, whose music interests us most in the twentieth. A difficulty in interpreting his registration instructions lies in understanding the generally stable atmosphere prevailing in the world of organ design, while remaining sensitive to changes in taste bearing particularly upon the performance of composed music. It must concern us that Dom Bedos' work reflected contemporary opinion, as opposed to the taste of the forgotten master, LeBègue, who had been dead for 68 years.

Before approaching the details of specification which governed the ensembles of the French classical instrument, some general

3. The 17th century must also have seen its share of storms and battles, as shown in the contract for an organ for Notre-Dame, Châlons-sur-Marne, 1635–39: "Et une pédale tirant dix-sept touches du clavier pour imiter le bruit de tonnerre" (quoted from Louis Grignon, *Vieux Orgues, vieux organistes* [Châlons-sur-Marne, 1879], p. 26).

4. Mercier in the *Tableau de Paris*, as quoted in Dufourcq, *La Musique d'orgue français de Jehan Titelouze à Jehan Alain*, p. 121.

5. Dom Bedos de Celles, *L'Art du facteur d'orgues*, 3, 523, n.a.

characteristics which guided builders of the period under discussion should be reviewed.

First of all, the main case of a French organ was not subdivided.[6] Behind the carved front, dark and austere when compared to the brilliantly decorated cases in the lighter churches of northern Europe, the unpartitioned interior was closed from view by Montre pipes of tin.[7] This case, of which the smaller Positif-à-dos was a diminutive reflection, was always shallow and high, not unduly broad. Its sides, ceiling, and back served to define the space occupied by the pipes and chests, and to reflect sound. While its dimensions varied as the years progressed, there was apt to be a balanced relationship between the internal tonal structure of the organ and the visual effect of the case itself as a piece of furniture in the church. Thus the eye and the ear played important roles in determining the appropriate size for instruments.

Secondly, these conditions for development of the instrument within the space outlined by the main case, complemented by the Positif-à-dos, suggest correctly that the French classical organ did not consist of full and contrasting ensembles for each keyboard. Even the physically distinct Positif, which was an organ in itself, did not apparently function musically as a foil to other manual divisions in the same sense that we encounter it in northern European instruments. That is, the Positif was the concertino of the French organ, while the north European Rückpositiv had risen to the position of equal partnership in its relationship to the Hauptwerk.

The French organ grew beyond the earlier Italian one-manual Ripieno concept, but the notion was never discarded that it was founded primarily upon one plenum, located on the main manual —the Grand Plein Jeu. With the Positif always coupled into the

6. It was customary, on the other hand, in northern Europe to find instruments with partitioned interiors; the dimensions of the separate divisions corresponded very closely to the tonal plan of the organ, and each of the separate divisions, or ensembles, was controlled by its own keyboard. The contrast between the unsubdivided case typical of French classical organs and the carefully partitioned cases of northern Europe constitutes perhaps the most important basic difference in structural design between the two types.

7. See Fig. 9.

Grand Plein Jeu according to the notations of the composers, we can draw the same basic conclusion for the tonal structure of these instruments as we have already noted for the casework—namely, that the French organ was one ensemble, the north European several.

Finally, the visual appearance of the case was not altered by the addition of a third, fourth, or fifth manual keyboard. While one could often see the basic layout of north European organs in the fronts of their cases, manuals beyond the Grand Orgue and Positif in French organs were added mainly for convenience in changing sonorities. Indeed, the Récit and Echo were never complete in their compass, ranging from two to three octaves only.

The Plein Jeu

Among the many attributes which differentiate the sounds of classical French organs from other instruments built during the same period, the most singular is the Plein Jeu. As with the ancient stopless instruments of the fifteenth century, the Plein Jeu was the organ. The proliferation of registers contributing color, brilliance, or contrast, which were incorporated in the instrument from time to time, tended to become stabilized during the seventeenth century; and the use of colorful flute and reed stops occupied the attention of composers. But the Plein Jeu always remained, and still is, the sine qua non of the instrument.[8]

The ingredients of a Plein Jeu for an organ built upon a sixteen-foot Principal were:

Grand Orgue +	Positif
16 Montre	8 Montre
16 Bourdon	8 Bourdon
8 Montre	4 Prestant
8 Bourdon	2 Doublette
4 Prestant	Fourniture

8. One encounters organs built in the 20th century with alleged French characteristics—i.e. "French reeds," Cornets, wide scaled mutations, etc., included in a specification and design that could not be less "French." But where is a modern organ with a classical French Plein Jeu?

2 Doublette	Cymbale
Fourniture	
Cymbale	

For a somewhat smaller instrument, the Montre 16′ of the Grand Orgue and Montre 8′ of the Positif were omitted, with appropriate adjustments to the mixtures. Otherwise, the Plein Jeu was the same. For even the smallest organs, reductions would be made down to a one-manual instrument without Positif, for which the Plein Jeu would consist of:[9]

8 Bourdon
4 Prestant
2 Doublette
Cymbale

Extra stops in such an instrument would be cut down to a minimum in order to preserve the integrity of the essential Plein Jeu.

The use of Bourdons and Flûtes at the fundamental pitches (16′ and 8′) in the plan of the Plein Jeu stemmed from the southern Netherlands but had its historical origins in the doubled principal ranks of the ancient Fournitures. When these Fournitures were rebuilt with registers, the doubled ranks had been replaced by Bourdons. Almost never, from the end of the sixteenth century (Gisors) to the end of the classical period, were the Bourdons excluded from the Plein Jeu.[10]

The classical Plein Jeu[11] was the trademark of French organs; and the stability of the instrument through such a long period was possible only in the context of the perfectly balanced plan of this plenum. As long as no disturbing tendencies upset this structural concept, which depended upon the delicate relationships between

9. See Dom Bedos, *L'Art du facteur d'orgues*, 3, 496.

10. An exception was the "plain jeu" for the organ of Rodez Cathedral, 1627, which was described in the contract as containing only the narrow-scale stops. See Dufourcq, *Documents inédits*, 1, 167–69, Doc. 247.

11. The spelling "plein" (full) is a corruption of the ancient "plain," which meant "unified," or "balanced,"

fundamental pitches and certain stressed overtones in the ensemble, there could be a degree of flexibility exercised in the use of the "jeux de détail," the mutations and reed stops. Also, the classical plan was not compromised by other variable factors, such as wind pressure, scaling and voicing, and pitch,[12] so long as reasonable limits were respected.

Some French builders early in the seventeenth century had experimented with the use of Tierce ranks intended for the Plein Jeu. These were separate, narrow-scale stops made of tin. However, the strong French predilection for wide-scale Tierces won the day. Before Racquette provided Mersenne with his renowned lists of registrations for the *Harmonie universelle* (1636), at least two examples of organs with Tierce Pleins Jeux existed in Paris:

> Minutier Central Fonds XXVI, No. 53, 23 Janvier 1628, as quoted in P. Brunold, *Le Grand Orgue de Saint-Gervais de Paris*, Paris, 1934: Fault faire un Jeu de tierce En la place du flajeollet Laquelle sera faicte destain et qui sera ouverte pour servir a mettre dans le plein Jeu.

> Arch. nat., Minutier central, XC, 37, 20 Juillet 1632, as quoted in P. Hardouin, "Le Doyen des buffets d'orgues parisiens," *L'Orgue*, No. 110, 1964, p. 58: Item ung jeu de Tierce dont le corps sera d'estain . . . lesd. jeux susnommez serviront pour le plain je. [In the same instrument, there was also a wide-scale Tierce]: Item une tierce de grosse taille faicte de plomb.

The balance of the Plein Jeu depended not only upon the use of 16′ pitch along with 8′ for fundamental,[13] and the vertical strength of the 4′ and 2′ principals, but especially upon the composition

12. Fellot concludes that slightly higher wind pressure in France may have been employed because of the different technique of voicing. Whereas the Germans used "open toe" voicing, the French did not. The pitch of 17th- and 18th-century organs was generally about a whole tone lower than today's standard.

13. I.e. for organs equipped with Bourdon 16′, or Bourdon and Montre 16′, on the Grand Orgue.

of the Fourniture and Cymbale,[14] which supplied both brilliance and stability to all ranges of the keyboard. The Fourniture and Cymbale of the Grand Orgue and Positif were designed to complement each other: the omission of either one would have spoiled the Plein Jeu. Only in small organs was a single mixture (Cymbale) considered sufficient.

The plan for these mixtures offered by Dom Bedos demonstrates the general approach used by most classical French builders for many decades before the publication of *L'Art du facteur d'orgues*. Since it is the simplest and most accessible explanation of what classical Fournitures and Cymbales were like, I give it here. If the actual Pleins Jeux in surviving instruments from the seventeenth and eighteenth centuries do not uniformly bear out every detail of Dom Bedos' recommendations, they will express, often in more complicated patterns, the same general objectives. At no time in the organ's history have builders shown a consistent inclination to copy the mixture dispositions laid out by their predecessors, for here is one of those areas where the artist-builder feels free to move about imaginatively.

Dom Bedos outlined a relation between the number of ranks for the Fourniture and the Cymbale; that is, they were sometimes equal in number, or the Cymbale had one or two fewer than the Fourniture (but never more).[15]

14. With respect to the attitudes of builders on the subject of mixture composition, an entertaining comment is found in the contract for rebuilding the organ for the church of Saint-Vivien, Rouen, in 1659:

"Plus, il faut faire un jeu de fourniture de quatre tuyaux sur marche d'octave en octave, les corps d'estain et les piedz d'estoffe à la place de celle qui y est laquelle ne vaut rien a raison qu'elle est plene d'unissons. Plus, un jeu de cymballe de trois tuyaux sur marche de quarte en quarte, les corps d'estain et les piedz d'estoffe à la place de celle qui y est la quelle ne vaut rien. [Further, a fourniture must be made with four ranks using octave repetitions, the pipe bodies of tin and feet of common metal, in place of the one there at present, which is worthless, because it is full of unisons. Further, a cymballe stop with three ranks and fifth repetitions, the bodies of tin and feet of common metal, in place of the present one which is worthless]" (quoted from Dufourcq, *Documents inédits*, 2, 222, Doc. 286).

15. The Cymbale with nine ranks recommended by Dom Bedos for a large organ with Montre 32′ on the Grand Orgue is a theoretical exception to this rule, which shows an expansion of the theory apparently never put into practice. At times the resources of the Fourniture and Cymbale were combined on one register, as the Plein

Only unisons and fifth-sounding overtones were employed in the Plein Jeu, a rule followed by all French builders from the mid-seventeenth century.[16] A pitch ceiling of $\frac{1}{8}'$ (fifth C for a 2' stop) was not exceeded. The Cymbales could be expected to have a lower pitch range than their northern counterparts, and generally repeated in fifths and fourths. The Fournitures, on the other hand, starting at lower pitch levels than the Cymbales, were repeated at the octave, and much less frequently.

Within the compositions of Fourniture and Cymbale given in Table 11 for a large organ with Montre 32'[17] are contained all the necessary mixture compositions for smaller organs. These may be found by counting the appropriate number of ranks, starting with the highest in pitch (right to left) for each mixture. The recommended number of ranks for each mixture for various sizes of instruments appears in the sample specifications, in the third volume of Dom Bedos' treatise.[18]

According to Bedos' system of breaks, the Fourniture and Cymbale of the Grand Orgue in an instrument based upon a Montre 16' would be five ranks each. Their compositions are shown in Table 12. For the composition of the mixtures of the Positif, the same method would be used, with the results shown in Table 13.

For an "ordinary" organ with Montre 8' (plus Bourdon 16'),[19] the Fourniture of the Grand Orgue is given four ranks, the Cymbale three. Thus, as can be seen from Table 13, in the analysis of the Positif mixtures with the same number of ranks, the Fourniture retains harmonics of the 16' series from f' ($5\frac{1}{3}'$ is the third harmonic of the 16' series). But, it will be noticed, for a "small 8'" organ,[20]

Jeu VII in the Positif of the organ in the Cathedral of Poitiers (1791). See Fellot, *L'Orgue classique*, pp. 55–56. For more extended discussion of mixture compositions in old French organs, see also J.-A. Villard, "Qui était Francois-Henri Clicquot?" *Bull. Assoc. F.-H. Clicquot*, No. 1–2 (1962–63), pp. 13–32.

16. A recently discovered exception to this rule is the organ of Gimont, built by Godefroid Schmidt in 1772, for which a Tierce Cymbale was used in the Grand Orgue. (See Fellot, p. 51.)

17. See Dom Bedos, *L'Art du facteur d'orgues, 1*, Pl.17.

18. Ibid., *3*, 489–96.

19. Ibid., p. 493.

20. Ibid., p. 494.

TABLE 11. Breakdown of Fourniture and Cymbale for 32' Organ as Described by Dom Bedos (Pl. 17)

Fourniture VII

C (key 1)	$4'—2\frac{2}{3}'—2'—1\frac{1}{3}'—1'—\frac{2}{3}'—\frac{1}{2}'$
f (key 18)	$8'—5\frac{1}{3}'—4'—2\frac{2}{3}'—2'—1\frac{1}{3}'—1'$
f' (key 30)	$16'—10\frac{2}{3}'—8'—5\frac{1}{3}'—4'—2\frac{2}{3}'—2'$

Cymbale IX

C	$4'—2\frac{2}{3}'—2'—1\frac{1}{3}'—1'—\frac{2}{3}'—\frac{1}{2}'—\frac{1}{3}'—\frac{1}{4}'$
c	$5\frac{1}{3}'—4'—2\frac{2}{3}'—2'—1\frac{1}{3}'—1'—\frac{2}{3}'—\frac{1}{2}'—\frac{1}{3}'$
f	$8'—5\frac{1}{3}'—4'—2\frac{2}{3}'—2'—1\frac{1}{3}'—1'—\frac{2}{3}'—\frac{1}{2}'$
c'	$10\frac{2}{3}'—8'—5\frac{1}{3}'—4'—2\frac{2}{3}'—2'—1\frac{1}{3}'—1'—\frac{2}{3}'$
f'	$16'—10\frac{2}{3}'—8'—5\frac{1}{3}'—4'—2\frac{2}{3}'—2'—1\frac{1}{3}'—1'$
c''	$21\frac{1}{3}'—16'—10\frac{2}{3}'—8'—5\frac{1}{3}'—4'—2\frac{2}{3}'—2'—1\frac{1}{3}'$
f''	$32'—21\frac{1}{3}'—16'—10\frac{2}{3}'—8'—5\frac{1}{3}'—4'—2\frac{2}{3}'—2'$

TABLE 12. Composition of Grand Orgue Fourniture
and Cymbale for Montre 16', According to Dom Bedos

Fourniture V

C	2'—1⅓'—1'—⅔'—½'
f	4'—2⅔'—2'—1⅓'—1'
f'	8'—5⅓'—4'—2⅔'—2'

Cymbale V

C	1'—⅔'—½'—⅓'—¼'
c	1⅓'—1'—⅔'—½'—⅓'
f	2'—1⅓'—1'—⅔'—½'
c'	2⅔'—2'—1⅓'—1'—⅔'
f'	4'—2⅔'—2'—1⅓'—1'
c''	5⅓'—4'—2⅔'—2'—1⅓'
f''	8'—5⅓'—4'—2⅔'—2'

TABLE 13. Composition of Positif Mixtures for 16'
Organ, According to Dom Bedos

Fourniture IV

C	1⅓'—1'—⅔'—½'
f	2⅔'—2'—1⅓'—1'
f'	5⅓'—4'—2⅔'—2'

Cymbale III

C	½'—⅓'—¼'
c	⅔'—½'—⅓'
f	1'—⅔'—½'
c'	1⅓'—1'—⅔'
f'	2'—1⅓'—1'
c''	2⅔'—2'—1⅓'
f''	4'—2⅔'—2'

the Fourniture of the Grand Orgue has dropped to three ranks,
which accommodates it to a Plein Jeu having no Bourdon 16'.

A most important feature of the classic French Fournitures and
Cymbales was their habitual accommodation of harmonics of both
the 16' and 8' series and of the 32' series where appropriate. This
was proven not only in the remarks of Dom Bedos, written late in
the eighteenth century, but in the oldest known examples of
seventeenth-century Pleins Jeux still surviving into the post-World

War II era. In the instrument at the Church of Saint-Sauveur du Petit-Andely, built in 1674 by R. Ingout, the composition of all the mixtures of the Grand Orgue and Positif corresponded exactly to the recommendations of Dom Bedos written a century later.

A few years later, Jean de Joyeuse constructed the renowned instrument of the Cathedral of Auch (1688), which survived "restoration" until the 1950s. At that time the builder Gonzalez replaced and respecified the entire Plein Jeu, evoking outraged cries from those interested in preserving intact France's most important organ monument from the seventeenth century. The composition of the original Plein Jeu of the Grand Orgue at Auch was given by Dufourcq in 1934 [21] (see Table 14).

TABLE 14. Composition of the Original Fourniture and Cymbale of the Grand Orgue at Auch, 1688

Fourniture VI

C	$2'—1\frac{1}{3}'—1'—\frac{2}{3}'—\frac{1}{2}'—\frac{1}{3}'$
F#	$2\frac{2}{3}'—2'—1\frac{1}{3}'—1'—\frac{2}{3}'—\frac{1}{2}'$
c	$4'—2\frac{2}{3}'—2'—1\frac{1}{3}'—1'—\frac{2}{3}'$
f#	$5\frac{1}{3}'—4'—2\frac{2}{3}'—2'—1\frac{1}{3}'—1'$
c'	$8'—5\frac{1}{3}'—4'—2\frac{2}{3}'—2'—1\frac{1}{3}'$
f#'	$10\frac{2}{3}'—8'—5\frac{1}{3}'—4'—2\frac{2}{3}'—2'$

Cymbale IV

C	$\frac{2}{3}'—\frac{1}{2}'—\frac{1}{3}'—\frac{1}{4}'$
F#	$1'—\frac{2}{3}'—\frac{1}{2}'—\frac{1}{3}'$
c	$1\frac{1}{3}'—1'—\frac{2}{3}'—\frac{1}{2}'$
f#	$2'—1\frac{1}{3}'—1'—\frac{2}{3}'$
c'	$2\frac{2}{3}'—2'—1\frac{1}{3}'—1'$
f#'	$4'—2\frac{2}{3}'—2'—1\frac{1}{3}'$
f#''	$5\frac{1}{3}'—4'—2\frac{2}{3}'—2'$

It is not unusual that the Fourniture would be given more numerous breaks than would be possible under the ancient system of octave repetitions recommended by Dom Bedos and doubtless carried out in many earlier instruments. This was accomplished by the introduction of fifth repetitions to the Fourniture, as in

21. See Dufourcq, *Esquisse* (as recorded by Gonzalez).

Auch (1688). The result was that the Fourniture departed in the bass from a higher pitch ceiling ($\frac{1}{3}'$ instead of $\frac{1}{2}'$), but arrived at the same arrangement at the top of the compass. The introduction of a break in the first octave of the Fourniture for the Grand Orgue at Auch, necessitated by the "plagale" system of repetitions, changed the harmonic plan of the bass octave in that the twelfth ($2\frac{2}{3}'$) entered very early. This narrow-scale twelfth, which was not favored as a separate register in France, normally did not figure at all in the bass octave or octave and a half of the classic Plein Jeu.[22]

The compositions of Fournitures and Cymbales tended to give strength and clarity to the low range of the Plein Jeu by stressing unison pitches and high mutations (Dom Bedos started a 16' Plein Jeu with 16', 16', 8', 8', 4', 2', 2', $1\frac{1}{3}'$, 1', 1', $\frac{2}{3}'$, $\frac{2}{3}'$, $\frac{1}{2}'$, $\frac{1}{2}'$, $\frac{1}{3}'$, $\frac{1}{4}'$). Assuming that the medium range[23] was ideally arranged, the treble tended to be given an extraordinarily large number of doubled ranks; nor were the pitches in the treble pushed as high as possible. Indeed, the Cymbale tended merely to double the pitches already given to the Fourniture for the top octave or even two octaves of the keyboard. Thus, in the top section of the keyboard, the Cymbale provided stability rather than brilliance.[24]

The breaks in mixtures, while they were necessary in order to stay within practical pitch levels, provided the opportunity for stabilizing and enriching certain ranges of the keyboard which would otherwise have been wanting, due to the limitations of the medium. The more remarkable it is, then, that within the extremely wide range of possibilities open to builders for treatment of mixtures, there was little tendency from the mid-seventeenth to the late eighteenth century in France to redefine the nature of Fourni-

22. See below, Table 15, the composition of the Plein Jeu for the organ at Saint-Maximin, where the $2\frac{2}{3}'$ starts in the Grande Fourniture II at low C! In this instance the $2\frac{2}{3}'$ could be put on or off without disturbing the Plein Jeu.

23. Fellot calls this central section "la bonne région."

24. The time-honored practice of multiple doublings of pitches, dating back to the Gothic Blockwerk (see Table 1), may be explained in the tendency of large Gothic churches to absorb high frequencies. For additional information, see Poul-G. Andersen, *Orgelbogen* (Copenhagen, 1955), pp. 69 ff.; and Christhard Mahrenholz, *Die Orgelregister* (Kassel, 1930), pp. 215 ff.

tures and Cymbales or to reassess the manner in which they contributed to the elegance of the Plein Jeu.

Proof of the ability of imaginative builders to work within the boundaries of the classic Plein Jeu can still be tested in the noble instrument of Jean-Esprit Isnard, built for the Church of Saint-Maximin (Var), 1772–73. The provision of Fournitures Petites and Grandes with fifth repetitions adds flexibility to the usual scheme. Note the high pitch ceilings for the Cymbales.

The full view of Saint-Maximin's Plein Jeu, combining the resources of the Positif with those of the Grand Orgue, appears in Table 15.[25]

The Flutes

It has been made evident that the Bourdons 16′ and 8′ in the Grand Orgue always served to enrich the Plein Jeu. But equally essential were their functions as foundations for the chorus of flute stops. All the combinations of wide-scale stops, either on the Grand Orgue or the Positif (or the Echo, which occasionally contained separate ranks of flutes), commenced with the Bourdon 8′ as foundation, often combined on the Grand Orgue with the Bourdon 16′. It was generally true that each manual was provided with a Cornet, appearing either as a five-rank half stop or subdivided into its component pitches as separate registers: 8′, 4′, $2\frac{2}{3}$′, 2′, and $1\frac{3}{5}$′.[26] These were provided in flute scales on the Grand Orgue of large instruments, but the Positif and Echo usually depended upon some principal stops to fill out the series of pitches.

Two flute registers with pitches higher than those included in the Cornet were inherited from the sixteenth century—namely, the Larigot $1\frac{1}{3}$′, or Petit Nazard, and the Flageolet 1′, or Sifflet. While the Larigot was apt to be included in the Jeu de Tierce,[27] the

25. For particulars concerning this instrument, see Marie-Réginald Arbus, *Une Merveille d'art provençal* (Aix-en-Provence, 1955).

26. The Cornet V (as a rule 25 notes, from middle C) appeared on the Récit, Grand Orgue, and Echo, but only rarely on the Positif, and not until the 18th century. These were distinctively named, respectively, Cornet séparé (indicating a separate wind supply from that of the Grand Orgue), Grand Cornet, and Cornet d'Echo.

27. See below.

TABLE 15. Composition of the Complete Grand Plain Jeu at Saint-Maximin, 1773

Positif

Cymbale III	$\frac{1}{4}'$	$\frac{1}{2}'$	$\frac{2}{3}'$	$1\frac{1}{3}'$
	$\frac{1}{3}'$	$\frac{2}{3}'$	$1'$	$2'$
	$\frac{1}{2}'$	$1'$	$1\frac{1}{3}'$	$2'$
Fourniture III	$\frac{2}{3}'$	$1\frac{1}{3}'$	$2'$	$2\frac{2}{3}'$
	$1'$	$2'$	$2\frac{2}{3}'$	$4'$
	$1\frac{1}{3}'$	$2\frac{2}{3}'$	$4'$	$5\frac{1}{3}'$
	C	g	g′	g″

Doublette 2'
Prestant 4'
Bourdon 8'
Montre 8'

Grand Orgue

Cymbale IV	$\frac{1}{3}'$	$\frac{1}{2}'$	$\frac{2}{3}'$	$1'$	$1\frac{1}{3}'$	$2'$
	$\frac{1}{2}'$	$\frac{2}{3}'$	$1'$	$1\frac{1}{3}'$	$2'$	$2\frac{2}{3}'$
	$\frac{2}{3}'$	$1'$	$1\frac{1}{3}'$	$2'$	$2\frac{2}{3}'$	$4'$
	$1'$	$1\frac{1}{3}'$	$2'$	$2\frac{2}{3}'$	$4'$	$5\frac{1}{3}'$
Petite Fourniture IV	$\frac{1}{2}'$	$\frac{2}{3}'$	$1'$		$1\frac{1}{3}'$	$2'$
	$\frac{2}{3}'$	$1'$	$1\frac{1}{3}'$		$2'$	$2\frac{2}{3}'$
	$1'$	$1\frac{1}{3}'$	$2'$		$2\frac{2}{3}'$	$4'$
	$1\frac{1}{3}'$	$2'$	$2\frac{2}{3}'$		$4'$	$5\frac{1}{3}'$
Grande Fourniture II	$2'$	$2\frac{2}{3}'$	$4'$		$5\frac{1}{3}'$	$8'$
	$2\frac{2}{3}'$	$4'$	$5\frac{1}{3}'$		$8'$	$10\frac{2}{3}'$
	C	c	c′	a′	c″	g″

Prestant 4'*
Bourdon 8'
Montre 8'
Bourdon 16'
Montre 16'

* The omission of the Doublette 2' is not typical.

Flageolet had all but disappeared from use by the second half of the seventeenth century.[28]

28. It is significant to notice that the pitch ceiling firmly established for overtones employed in the Fourniture and Cymbale was exceeded in both the Larigot and Flageolet. Thus it is quite evident that considerations of musical texture were very strong in influencing the organ builders' choices in the delicate matter of pitch.

Around 1660, builders began to favor the use of mutation ranks which strengthened the 16′ fundamental. The first to appear was the Double Tierce $3\frac{1}{5}'$,[29] but the completion of the 16′ series of harmonics with the Nazard $5\frac{1}{3}'$ did not apparently occur until the eighteenth century, notwithstanding the fact that a "Gros Nasard" had been mentioned by Mersenne in 1636.

Thus, just as the Plein Jeu consisted of an orderly and systematic arrangement of diapason stops made of tin, from the Montre 16′ to the Cymbale, reinforced by the flute fundamentals, so also the Jeux Flûtés for each section of the organ were distributed with a rational grouping, or allocation, which emphasized the need for such arrangements in certain musical textures. The flute voices of the Grand Orgue were collectively referred to as the Grand Jeu de Tierce or the Jeu de Tierce du Grand Orgue; those of the Positif were the Petit Jeu de Tierce or the Jeu de Tierce du Positif. The Récit, with only twenty-five keys, was usually restricted to a Cornet V. But the Echo,[30] on the other hand, with the somewhat more distinctive role of a reflection of the Grand Orgue or Positif, was occasionally treated more generously. Perhaps its most expansive treatment is found in the contract signed in 1688 by Jean de Joyeuse, which specified the Echo with its own Plein Jeu and a complete Cornet décomposé, as well as a reed voice:

29. The term Grosse Tierce was also applied to the stop pitched at $3\frac{1}{5}'$. But some builders used this same name for the Tierce $1\frac{3}{5}'$, in order to differentiate it from the narrow scale seventeenth, as occasionally found in organs earlier in the century (Petite Tierce).

30. The Echo, located under the main chest like a north European Brustwerk, was never liberated, even though at certain moments it seemed to be on the verge of a new evolution. The unconventionally rich development of Auch's Echo cries for opening the casework with doors—an idea that did not seem to appeal to French builders. One is astonished, in the light of this story, to read a comment from Dijon, 1738, Saint-Nicolas: "d'enfermer le cornet d'écho pour l'éloigner et que la boette s'ouvre pour la rapprocher quand on voudra" (quoted from Jacques Gardien, *L'Orgue et les organistes en Bourgogne et en Franche-Comté au 18e siècle* [Paris, 1943], p. 48).

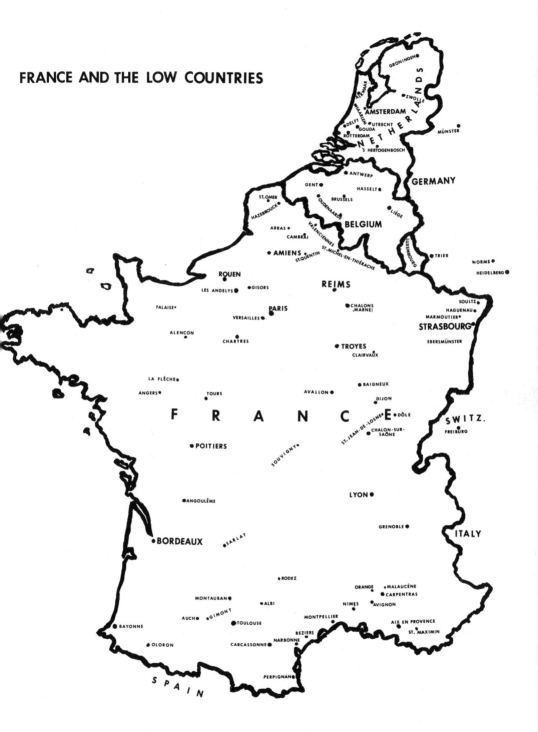

Fig. 1. Map of France and the Low Countries

Fig. 2. Saenredam painting of the interior of Bavokerk, Haarlem (1636), showing
Trompes (Bordunen)

Fig. 3. Nineteenth-century lithograph of the organ at Amiens Cathedral (1549)

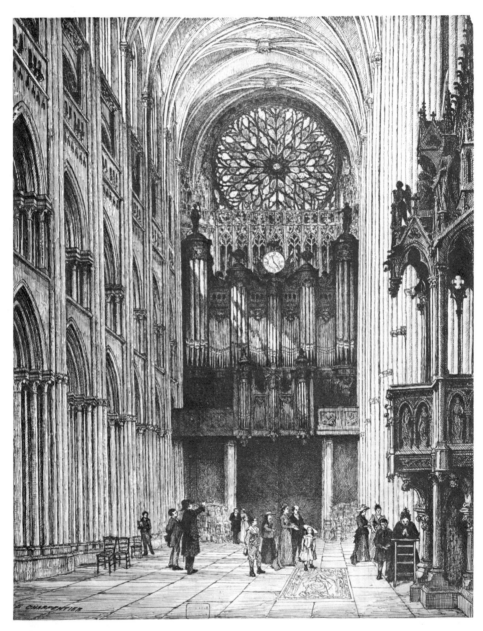

Fig. 4. Nineteenth-century print of the interior of Rouen Cathedral, looking west

Fig. 5. Early sixteenth-century organ case at Lorris-en-Gatinais (Loiret)

PROPOSITION XXXI.

Expliquer tous les Ieux tant simples que composez des Orgues les plus accomplis, & les plus grands qui se facent maintenant.

ENCORE que i'aye defia parlé des differens jeux de l'Orgue, neantmoins cette Propofition fuppleera ce qui pourroit auoir efté obmis, car elle contient la plus grande multitude des jeux, que les plus excellens Facteurs mettent dans les plus grands Orgues de l'Europe, quoy que les fiecles à venir puiffent en adioufter plufieurs autres, puis que l'imagination des hommes ne s'eft pas encore bornée en ce fuiet.

Or ie marque chaque Ieu par les lettres de l'Alphabet, afin qu'elles puiffent feruir pour entendre les jeux compofez que i'adioufte apres les jeux fimples, dont le premier, qui appartient au grand jeu, duquel nous parlerons premierement, s'appelle la Montre.

Table des fimples Ieux des grands Orgues.

A La Montre, dont le plus gros tuyau eft de feize pieds ouuerts, & confequemment le dernier, qui fait la Vingt-neufiefme auec le premier, a feulement vn pied de long: ils font tous d'eftain.

B Le Bourdon eft de huict pieds bouchez, & eft de bois, ou d'eftoffe, il fait l'vniffon auec la Montre, mais il eft plus doux, parce qu'il eft bouché.

C L'autre Bourdon eft de quatre pieds bouchez, ou de huict ouuerts en façon de fleute, il eft à l'Octaue des precedens, & peut eftre d'eftain, ou de bois.

D Le Preftant eft de quatre pieds ouuerts, à la Quinziefme de la Montre, ou de deux pieds bouchez; & s'appelle ainfi, parce qu'il fert à regler le ton de l'Orgue, à raifon qu'il eft proportionné à la voix des hommes.

E La Doublette eft de deux pieds ouuerts, à la Vingt-deuxiefme de la Montre.

F Le Flajollet eft d'vn pied ouuert, & eft à la Vingt-neufiefme de la Montre, il fe doit iouër tout feul naturellement auec le 4 pieds bouchez.

G Le Nazard eft d'enuiron cinq pieds ½, & eft bouché, ou à cheminée: il eft à la Douziefme de la Montre: & eft de plomb.

H Vn autre Nazard à l'Octaue du precedent, d'enuiron deux pieds & ½, bouché ou à cheminée.

I La Fleute d'Allemand a quatre pieds, & eft à cheminée, c'eft à dire que fon corps a deux groffeurs, dont l'vne commence à la bouche du tuyau, & finit au tiers de la longueur, iufques où il a la groffeur d'vn tuyau bouché de mefme longueur, & la cheminée a les deux autres tiers en longueur, & la groffeur de deux pieds ouuert. Or fi l'on fait cette Fleute de quatre pieds de long, le tiers du corps aura quatre pouces en diametre, & les deux autres tiers faits en cheminée auront deux pouces en diametre.

L La Tierce eft enuiron d'vn pied, fept pouces ouuerts, & eft à la Tierce du C fol, de deux pieds ouuerts.

M La fourniture a quatre tuyaux fur marche, dont le premier eft quafi d'vn pied & demy ouuert, le fecond eft d'vn pied en C fol, le troifiefme de huit

I i

Fig. 6. A page from Mersenne's *Harmonie universelle* (1636), the "Sixth Book of the Organ," revealing the omission of a Montre 8′ from the stop list of the Grand Orgue

Fig. 7. Title page of LeBègue's *Premier Livre des pièces d'orgue* (1676)

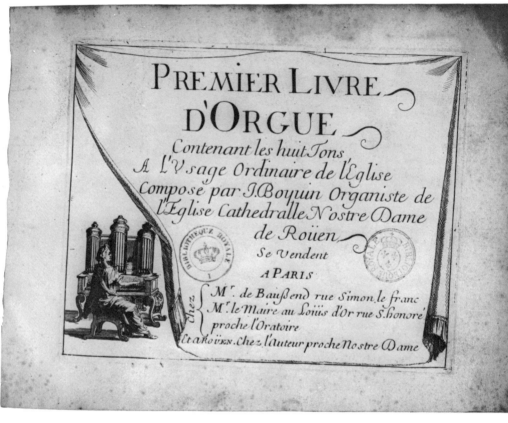

Fig. 8. Title page of Boyvin's *Premier Livre d'orgue* (1689)

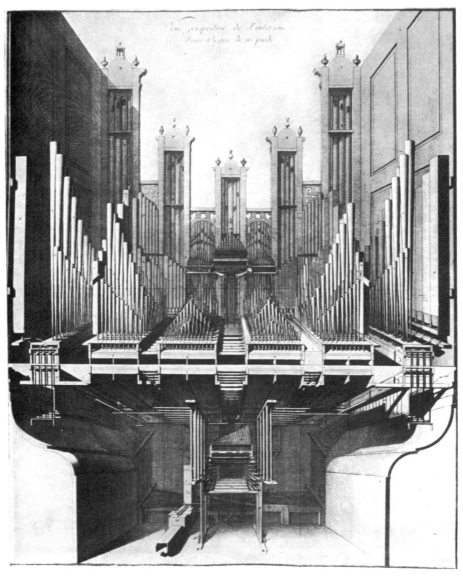

Fig. 9. The interior view of an organ based on a 16′ Montre, Pl. 50 from *L'Art du facteur d'orgues* (1766–70), by Dom Bedos de Celles

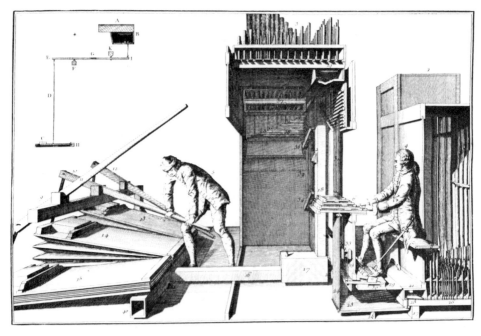

Fig. 10. From Dom Bedos, *Facteur d'orgues,* Pl. 52

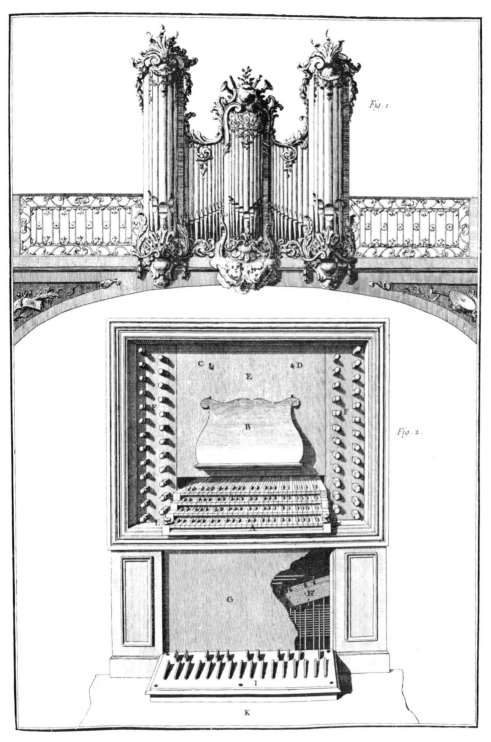

Fig. 11. Decorated case of a Positif and the console (fenêtre) with typical pedal keys, from Dom Bedos, *Facteur d'orgues,* Pl. 33

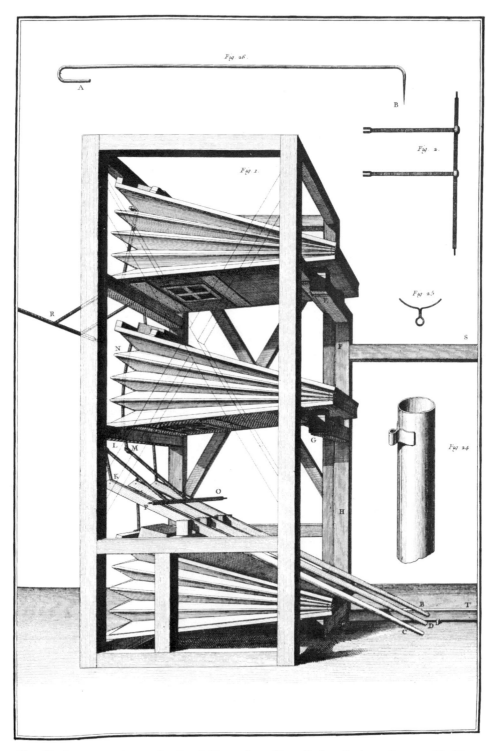

Fig. 12. An arrangement of splint bellows, from Dom Bedos, *Facteur d'orgues,* Pl. 75

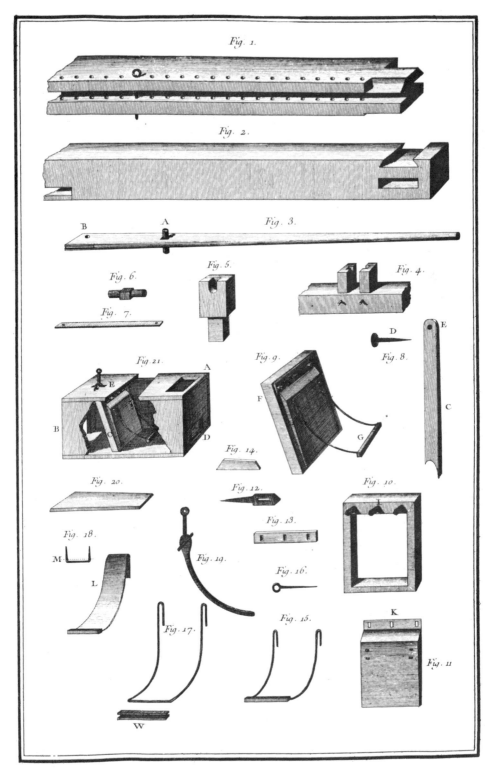

Fig. 13. Parts of the Tremblant doux (Figs. 9-21), from Dom Bedos, *Facteur d'orgues,* Pl. 49

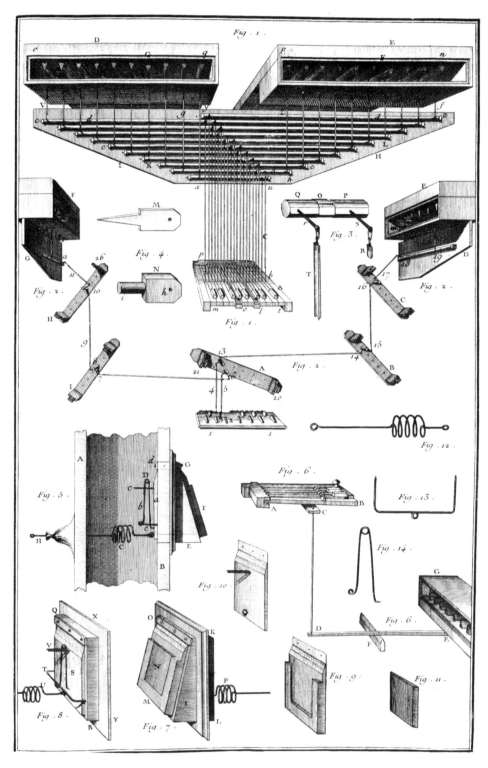

Fig. 14. Parts of the Tremblant fort (Figs. 5-12), from Dom Bedos, *Facteur d'orgues,* Pl. 46

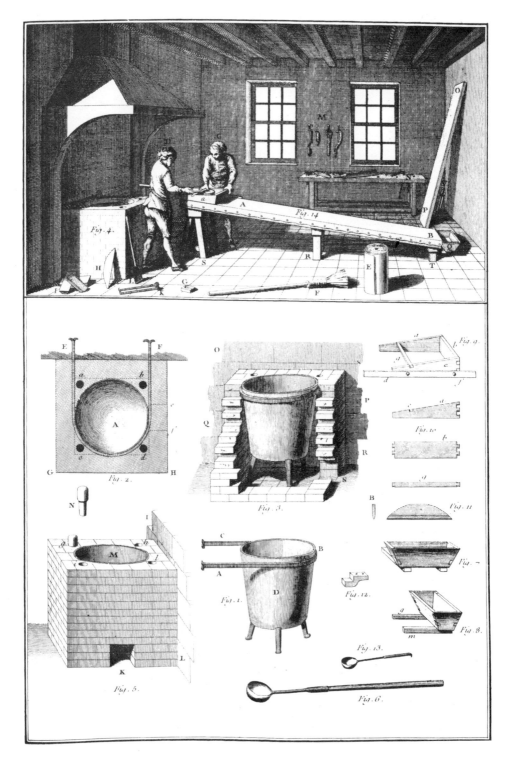

Fig. 15. Technique of pouring pipe metal, from Dom Bedos, *Facteur d'orgues*, Pl. 64

Fig. 16. The organ at Poitiers Cathedral, built by François-Henri Clicquot (1790)

Echo, 37 keys

Bourdon à cheminée
Prestan
Doublette
Nasard
Tierce
Fourniture III
Cymbale III
Voix humaine

It would not be expected that both the Grand Jeu de Tierce and the Petit Jeu de Tierce would be given a complete series of flute ranks, due to the limitations of size in divisions. The Prestant 4' and Doublette 2' of the Positif usually served dual functions, while the richest endowment of flutes was reserved for the Grand Orgue.

In Paris, in 1660, a new Grand Orgue built by Enoc for the Chapelle des Jacobins shows an extraordinarily lavish supply of flute colors[31] (see Table 16). The series is practically complete,

TABLE 16. Composition of the Grand Orgue, Chapelle des Jacobins, Paris, 1660

8 Montre	16 Bourdon	8 Trompette
4 Prestant	8 Bourdon	4 Clairon
2 Doublette	$3\frac{1}{5}$ Grosse Tierce	8 Cromorne
IV Fourniture	4 Flute	8 Voix humaine
III Cymbale	$2\frac{2}{3}$ Nasard	
	2 Quarte de nasard	
	$1\frac{3}{5}$ Tierce	
	$1\frac{1}{3}$ Larigot	
	1 Flageolet	

save only for the Gros Nasard $5\frac{1}{3}'$. The development of flute stops for the different sections of the organ over the entire period under discussion is neatly summed up by Fellot[32] (see Table 17). The

31. Quoted from Dufourcq, "Recent Researches into French Organ Building from the Fifteenth to the Seventeenth Century," *The Galpin Society Journal, 10* (May 1957), 72.
32. *L'Orgue classique*, p. 32.

TABLE 17. The Development of Flute Stops

Preclassical Distribution
(before the wide-scale Tierce, ca. 1630)

Grand Clavier	Positif	Pédale
8' Bourdon (Flûte in the Midi)	8' Bourdon	8' Flûte (12' and 16' in the Midi)
4' Flûte	4' Flûte allemande	4' Flûte
2⅔' Quinte-flûte	2⅔' Quinte-flûte	
2' Flageolet (or 1')	1⅓' Larigot (rare)	
1⅓' Larigot	Cornet (rare)	
1' Sifflet	Sesquialtera (very rare)	
Cornet à Boucquin V (dessus)		

First Classical Period
(*grand siècle*, before the appearance of *Dessus de Flûte* 8')

Grand Clavier	Positif	Récit
16' Bourdon	8' Bourdon	Cornet V
8' Bourdon	4' Flûte	
4' Flûte	2⅔' Nasard	**Echo**
3⅕' Double-Tierce (end 17th c.)	2' Quarte de nasard	Cornet V
2⅔' Nasard	1⅗' Tierce	
2' Quarte de nasard	1⅓' Larigot	**Pédale**
1⅗' Grosse Tierce		
1⅓' Larigot (rare)		8' Flûte (rarely 16', in Midi)
1' Sifflet or Flageolet		4' Flûte
Cornet V (dessus)		

After Louis XIV (1715)

Grand Clavier	Positif	Récit
16' Bourdon	8' Bourdon	Cornet V
8' Bourdon	8' Dessus de Flûte	
8' Dessus de Flûte	4' Flûte (very rare)	**Echo**
5⅓' Gros Nasard (ca. 1750, rare)	2⅔' Nasard	Cornet V
4' Flûte (rare)	2' Quarte de nasard (rare)	Flûte 8'
3⅕' Grosse Tierce	1⅗' Tierce	
2⅔' Nasard	1⅓' Larigot	
2' Quarte de nasard	Dessus de Cornet V (in large instruments)	**Pédale**
1⅗' Tierce		8' Flûte (16', rare at the end of 18th c.)*
1⅓' Larigot (very rare)		4' Flûte (Nasard, Quarte, rare)
Grand Cornet V		

* Flutes at 16' pitch were sometimes found in the south. But even Dom Bedos, who worked in that region, recommends them only for instruments with a 32' Grand Orgue.

gradual disappearance of the higher pitched flutes can be observed taking place during the course of the period of greatest stability. The 1′ was the first to go,[33] then the 1⅓′ Larigot dropped out of the Grand Orgue, and the Prestant 4′ and Doublette 2′ were required to serve the flute choruses more and more frequently.

The specification for the organ of the Chapelle de l'Ecole Militaire, Paris, 1772, built by Adrien L'Epine,[34] reveals the shift of interest in flute colors (see Table 18). The Bourdons, of course,

TABLE 19. Paris, Chapelle de L'Ecole Militaire, 1772, Builder: Adrien L'Epine

Grand Orgue, 51 keys

8′ Montre	8′ Dessus de flûte alle-	8′ Trompette
8′ Bourdon	mande (30 pipes)	4′ Clairon
4′ Prestant	2⅔′ Nazard	8′ Basson, or Voix hu-
2′ Doublette	2′ Quarte de nazard	maine allemande
IV Fourniture	1⅗′ Tierce	
IV Cymbale	V Cornet (two octaves)	

Récit

V Cornet
8′ Trompette

Positif

8′ Bourdon	8′ Dessus (39 pipes plus 12	8′ Cromorne
4′ Prestant	à cheminée or à fuseau)	8′ Hautbois (30 pipes,
2′ Doublette	2⅔′ Nazard	E to D)
III Fourniture	1⅗′ Tierce	
III Cymbale	1⅓′ Larigot	

Pédale, 34 keys (F to D)

8′ Flûte, 27 pipes
4′ Flûte, 27 pipes
8′ Trompette, 34 pipes
4′ Clairon, 34 pipes
Two tremblants, one strong and one weak.

33. By the mid-18th century the Sifflet 1′ was considered useless, as is shown in the language of the contract for rebuilding completely the organ at the church of Saint-Nicaise, Rouen, 1751: "la grosse range de fourniture de quarante huit tuyaux . . . laquelle sera posé à la place au jeu de siflet, jeu inutile, qui sera refondu" (quoted from Dufourcq, *Documents inédits*, 2, 362, Doc. 411).
34. Quoted from ibid., 2, 408–12, Doc. 437.

were always stopped.[35] But "Flûte" was also used for closed pipes. Until the introduction of the Dessus de Flûte 8', it was not customary for Flûtes 8' or 4' to be open. The Bourdons could have wooden basses and metal trebles, or the trebles could be à cheminée. The Flûte 4' was usually a chimney flute. The bass of the Nazard was apt to be stopped or à cheminée, while the trebles were tapered or open. Builders used common metal (étoffe) or lead for all metal flute pipes and even some principals, but the Montres were of tin. Flutes in the pedal were usually made of wood, but could be closed, à cheminée, or open.

Harmonic pipes have not been discussed here because they were not in general use in France during this period. But there is some indication of activity in this regard, extending from the mid-seventeenth century to Dom Bedos:

> Contract concerning the organ at Nîmes Cathédrale, 1643:[36] la neufièsme sera la fleute de huict piedz parlant de quatre et d'estophe.

> Organ of St. Cande le Vieil, Rouen, 1725:[37] plus de 2 bourdons de 4 pieds bouché et de 8 pieds en résonnance, d'une flute de 8 pieds bouché et de 4 pieds en résonnance.

> Dom Bedos, L'Art du facteur d'orgues, p. 51: Un autre Jeu à Bouche, qui n'est pas encore bien commun en France, c'est la basse de Viole, qu'on fait en étain, et auquel on donne toute l'étendue du Clavier. . . . C'est un 8 pieds pour la hauteur des tuyaux; mais pour la grosseur, on suit la taille du Prestant. Il est assez difficile de le mettre au point qu'il faut pour qu'il imite vraiment la basse de Viole. Quoique ce soit un 8 pieds, on le fait Octavier, & il parle à l'unisson du Prestant. [Another flue stop which is still not common in

---

35. At least, almost always. Cf. Dufourcq, Documents inédits, 2, 210, Doc. 281, Rouen Saint-Denis (1688): "(Pedalle) Un jeu de bourdon de huit pieds ouvert . . . le tout de bon bois de chesne"; p. 219, Doc. 284, Rouen Saint-Herbland (1685): "(Pedalle) un bourdon de huit pieds ouvert, tous de bois de chesne"; p. 361, Doc. 411, Rouen, Saint-Nicaise (1751): "Les quatre jeux seronts: bourdon de huit pieds ouvert."

36. See ibid., 2, 309, Doc. 361.

37. Ibid., 2, 345, Doc. 395.

France is the basse de Viole, made of tin and extending over
the whole keyboard. . . . It is 8′ according to pipe lengths;
but as to diameter, it follows a Prestant scale. It is rather
difficult to bring it to the point necessary for really imitating
a basse de Viole. Though it is 8′, it is made to speak the octave,
and sounds at the unison with the Prestant.]

The Reeds

Although reeds of many varieties had been in use in the sixteenth
century, a "classical" selection seemed to govern the choice of most
builders after the early part of the seventeenth century.

Grand Orgue: Trompette 8′, Clairon 4′, Voix humaine, 8′
Positif: Cromorne 8′
Récit: Trompette 8′ (occasionally)
Pédale: Trompette 8′

In some large instruments the Echo might have been supplied
with a Cromorne (cf. Saint-Louis-des-Invalides, Paris, 1679) or a
Voix humaine (Rodez Cathedral, 1676); and the Grand Orgue
might be given an extra Cromorne, and the Positif an extra Voix
humaine (Rouen Cathedral, 1689). But until the eighteenth century, the arrangement of reeds remained quite stable.

Practically all the music from the period fits the scheme just
mentioned: the full-length trumpets served in the manuals for
audacious melodies in the bass or soprano, or for the Grand Jeu;
the half-length Cromorne on the Positif functioned in ensemble as
an echo in the Grand Jeu and in melodies of a more contemplative
character (bass, tenor, or soprano); and the Voix humaine, one
quarter length or less, was always used with the Bourdon 8′ and
Tremblant doux in tender airs and chords. The Trompette de la
Pédale was invariably the most brilliant and penetrating, in order
that it might serve a primary function of sounding the *cantus firmus*
against the Plein Jeu as accompaniment. It is curious that the idea
of using 16′ reeds (cf. sixteenth century) did not seem to appeal to
builders until about 1690, when we have the earliest examples of
the Bombarde 16′. Indeed, in 1679 it appears that the renowned
LeBègue prevailed against the inclusion of a Trompette 16′ for the

organ built by Thierry at the Hôtel des Invalides, Paris:[38] "Pour la trompette de 16 p. comme ce jeu est inusité en France et fort grossier, lequel aussy ne se peut faire qu'avec une forte quantité d'étain, si on juge à propos de le supprimer et substituer à sa place une voix humaine cela ne seroit pas mal."

Eventually, the appeal of "les grandes batteries" brought more and more trumpets, so that a large instrument in the mid-eighteenth century could be expected to contain at least one trumpet 8' per keyboard. Furthermore, a fifth manual was added, the Bombarde, placed above the Grand Orgue and permanently coupled to it. At Saint-Gervais, Paris, 1768, this manual controlled only the single stop, Bombarde 16', while at Notre-Dame de Paris, 1733, François Thierry gave the Bombarde (operating for the Grand Orgue) four powerful reed voices:

16' Bombarde
8' Trompette
8' Trompette
4' Trompette

At Saint-Martin, Tours, LeFèbre built an immense instrument, which contained a Montre 32' on the Grand Orgue and complete families of Trompettes on both the Grand Orgue and the Bombarde manuals. "Les grandes batteries" for this organ included so many trumpets that they are best viewed in the context of the entire list of stops[39] (see Table 19).

The extravagant layout of the Tours instrument, with its over-supply of flutes and its congestion of trumpet stops, is typical of an important difference between the language of Dom Bedos in the late eighteenth century and that of the composers a hundred years earlier, both describing the proper combinations to use for certain musical textures. It is unquestionably true that organs built during the earlier period, which was more musically productive, were not saturated with either trumpets or flutes. The reader will be well advised to interpret Dom Bedos' words with a continuing reference to this rather marked contrast. A specification is found in Table 20

---

38. This portion of the text of LeBègue's letter is quoted from N. Dufourcq, *Nicolas LeBègue* (Paris, 1954), p. 57.

39. Specification given as quoted in Dufourcq, *Esquisse*, p. 437.

TABLE 19. Saint-Martin, Tours, 1761, Builder: J. B. N. LeFèbre

Grand Orgue (53 keys)

32′ Montre	8′ I Flûte	I Trompette
32′ Bourdon	8′ II Flûte	II Trompette
16′ Montre	5⅓′ Gros nasard	I Clairon
16′ Bourdon	2⅔′ Nasard	II Clairon
8′ Montre	Quarte de nasard	
8′ Bourdon	Grosse Tierce	
4′ Prestant	Tierce	
2′ Doublette	Larigot	
VI Grosse fourniture	Cornet	
V Petite fourniture		
IV Cymbale		

Bombarde

Bourdon	Cornet	Bombarde
Prestant		I Trompette
		II Trompette
		Clairon

Récit (32 keys)

Cornet	Trompette

Echo (29 keys)

Cornet

Positif

8′ Montre	Cornet	Trompette
16′ Bourdon	8′ I Flûte	Clairon
8′ Bourdon	8′ II Flûte	Voix humaine
4′ Prestant	Nasard	Cromorne
2′ Doublette	Quarte de nasard	
V Fourniture	Tierce	
IV Cymbale	Larigot	

Pedale (36 keys, including "ravalement")

16′ Flûte	4′ I Flûte	24′ Bombarde
8′ I Flûte	4′ II Flûte	I Trompette
8′ II Flûte	5⅓′ Gros nasard	II Trompette
	2⅔′ Petit nasard	I Clairon
	Quarte de nasard	II Clairon
	Grosse tierce	
	Petite tierce	

TABLE 20. Saint-Denis, Rouen, 1688–98, Builders: Clément
and Germain Lefebvre

Grand Orgue (48 keys)

16' Bourdon (2 octaves wood)	4' Flûte, stopped (common metal)	8' Trompette
8' Montre (tin)	2⅔' Nasard (metal)	4' Cleron
8' Bourdon (1 octave wood)	1⅗' Grosse tierce (metal)	8' Voix humaine
4' Prestant (tin)	V Cornet	
2' Doublette (tin)		
IV Fourniture	Two *tremblans*, *à vent doux* and *à vent perdu*	
III Cymbale		

Cornet de Récit (from middle C)

V Cornet	8' Trompette

Cornet d'Echo (from second F)

8' Bourdon	2⅔' Nasard	8' Cromorne
4' Prestant	1⅗' Tierce	8' Voix humaine
2' Doublette		
III Fourniture		

Pedalle (29 keys)

8' "Un jeu de bourdon de huit pieds ouvert" (wood)	8' Trompette
4' Flûte, open (1 octave wood)	

Positif (48 keys)

8' Bourdon (1 octave wood)	4' Flûte, stopped (common metal)	8' Cromorne
4' Prestant (tin)	2⅔' Nasard (metal)	
2' Doublette (tin)	2' Quarte de nasard (metal)	
III Fourniture	1⅗' Grosse tierce (metal)	
II Cymbale	1⅓' Larigot	

for a new organ for the Church of Saint-Denis in Rouen,[40] started
in 1688 but not completed until ten years later, when the organist
of the Cathedral, Jacques Boyvin, finally declared the terms of the
contract fulfilled. Doors were to be supplied for both the Grand
Orgue and Positif, with hinges for opening and closing, and painted
on the inside with fleurs-de-lis.

40. Taken from Dufourcq, *Documents inédits*, 2, 210, Doc. 281.

5. Registration in the Classical Period (1665–1770)

In order to gain a thorough understanding of the practical aspects of registration among French organists during the classical period we rely heavily on the prefaces which some composers included in their collections of organ music. These prefaces often give helpful instructions to the organist concerning the registration and stylistic performance of the pieces. In addition, several theoretical treatises written in this period give similar instructions for organists.

These two kinds of sources will provide our chief information about the registration of French organ music after Mersenne (1636) and before the Revolution (1789).[1] Listed together, the sources are these:

> Guillaume-Gabriel Nivers, Preface to *Premier Livre d'orgue*, 1665
> Nicolas LeBègue, Preface to *Premier Livre d'orgue*, 1676
> Anonymous text from *Second Livre d'orgue* of LeBègue, 1678
> Nicolas Gigault, Preface to *Livre de musique pour l'orgue*, 1685
> André Raison, Preface to *Livre d'orgue*, 1688
> Jacques Boyvin, Preface to *Premier Livre d'orgue*, 1689
> Gilles Juillien, Preface to *Livre d'orgue*, 1690
> Lambert Chaumont, Preface to *Livre d'orgue*, 1695
> Gaspard Corrette, Preface to *Messe du 8ᵉ ton*, 1703
> Anonymous text, "Anonyme de Tours," ca. 1710–20
> Michel Corrette, Preface to *Premier Livre d'orgue*, 1737
> Anonymous text, *La Manière très facile pour apprendre la facture d'orgue*, 1746 (Caen)
> Dom Bedos de Celles: *L'Art du facteur d'orgues*, 1766–70

1. Gravet points to an early 19th-century document of little importance here. See *L'Orgue*, No. 100, pp. 255 ff., in which is reprinted a section of Guillaume Lasceux, *Essai de théorique et pratique sur l'art de l'orgue*, 1809: "Mélange des Jeux, pour les différens morceaux que l'on traite sur l'orgue." These instructions merely reflect the breakdown of the classical style in an unproductive period.

A span of almost three decades will be noticed from the time of Mersenne's treatise to that of Nivers' preface. It was during this period that the gradual adoption of a "new" style of composition took place, modeled after the lute and harpsichord techniques being developed by the Gaultiers and de Chambonnières. But this new melodic style was not entirely new, and its appearance did not mean that the older polyphonic style was completely forgotten. In the registrations of Mersenne, and those of the sixteenth century as well, there was evidence of a melodic style. And music with polyphonic texture was still being written late in the seventeenth century. If Racquette, in the early seventeenth century, composed a dozen duets for the organ, a "new" technique which remained very popular until the end of the eighteenth century, we must also take notice of the *Fugues and Caprices* of François Roberday (1660), which seem not at all related to the new, decorative French style, but rather reminiscent of Froberger's pieces, or even Frescobaldi's.[2] In the meantime, Louis Couperin, pupil of the great harpsichordist Chambonnières, was composing organ pieces and little dances in the new fashion as early as 1650.

Although there is little information contributing to our knowledge of the habits of French organ players in registering music during these thirty years, some interesting observations are found in Trichet's *Traité des instruments de musique* (ca. 1640).[3] Trichet takes Mersenne to task for suggesting that the organ, being the most nearly perfect of instruments, should plead for a new invention which would make it possible for the pipes to speak vowel and consonant sounds. Trichet's purpose is not to invent but merely to understand a complex musical instrument:

> Does it not suffice to have found a way that in the same organ may be heard something more than thirty different kinds of registrations and several hundred pipes all sounding different, but nevertheless in tune with each other? One can hear the

2. It should not go unnoticed that Froberger spent two years in Paris, 1652–53.

3. See Pierre Trichet, *Traité des instruments de musique* (Neuilly-sur-Seine, 1957). Refer also to the "Mémoire pour tirer des jeux de mustation" (ca. 1660), from Saint Bavo Church, Ghent, which is given a thorough-going analysis by Vente in *Die brabanter Orgel*, pp. 163–64.

song of the lark, the twittering of the nightingale, the drone of the pedals ("bourdonnement"), the noise of drums, trumpet fanfares, the echoing of clerons, the clanking of cymbals, the tolling of bells, the buzzing ("nazardement"), the grating sound of the régales or voix humaines; in short the sound of almost all musical instruments, such as the playing of soft flutes, fifes, flageolets, arigots [kind of fife], oboes, bassons, cornets, cromornes, musettes, violins, with the stops montre, prestant, doublette, tiercette, gros bourdon, petit and fort nazard, otherwise called jeu renversée [cf. Mersenne]. To this the tremblant may be added, which is not a real stop, just as black and white are not true colors, but can be combined with other colors giving them a new luster and diversity. All these stops can be heard in many ways, or all together if desired, or by combining them and separating them alternately.

We can also gather some information for this period from the titles of organ pieces, which often prescribed their registration. Gravet points to two undated, anonymous manuscripts which contain pieces with titles indicating registrations.[4] More pertinent, however, are the titles of a number of dated organ works by Louis Couperin, recently discovered by Guy Oldham in London.[5] When these pieces are finally released to the public, Louis Couperin will take his proper place in the front line of composers who contributed to the important stylistic development of the mid-seventeenth century. It is reassuring to observe that Couperin's registrations, judging from the titles, must not have differed radically from those of Nivers in 1665:

No. 20 Fugue sur le Cromhorne (1656)
No. 29 Fugue quil fault Jouer dun mouvement fort lent sur la tierce du Grand Clavier avec le tremblant lent (1665)
H 1 Fantaisie sur le Jeu des haubois (1654)
H 2 Fantaisie sur le mesme Jeu (1654)

4. These are: a manuscript found in the Bibliothèque Sainte-Genevieve, and another from the Bibliothèque de Tours, No. 825. See Gravet, p. 215.

5. The titles are given in Guy Oldham, "Louis Couperin, a New Source of French Keyboard Music of the Mid-Seventeenth Century," *Recherches* (1960), pp. 51–59.

No. 57 Fantaisie sur le Cromhorne (1665)

No. 58 Fantaisie sur La tierce du Grand Clavier avec le tremblant Lent

No. 63 Fugue sur la tierce du Grand Clavier (1656)

No. 64 Fugue sur La tierce (1657)

No. 65 Fugue sur le Cromhorne (1658)

We turn now to the period following these thirty years for which there is relatively little information. As we shall see, the prefaces and treatises already listed provide a large body of information pertinent to registration and musical style. There are, however, two other areas from which related information can be drawn: the music itself, and contracts for organs built in this period.

As in the music of Louis Couperin mentioned above, we find that in all the organ music of this period the title (or subtitle) of a piece is often an indication of its proper registration. Occasionally the titles provided options with respect to choice of stops, such as: "Concert de Flûtes, ou Fond d'orgue," "Basse et dessus de Trompette ou de Cornet séparé, en Dialogue," or "Récit grave de Nazar, ou de Tierce, ou de Cromorne." The most usual titles, such as Grand Jeu, Fugue, Tierce, Flageolet, Basse de Trompette, and so on, are explained, often at some length, in the prefaces written by the composers, as well as in the theoretical treatises which discuss organ registration. Occasionally, though, we find an unusually specific or different title. Only the unusual indications need now draw our attention individually, and these are quite rare:

> Nivers (1667): "La Prose de la feste du très sainct Sacrement"; "Sit laus plena" with Petit Plein-Jeu vs. Dessus de Trompette; "Dogma datur," with Plein-Jeu (Petit) vs. Basse de grosse Tierce; "Laudis Thema," with Basse de Trompette accompanied with Plein-Jeu. More examples of the same registrations in the same book (II).

> Boyvin (1689): "Petit Dialogue en Fugue sans Tremblant."

> François Couperin (1690): "Dialogue sur les Trompettes, Clairon et Tierces du G.C. Et le bourdon avec le larigot du positif," and again: "Dialogue sur la Trompette du grand Clavier, et sur la montre, le bourdon, et le nazard du positif."

DeGrigny (c. 1700): Fugues à 5, indicating the two highest voices for the right hand on the Cornet, the next two for the left hand on the Cromorne, and Pédalle. Also, note: "Dialogue à deux tailles de Cromorne et deux dessus de Cornet," the same registration being used for a different musical texture.

Daquin: "Noel sur les jeux d'anches sans tremblant"; "Noel en Musette, en dialogue, et en duo," with indication in the score for the left hand on "Cromhorne avec le Bourdon."

Dandrieu (1739): "Duo en cors de chasses sur la Trompète."

Alongside the registrations with which the composers titled their pieces, we frequently find directions about the interpretation of the works. These interpretive aids, extremely valuable if they originate from the composer, are far too numerous to list completely.[6] Here are a few examples:

Boyvin: "Dessus de Tierce en vitesses et accords"
Raison: "Petit plein jeu: legèrement"
DuMage: "Duo: fort gai"
Dandrieu: "Fugue: majesteusement"
              "Duo: gaiment et flaté"
              "Tierce en taille: fièrement"
Jullien: "Cromorne en taille: gravement"

In addition, one occasionally finds hints about the application of notes inégales, such as:

Dandrieu: "Musète: naïvement et louré"
              "Dialogue: gravement et pointé"
Jullien: "Fugue renversée: gravement, sans pointer les croches"

Even more arresting is the instruction given by Nivers in his second book (1667), in which he distinctly directs the player to change style according to his option for registration:

Nivers: "Couplet en Récit de Voix Humaine, gravement: ou de Cromhorne, plus légèrement"

6. See Appendix C, where particular attention is directed to the remarks on interpretation by LeBègue, Raison, Chaumont, G. Corrette, and Dom Bedos, showing a sensitive balance between performing style and registration.

Finally, one must note inconsistencies in nomenclature, which could lead to incorrect interpretation in terms of registration. For instance, what Nivers called "Fugue grave" does not correspond in musical texture to Couperin's "Fugue," or to the "Fugue grave" for which Dom Bedos counsels the use of trumpet reeds. The Nivers "Fugues," and possibly also the Louis Couperin "Fantaisies" and "Fugues," would be better recognized today as "Récits de Cornet," "Récits de Voix humaine," and so on. Here are some examples:[7]

> Nivers (1667): "Fugue grave sur le sujet de l'hymne précé-
> dente, en Récit de Voix humaine"
> "Fugue . . . en Récit de Cromhorne"
> "Fugue," indications in score for "Jeu doux"
> and "Basse de Trompette"

In the category of builders' contracts for instruments, we have already noticed the early habit to list stops in groups, especially those belonging to the Plein Jeu.[8] It hardly needs to be mentioned that the best builders must have been constantly sensitive to the particular needs of musical textures. Indeed, the system provided that the musicians would have the last word, as we have already observed[9] at Saint-Denis, Rouen, where Boyvin withheld approval of the organ for ten years after the signing of the contract. Contracts often included references to musical textures which would be served by certain orders of stops or by careful voicing of families. Comments of this kind do not provide us with a fundamental under-

---

7. In the Schola Cantorum edition of Nivers' *Second Book* (1667), annotated by Dufourcq, one encounters a host of outlandish suggestions for the registrations of these "Fugues," which are confusing enough in themselves. Fugal registrations such as those listed below in that edition are without historical foundation:

> Grand Plein-Jeu, Anches Récit ("Offerte en fugue . . .")
> Fonds 8
> Fonds 8-4-2
> Montre 8
> Principaux 8-4-2
> Fonds 8-4
> 8-2
> Principaux 8

8. See Dufourcq, *Documents inédits:* Doc. 182 (1614), 187 (1632), 206 (1580), 212 (1624), 215 (1629), 247 (1627), 287 (1659), 309 (1649), 310 (1658), and 313 (1679).

9. See above, p. 92.

standing of habits of registration, but they are a valuable supplement to the primary sources. Here are some examples:[10]

> 1586, Couvent des Augustins:[11] une flutte de six piedz, bouchée, pour jouer avec le jeu de cornetx.

> 1629, Tréguier, Cathédrale:[12] Plus une flutte sonnant quatre pieds, pour servir de flutte d'alleman faicte de plomb. Plus unne quinte flutte pour servir de nazart . . .

> 1632, St. Godard, Rouen:[13] Item, une quinte fluste, pour servir de nazard, de trois pieds. . . . Item, ung jeu de régalles pour servir de voix humaine.

> 1669, St.-Médéric, Paris:[14] Plus il faut faire un bon tremblant lent pour jouer les voix humaines.

> Early eighteenth century, Carpentras, Cathédrale:[15] On faira de plus un tremblant doux pour toucher avec la voix humaine.

> 1725, St.-Candle le Vieil, Rouen:[16] Sur ce qui a été répresenté de faire en neuf un cornet de recit de 5 tuyaux sur chaque touche et de 25 touches, lequel cornet sera d'un bonne harmonie convenable pour jouer le duo et les grands jeux.

Among France's great organ builders of the late seventeenth century, Jean de Joyeuse (ca. 1635–98) was perhaps the wordiest, and he also held the post of organist at the church of Saint-Nazaire, Carcassonne. His Parisian training and his musical background seemed to tempt him to pontificate in contracts for organs, all of which were built in the southern part of the country. Excerpts from some of his contracts, appearing below, hold special interest today to anyone interested in the historical relationship between

---

10. See also above, pp. 50–54, for comments about Nazards in contractual documents.

11. See Dufourcq, *Documents inédits*, *1*, 142, Doc. 222.

12. Ibid., *1*, 133, Doc. 215.

13. Ibid., *1*, 111, Doc. 187.

14. Arch. nat., Min., cent., CXII, 356, as quoted in Dufourcq, *Nicolas Le Bègue*, p. 151.

15. Dufourcq, *Documents inédits*, 2, 329, Doc. 378.

16. Ibid., 2, 346, Doc. 395, n. 1.

musicians and organ builders, and in the results this partnership
produced.[17]

1. Augmentation and repair of the organ for the church of
St.-Nazaire, Béziers, 1679 (Arch. Dép. Herault, G 331):

13. Plus il faut démonter, netoyer et faire parler tous les
tuyaux du jeu de la quarte de nazard et luy donner un son
propre pour estre mis avec la tierce et le nazard. [Further,
all the pipes of the quarte de nazard must be taken out,
cleaned, and made to speak, and given a sound appropriate
for use with the tierce and nazard.]

14. Plus il faut faire jeu de tierce neuve et de grosse taille
les corps d'estin et les pieds d'estoffe à la place de celle quy
y est à présent et luy donner un son convenable pour estre
mis avec la quarte et le nazard. [Further, a new wide-scale
jeu de tierce must be made with bodies of tin and feet of
common metal, in place of what is not there, and it must
be given a sound compatible with the quarte and the
nazard.]

[Pédalle] 34. Plus il faut faire un jeu de pedalle de flûte
de huict pieds et de grosse taille pour pouvoir jouër des
trio. [Further, a flûte 8' must be made for the pedal, of
large scale, for playing trios.]

35. Plus sera fait à neuf un jeu de pédalle de trompette
sonnant huict pieds, les corps d'estin de grosse taille . . .
ce jeu servant beaucoup pour fortifier de beaucoup les
plains jeux et pour battre un plain chant en basses, un
plain chant en taille, et pour battre les responds. [Further,
a new trompette 8' will be made for the pedal, of large
scale, bodies of tin . . . this stop serving greatly to fortify
the plains jeux and for playing the plain chant in the bass,
plain chant in the tenor, and for sounding the responses.]

[Eco] 44. Plus il faut faire à neuf une cimballe à deux
tuyaux sur marches, les corps d'estin, les pieds d'estoffe,
et d'une composition avec la fourniture pour respondre et

17. The complete texts from which the following excerpts are taken appear among
the Pièces justificatives, in N. Dufourcq, *Jean de Joyeuse* (Paris, 1958), pp. 37 ff.

au plain jeu et au plain jeu de positif. [Further, a new cimballe must be made with two ranks, with bodies of tin and feet of common metal, and with such a composition as to complement the fourniture and the plain jeu, and the plain jeu de positif.]

2. Contract for the organ at St.-Michel, Carcassonne, 1684 (Arch. Dép. Aude, 3 E 1115, f° 527 v°):

[Cornet d'eco] Plus sera fait vingt cinq gravures dans les deux saumiers de la grande orgue, qui serviront pour faire jouer quand on voudra la bas de trompete en pedale et la montre de la grand orgue aussy, affin de jouer le plain chant en pedale et de trieaux. [Further, twenty-five wind channels will be made in the two chests for the grand orgue, which will be used to allow the bass of trompete en pedale and the montre of the grand orgue together when desired, in order to play plain chant in the pedal and trios.]

3. Augmentation of pedal for St.-Michel, Carcassonne, 1687 (Arch. Dép. Aude, 3 E 1116, f° 270 v°):

Et sur les deux saumiers seront posés premièrement un jeu de pédalle de flute sonnant huit pieds ouvert, le tout de très bon bois comme dit est et de grosse taille; le dit jeu sera d'une forsse convenable pour acompaigner l'hors qu'on jouera des trios et tiersses en taille.

Plus sera fait un jeu de pédalle de trompete sonnant huict pieds de grosse taille . . . la dite pédalle sera fort esclatante, affin d'estre entendue distinctement avec le plain jeu lorsqu'on jouera des plain chants et grands jeux. [And first an open 8′ pédalle de flute will be placed on the two chests, of large scale and made entirely of wood; this stop will be strong enough for accompanying when playing trios and tiersses en taille. In addition there will be a large scale pédalle de trompete 8′ . . . this pedal stop will be very brilliant, in order to be heard distinctly against the plain jeu when playing plain chants and grands jeux.]

4. Proposition for the organ at Auch, Cathédrale, 1688 (Auch, Etude de Maitre Mir., 29 janvier, 1688):

Plus un jeu de voix humaine sonnant à l'unisson de la trompette . . . tout le dit jeu sera aussi prompt à parler et bien
égal de l'armonie et du son, sans qu'aucuns des dits tuyaux
changent de son ny de ton, quand y mettra le tremblant.

Plus un jeu de fourniture de six tuyaux sur marche . . .
le dit jeu sera fait d'une composition comme sont les
meilleurs plains jeux de la ville de Paris.

Plus un jeu de cimbale de quatre tuyaux sur marche . . .
et d'une composition proportionée au jeu de fourniture.
[Further, a voix humaine stop, sounding at the unison with
the trompette . . . this entire stop must also be prompt
in speech, and very even in quality and intensity, without
any change in timbre among the pipes when the tremblant
is applied to it. Further, a fourniture with six ranks . . .
which will have a composition just like the best plains jeux
in the city of Paris. Also, a cymbale with four ranks . . .
and with a composition complementing that of the
fourniture.]

Plus sera fait deux sommiers de pédales . . . et posé sur
les dits deux sommiers quatre jeux, scavoir un jeu de pédale
de flute de huit pied ouvert . . . et le dit jeu poussera
beaucoup afin d'etre entendue distinctement lors qu'on
jouera de trio et tierce en taille, . . . une pédale de trompete . . . la dite pédale sera fort éclatante afin d'estre
entendue distinctement lors qu'on jouera les plains jeux
ensemble . . .

Plus sera fait un jeu de cornet séparé sur un clavier à
part pour faire des ècos et jouer des trios à la mode de Paris.
[Also, two pedal chests will be made . . . upon which
will be placed four stops, namely, an 8′ open stop called
pédale de flûte . . . and this stop must be pushed a good
deal so that it may be heard distinctly for playing trios and
tierce en taille . . . and a pédale de trompete . . .
which will be very brilliant, so that it may be heard distinctly when playing together with the plain jeux . . .
Further, a jeu de cornet séparé will be made with a separate keyboard, for making echoes and playing trios according to the fashion in Paris.]

Sera fait aussi un clavier de pédale de vingt six touches commanceant en C sol ut fa tout en bas et finissant en D la ré sol au dessus de la clef de sol ut fa . . . Le dit clavier de pédale étant fait pour jouer des plains chant, tierce en taille, et trio, comme l'ont fait à Paris. [Also, a pedal keyboard will be made with twenty-six keys starting on C sol ut fa in the bass and ending on D la re sol above the key sol ut fa . . . this pedal keyboard being made for the purpose of playing plain chant, tierce en taille, and trio, just as is being done in Paris.]

5. Rebuilding the organ at Perpignan Cathédrale, 1688 (Arch. Com de Perpignan; BB 71, 1688, 19 avril):
[Positif] Plus un jeu de flute sonnant quatre pieds et a l'unisson du prestant, qui est un jeu pour acompagner a la musique avec le bourdon. [Also, a flute 4′ at the unison with the prestant, a stop which used to accompany music along with the bourdon.]

[Pedalle] De plus il est aussy fort necessaire pour la perfection de la dite orgue de faire des pedalles comme il s'ensuit, pour pouvoir joüer des plain jeux, des trios et des tierces en taille, de la maniere qu'on a de coutume de joüer dans les orgues de Paris . . .
Premierement, un jeu de pedalle de flute de huit pieds ouvert de grosse taille . . . lesquels parleront distinctement pour pouvoir estre entendus quand on joüera des trios comme a desja été dit, etc.
Plus sera fait un jeu de pedalle de trompette de grosse taille . . . le dit jeu sera fort eclatant pour estre entendu distinctement lorsqu'on joüera les plain jeux, quand mesme les deux claviers seront tirés l'un sur l'autre et parleront promptement. [Furthermore, it is essential for the perfection of this organ that the pedal stops be made as follows, in order that one may play plain jeux, trios, and tierces en taille, in the way customary at the organs in Paris . . . First, an open 8′ pedalle de flute of large scale . . . speaking distinctly in order to be heard while playing trios, as has already been mentioned, etc. Also, a large scale pedalle

de trompette . . . this stop will be very brilliant so that
it will be heard distinctly for playing plain jeux, even with
the two keyboards coupled together, and they must speak
promptly.]

6. Rebuilding the organ for Narbonne Cathédrale, 1697
   (Arch. Dep. Aude, G 36, f° 137 v° août, 1697):
   Plus sera fait un jeu de pédale de fleute de grosse taille pour
   servir d'accompagnement quand on voudra jouer de tierce
   en taille, de trio, et autres accompagnemens . . .

   Plus sera fait un jeu de pédale de trompette de dix sept
   tuyaus, . . . Ce jeu est pour jouer de plains chans en
   basse et en taille et avec le plein jeu. [Also a large scale
   pédale de flute should be made to serve as accompaniment
   when desired for playing the tierce en taille, trio, and other
   accompaniments . . .

   Further, a pédale de trompette must be made with seventeen pipes . . . this stop is for playing plain chants in the
   bass and tenor, and with the plein jeu.]

I return now to a discussion of the primary sources of information given earlier in this chapter. The reader is urged to make frequent references to Appendix C, in which all the listed sources
appear in English translation.

An analysis of registration for organ compositions of the seventeenth and eighteenth centuries in France must be approached not
by a study of form, which in this music is not complex, but rather
by observing the close interrelationships among registration,
musical texture, and expression. The essence of the classical French
style of registration lies in this identity. Thus we would no more
expect a composer in this period to indicate a registration such as
Grand Jeu for a piece written in two voices, than to suggest that
a Voix humaine be performed "gaiment."

Nevertheless, within general stylistic boundaries we can observe
some flexibility of attitude toward the details. This is not in conflict
with the continuing respect for stylistic outlines; indeed, it provided
the yielding atmosphere without which the creative urge could
have been discouraged. The area of pliability is best understood

by comparing the apparently opposite attitudes of Nicolas LeBègue and André Raison:

Nicolas LeBègue, Preface to *Premier Livre d'orgue* (1676):
I hope particularly that all those who do me the honor of playing these pieces will want to play them according to my intentions, that is to say, with the correct combinations of stops and the proper tempo for each piece. . . . There are several pieces in this book which are not useful to organists whose instruments lack the stops necessary for their execution.

André Raison, "Au Lecteur," from *Livre d'orgue* (1688):
As I vary the choice of stops and manuals a great deal, it is not necessary that all my pieces be played exactly as they are marked . . . What is played on the Grand Clavier could also be played on the Petit, except that this must then be played in a lighter style. [The entire preface is devoted to a discussion of this sort of flexibility. But it should be remarked that the performer is always guided within the limits of the musical textures, and he is warned that even a change of manuals might mean a modification of his playing style.]

Raison even bows to the player who cannot manage the pedals, with the frequent annotation, "Pedalle de Flutte ou une 3e main [Pedal Flute or a third hand]." In the original edition of the *Messe du premier ton*, an alternate version of the "Autre premier Kyrie" is offered, transposed to suit a new arrangement of voices: "Autre premier Kyrie, pour un plein jeu accompagné d'une Pedalle de Trompette en Taille." with the later note: "Pedalle de Trompette d'une 3e main en touchant le petit plein jeu." He advises the inexperienced musician that the piece is written so that it works even without the annoying Trompette part: "L'jntention de l'Auteur est de jouer aussi le plein jeu sans la Pedalle [It is the composer's intention that the plein jeu may be played without the pedal part]."

Such comments are not confined to those composers who left us careful instructions for registration. Clérambault, for one, took the trouble to write his pieces so that the récits could be played on one-manual organs with split stops:

Louis-Nicolas Clérambault, *Livre d'orgue* (1710), "Avertissement": I have composed these pieces in such a way that they can be played as easily on a cabinet organ with split stops as on a large instrument; that is why in the Basse de trompette, and in the récits, the accompaniment does not pass the middle of the keyboard, nor the melodies of the Dessus and the Basse. Those who have large organs can play the accompaniments with the left hand an octave higher if they find them too low.

Further, Clérambault says, in the Grand Plein Jeu of the *Suite du premier ton*: "On pourra joüer cette Basse sur la pedale de Trompette si l'on veut [The bass can be played on the pedal Trompette, if one wishes]," and for the Dialogue sur les grands jeux: "Ceux qui n'auront point de Cornet séparé pourront se servir du Positif pour toucher le dessus dans les endroits qui sont doux. [Those who do not have a Cornet séparé may use the Positif for the dessus in the softer passages.]"

It appears that LeBègue's more rigid approach would have received support from the exacting Jean-Henri d'Anglebert, who included five fugues on the same subject and a Quatuor on the Kyrie in his *Pièces de clavecin* (1689). In the Preface, D'Anglebert said:

> I wanted to give also a sample of what I have done earlier for the organ; that is why I have simply included five fugues on the same subject, varied with different tempos, and have finished with a "quatuor sur le Kirie de la Messe." Since this piece is more worked out than the others, it can have its best effect on a large organ, and even on four different keyboards; I require three manual keyboards and pedals, having stops of equal strength but different character, in order to distinguish the entries of the parts.

In an attempt to organize the numerous details among the instructions for registration, a somewhat oversimplified grouping of pieces follows, categorized according to musical texture:

1. Broad textures
   a. Plein Jeu
   b. Grand Jeu

    c. Fugue

    d. Fond d'orgue

  2. Contrapuntal textures

    a. Duo

    b. Trio

    c. Quatuor

    d. Certain fugues

  3. Melodic textures

    a. Récits de dessus

    b. Récits en taille

    c. Récits en basse

  4. Composite textures

    a. Dialogue

    b. Offertoire

    c. Variations, chaconnes, passacaglias, etc.

The Broad Textures

There was almost never any disagreement about what made a Plein Jeu. The rich amplitude of the combined choruses of the Grand Orgue and Positif, developed over the centuries, included a uniquely balanced texture with the fullness of a 16′ fundamental and the controlled brilliance of mixtures which were neither strident nor piercing. The aggressive Trompette of the pedal could pierce its transparent fabric, but alone it filled the church with a sound which did not become tiresome. Thus the Preludes and Pleins Jeux of the classical period were scored with few rests and with close, slow-moving harmonic blending of four- or five-voice writing. There was no conflict about what sort of music sounded best on the Plein Jeu, and pieces written for that combination would seldom be performed on any other registration.[18] The Plein Jeu never allowed the intrusion of manual reed stops,[19] nor was it apparently used at all for the performance of fugues.

For the Grand Jeu, or Grands Jeux, no such uniformity is apparent. This registration, used for many Dialogues, Offertories, and

18. Nivers (from *Livre d'orgue*, 1675) mentions the possibility of playing Préludes on the "Plein Jeu de Tierce." Gigault (1685) allows Préludes on the reeds with grand tremblant.

19. Dom Bedos' suggestion that the Bombarde may be used in the Plein Jeu cannot be applied to music written generations earlier.

variations (composite textures), was dominated by the sound of the Trompette, or the Trompette and Clairon of the Grand Orgue, supported by some foundation stops. Perhaps the Cornet was used to strengthen the trebles of the reeds. Where the Positif was used, the sound of the Cromorne predominated. The Récit and Echo could add further variety, and the Pédale de Trompette often entered, even coupled to the Grand Orgue. Two important observations might be mentioned: first, that seventeenth-century composers frequently recommended the strong Tremblant in this combination, while Dom Bedos later decried its use at all; and secondly, that the Grand Jeu was a registration intended to show off the reeds, to which mixtures were never to be added. Chart 1 will supplement Appendix C in giving the reader a glance at all the advice from our primary sources.

According to all the evidence collected in Chart 2, pieces entitled "Fugue," whether Fugue grave or Fugue de mouvement, were customarily played on reed stops. However, even those composers who indicated only the Trompette or the Cromorne (Nivers, Gigault, Jullien) might have assumed that the player would draw the Trompette's "foundation" along with it, and the Cromorne's, as well. A review of many of these short pieces will show that the Fugue was normally, like the Grand Jeu, a vehicle for using reed sound. The term was used loosely, however, ranging from Louis Couperin and Nivers[20] to Gigault, who wrote a "Fugue du 1er Ton, poursuivie à la manière italienne, à 4 parties." This last piece is unique in its length and style, suggesting the possibility of a clearer, lighter registration. But there was usually a lack of contrapuntal interest in pieces called "Fugues," for which the excitement of the sound of the Trompette compensated. Nicolas DeGrigny expressed his disenchantment with this custom by writing five-part Fugues with considerable contrapuntal interest, and giving them an unusual registration: right hand, Cornet séparé; left hand, Cromorne, Pédale de Flûte. Jullien, in 1690, suggested that his Fugues, being written with special attention to voice clarity, might be played "en quatuor."

Finally, in the class of close-knit musical textures, we observe

20. See above, p. 98.

the Fond d'Orgue, which was always a combination of all the Flutes and Principals at 16′, 8′, and 4′ pitches, possibly coupling the Positif to the Grand Orgue. Gigault used the titles "Fond d'Orgue" and "Concert de Flutes" as dual options, because the texture of pieces bearing those titles was always apt to be thick and slow in motion. The chief differences between them were that the "Concert de Flutes" was quieter, using fewer stops than the "Fond d'Orgue," and that the "Concert de Flutes" included the Tremblant doux, which was never used for the "Fond d'Orgue."

Here are the recommendations that have come down to us for Concert de Flûtes":

J. Boyvin: (1689)	Bourdon and Fluste on both the Grand Orgue and the Positif, coupled. Tremblant doux.
G. Corrette: (1703)	Bourdon and Flûte on both the Grand Orgue and the Positif, coupled. Tremblant doux.
Anon. (Tours):	"Fluste, Prestant or Bourdon alone, or Montre alone on a small organ."
M. Corrette: (1737)	Grand Orgue, Bourdon and Montre Positif, Bourdon alone. Tremblant doux.
Anon. (Caen): (1746)	"Flute, two Flute Almande, Montre, Bourdon 4. Nothing else. The Tremblant doux. In the Pedalle, two flutes and Bourdons."

The Contrapuntal Textures

Charts 3, 4, 5, and 6, for Duos, Trios à deux dessus, Trios à trois claviers, and Quatuors, select most of the pertinent comments about these pieces from the primary sources in Appendix C. Dom Bedos emphasized the need for the performer to adjust his playing style to the speech characteristics and timbres of the combinations being used, doubtless having in mind that his readers would be improvising. Thus we do have valuable assistance of an interpretive nature in his remarks. There seemed to be general agreement that the Duo was a piece to be played boldly and lightly, and it will be noticed that no one recommends the Tremblant. Jullien says that Trios can be played on any of his Duo combinations as well. In the case of the Quatuor we encounter registrations which are repeated for use in certain melodic Dialogues, and there is an extraordinarily strong concentration upon all the standard melodic combinations, which must be delicately balanced for use in musical textures demanding distinctiveness and clarity of contrapuntal line.

With reference to the use of the Pédale in the Quatuor, which was specifically recommended only by Dom Bedos[21] among our primary sources, one should not be led to believe that the Quatuor was never played with pedal until after the middle of the eighteenth century. Both D'Anglebert[22] and Marchand, writing in the seventeenth century, required the use of the pedal for their Quatuors. Thus these charts, drawn up for convenient reference, should not be used to provide information on the frequency of use or the popularity of any particular manner of performance. Much of the published music of the period was written to accommodate organ players of little skill who lived in the provinces and needed help in choosing registrations.

Melodic Textures

Of all the registrations used for Récits,[23] the Cornets and Tierces were unquestionably the favorites. There was a fine distinction between these two terms, which can be observed in Chart 7.[24]

The Cornet usually meant a five-rank half-stop, commencing at middle C and comprising 8' (stopped), 4', $2\frac{2}{3}'$, 2', $1\frac{3}{5}'$, all in flute scales. Cornet V was always found on the Récit manual, and we have observed that its pipes were just above the chest for the Grand Orgue, but winded separately. The Grand Cornet V might have occupied space contiguous to the Cornet de Récit, but it was, of course, played from the Grand Orgue. The Cornet was not found in the Positif until late in the eighteenth century, and then only

21. Dom Bedos' frequent mention of the Jeu de Tierce of the "Pédalle" should not mislead the modern reader. Only in very rare instances did pedal sections of French organs before the 19th century have such full development.

22. See above, p. 106.

23. Récit refers both to the division of an organ and to the musical line sounding the melody.

24. For melodies in the soprano range, the use of the Cornet de Récit (Cornet séparé) and the Trompette de Récit was very frequent. These do not appear in Charts 7, 8, and 9 because they are single stops always used alone.

for large instruments; but it was always present where there was an Echo manual, and its pipes would then be located under the chest of the Grand Orgue, so that they would not speak out in any direction. Thus there were Cornets on the Récit, the Grand Orgue, and the Echo, with occasional appearances on the Positif.

The Tierce indicated a particular stop: $3\frac{1}{5}'$, $1\frac{3}{5}'$, or $\frac{4}{5}'$. But it also designated registrations using the Tierces. Thus the Grand Jeu de Tierce or the Petite Tierce du Grand Orgue were quite distinctly different from the Jeu de Tierce du Positif. It will be observed from Chart 7 that Tierce registrations on the Positif varied from a combination of four stops, sounding $8'$, $4'$, $2\frac{2}{3}'$, and $1\frac{3}{5}'$, to seven, with the full range of pitches for the Cornet plus the Larigot $1\frac{1}{3}'$. Because of its forward location, the Positif was a favorite choice for sounding the Jeu de Tierce in the tenor range (Tierce en Taille). On the Grand Orgue's $16'$ and $8'$ fundamental pitches, the Jeu de Tierce developed in a unique manner for bass melodies, with no parallel in organs of any other country. The Grand Jeu de Tierce[25] was made up of all the pitches of the Cornet, plus the Bourdon $16'$ and the $16'$ mutations when they appeared—namely, $3\frac{1}{5}'$ and $5\frac{1}{3}'$. Thus, by the late eighteenth century, Dom Bedos lists an astonishing array of ten to thirteen stops for the Grand Jeu de Tierce, ranging from $32'$ to $1\frac{3}{5}'$.

From the smallest Tierce of four stops, $8'$, $4'$, $2\frac{2}{3}'$, and $1\frac{3}{5}'$, the deletion of the most colorful element leaves a combination which was used both for Récits and for accompaniment (Jeu doux, see below)—namely, the Nazard, made of $8'$, $4'$, and $2\frac{2}{3}'$.

All the reeds were useful both in ensemble (Grand Jeu, Fugue, Voix Humaine, etc.) and in Récits. Charts 8 and 9 show the "foundation" of flue voices recommended as reinforcement for reed solos. It will be observed that the "foundation" was apt to be altered for the range in which the reed was expected to sound. For instance, the Trompette in a soprano melody would be used with a light "foundation" if played on the Grand Orgue, or quite alone when played en dessus on the Récit;[26] but a Basse de Trom-

---

25. As opposed to the Petite Jeu de Tierce du Grand Orgue, a combination for which the $16'$ fundamental was excluded.

26. The Petite Trompette on the Récit was found more frequently in the 18th than in the 17th century.

pette was quite another matter. Here, the "foundation" for the
reed ranged from just the Prestant 4' (Dom Bedos)[27] to a large
number of additional stops. Boyvin went to the extreme when he
recommended that the Basse de Trompette be played with a bass
registration like this:

> 8' Bourdon
> 4' Prestant
> $2\frac{2}{3}$' Nazard
> 8' Trompette
> 4' Clairon
> Cornet
> Tremblant fort

It is clear, however, that the normal "foundation" for Trompettes
and Cromornes was Bourdon 8' plus Prestant 4', while the Voix
Humaine was supported by the Bourdon 8' and Flûte 4'.

A curious vestige from the past lies in the combination of Bourdon
16' and Clairon 4', which survived from Mersenne ("le Cleron")
through the hands of Raison (1688) and Dom Bedos (1770) into
the Romantic era with César Franck.[28]

The accompaniments of Récits, like the melodies, varied a great
deal. Just as the solo parts were seldom played on single stops, so
also the accompaniments were almost always recommended with
two or more stops. Even used in the singular, Jeu Doux (= soft
stop, or soft registration) embraced a surprisingly wide variety of
combinations. Chart 10, on Jeu Doux, will serve as a reminder
that the normal procedure was to accompany melodies on the
Bourdon 8' with the Prestant 4', or the Flûte 4', at least until Dom
Bedos, who had a tendency to accompany Récits with as many 8'
stops as he could gather on a given keyboard. Dom Bedos takes a
paragraph to explain that accompaniments should, in his view,
be done on 8' sounds, unless they are too feeble. Then one can use
4' as well, but "never add 16' in this combination." Here he is in

---

27. Dom Bedos favored using Trompettes and Clairons together, but warned
strongly against "spoiling" the sound of reeds with the Tremblant, and suggests that
the "foundations" are useful for taking off the edge of reeds, especially the short ones.

28. See Franck, *Grand Pièce Symphonique*.

conflict with the composers who had suggested 16′ in Jeu Doux, especially for accompanying the Tierce en Taille.

There is such a wide variation among Jeu Doux that the modern performer is well advised to give this matter some special attention, for the choice of stops for accompaniment is frequently left to his taste. On the one hand, Boyvin suggests the Montre 8′ alone to accompany the Cromorne, and Michel Corrette the Bourdon 8′ for the Basse de Cromorne, while, on the other, Nivers directs that his Basses de Trompette should be accompanied with the Petit Plein Jeu. Between these two extremes we find Jeux Doux of motley sorts, employing an astonishingly large array of stops, according to the preferences of this or that writer:

List of Stops Recommended for the Various "Jeux Doux"
16′ Bourdon
16′ Montre
8′ Flute
8′ Montre
8′ Bourdon
4′ Flute
4′ Prestant
$2\frac{2}{3}$′ Nazard
2′ Doublette
$1\frac{1}{3}$′ Larigot

It is expected that a study of the charts provided in this section will serve the purpose of placing Dom Bedos in perspective. Since he was dealing with a tradition that enjoyed a long life, and since he treated it more fully than anyone else, there has been a habit in this century of allowing Dom Bedos alone to speak on the subject of registration. Yet he was writing many years after the productive period had ended. Perhaps one of his most significant remarks was made in the footnote for the subtitle in the section on registration: "Tastes have changed since that time [the late seventeenth century]. Because of different uses of stops and ways of treating them, certain alterations in those earlier combinations have been necessitated." As more attention is given to the advice of the composers, in the light of Dom Bedos' comment, the more remarkable it is that Dom Bedos himself, in describing a dying tradition, noticed how the evolutionary process had changed people's attitudes. Thus we find him in conflict with the composers, not only with respect to some relatively unimportant details, such as the use of the Nazard with the Cromorne, but in some major considerations, such as the inclusion of reed tone in the Plein Jeu or the use of the Tremblant fort in the Grand Jeu. This, of course, does not diminish the value of Dom Bedos' thinking, but increases it, as it demonstrates authoritatively the fact that he, like Mersenne, was living in a time of stylistic transition. He was carefully making a record of performing habits in an age that was soon to be quite forgotten. Since Dom Bedos, unlike Mersenne, was a specialist, there is no chance that we will ever find a more valuable document on the subject of registration than his chapter on the combinations of organ stops. For him the objectives went beyond the simple handling of registers to the delicate and demanding realm of musical expression. Thus, for the player today who dares to enter this sensitive area, Dom Bedos' words still hold unique and lasting value.

Chart 1. Le Grand Jeu

KEY:
- **G** = GRAND ORGUE
- **GP** = POSITIF AND G.O.
- **( )** = OPTIONAL
- **P** = POS. ONLY
- **X** = MANUAL NOT MENTIONED

Stop	NIVERS 1665	LE BÈGUE 1676	ANON. 1678	RAISON 1688	BOYVIN 1689	CHAUMONT 1695	G. CORRETTE 1703	ANON. TOURS c.1710	M. CORRETTE 1737	ANON. CAEN 1746	DOM BEDOS 1766-70
16'	X							X			
8' (OPEN)	X		G					X / X			
BOURDON 8	X	GP / G	GP	GP	GP / GP	GP / G / G	GP / GP	X / X	GP		
PRESTANT 4	X	GP / G	GP	GP	GP / GP	GP / G / G	GP / GP	X / X	GP / GP	GP	GP
DOUBLETTE 2	X	G	GP			G		X			
NAZARD $2\frac{2}{3}$	X	GP	GP	GP	GP	GP	GP	X / X	GP / GP	GP	
TIERCE $1\frac{3}{5}$	X	GP	GP	GP		GP	GP	X	GP / GP	GP	
QUARTE DE NAZ. 2		G	GP		G(P)	G					
CORNET	X	G / G	G	G	G / G	G / G / G	G / G	X	G / G	GP	GP
CROMORNE 8	X	P	P	P	GP / P	P	G / P	X / X	G / G	P	P
TROMPETTE 8	X	G / G	G	G	GP / G	G	G / G	X	P / P	GP	GP
CLAIRON 4	X	G / G		G	G / G	G / G	G / G		G / G	GP	GP
CORNET SÉPARÉ AND/OR ECHO		X	X	X	X		X	X	G / G		X
TREMBLANT FORT	X	X	X	X	X / X	X	X / X	X	X / X		
COUPLER (G.O.+POS)							X				X
PEDAL REEDS										X	X

Chart 2. Fugues

Source	Tremblant	Trompette 8	Clairon 4	Prestant 4	Jeu de Tierce	Bourdon 8	Cromorne 8	Nazard $2\frac{2}{3}$	Tierce $1\frac{3}{5}$	Fonds	Cornet	Bourdon 8	Cromorne 8	Prestant 4	Trompette 8	Clairon 4	Jeu de Tierce	Cornet	Manual Coupler	Péd. Reeds
DOM BEDOS 1766-70		X			X															
DOM BEDOS 1766-70		X	X	X							X		X	X	X				X	X
DOM BEDOS 1766-70										X		X	X	(FUGUE GRAVE)					X	
DOM BEDOS 1766-70		X	X	X	(FUGUE GRAVE)							X		X	X				X	X
ANON. TOURS 1710								X		X										
G. CORRETTE c. 1703		X		X		X						X	X	X					X	
CHAUMONT 1695	(FUGUE GAYE)			X		X		X	X											
CHAUMONT 1695		X	X	X		X		X				X	X	(SMALL ORGANS)						
JULLIEN 1690									X											
JULLIEN 1690		X¹																		
BOYVIN 1689												X	X	X						
BOYVIN 1689		X		X		X						X							X	
GIGAULT 1685		X																		
ANON. 1678		X				X														
LE BÈGUE 1676		(SMALL ORGANS)			X	X														
LE BÈGUE 1676		X	X	X		X														
NIVERS 1665	X			X																

GRAND ORGUE — POSITIF — PÉD.

Chart 3. Le Duo

KEY:
L = LEFT HAND
R = RIGHT HAND
1 = ALTERNATES
2 = 8,4,2⅔,1⅗ ONLY

	NIVERS 1667	LE BÈGUE 1676	RAISON 1688	BOYVIN 1689	CHAUMONT 1695	G.CORRETTE 1703	ANON.TOURS C.1710	M.CORRETTE 1737	ANON.CAEN 1746	DOM BEDOS 1766-70
RÉCIT										
CORNET SÉPARÉ	R	R	R		R			R R	R	R R R R
TROMPETTE 8										R
GRAND ORGUE										
16' FOUNDATIONS							SEE INSTRUCTIONS			
FONDS (16,8,4)								L		L
GRAND JEU DE TIERCE	L	L	L L	L	L	L			R² R¹	L
PETITE TIERCE DU GO		LR								R
TROMPETTE 8			L					LR		LR L
CLAIRON 4			L					LR		LR L
PRESTANT 4			L							LR
CORNET		R	L						R¹	
BOURDON 8										
COUPLER								X		X
POSITIF										
BOURDON 8									L L L	L L R¹ R¹
PRESTANT 4									L	L R R R¹
CROMORNE 8										L
JEU DE TIERCE	R	R	R² R	R² R²	R²	R²		L²	L²	L R
TROMPETTE 8										L
8, 8, FL.4, 2⅔										R
NAZARD 2⅔										

Chart 4. Trios à deux dessus

KEY:

1 = 8, 4, 2⅔, 1⅗ ONLY
2 = CHECK INSTRUCTIONS
( ) = OPTIONAL
L = LEFT HAND
R = RIGHT HAND

		LE BÈGUE 1676	GIGAULT 1685	RAISON 1688	BOYVIN 1689	CHAUMONT 1695	G. CORRETTE 1703	M. CORRETTE 1737	DOM BEDOS 1766-70
RÉC.	CORNET SÉPARÉ	R							
GRAND ORGUE	BOURDON 8								
	PRESTANT 4								
	GRAND JEU DE TIERCE	L R (FOR MEDIUM-SIZED ORGANS)	L				L	L	
	PETITE TIERCE DU G.O.	L R (FOR SMALL ORGANS)	L R[2]	L[1]			L	L	L
	VOIX HUMAINE + BDN. 8, FL. 4	L		L	R	L			
	TROMPETTE 8	L			L	L	L	L	L L
	CLAIRON 4, +16'								L
	TREMBLANT DOUX	X	X	X	X	X	X		
POSITIF	BOURDON 8	(R)		R		R	R	R R	R
	FLUTE 4	(R)		R		R	R	R	
	PRESTANT 4	(R)	R[2]				R	R	R
	CROMORNE 8	R	R[2] R		L	R	R	R	R
	JEU DE TIERCE	R[1]				R[1]			
	NAZARD 2⅔			R			R	R	R
	BOTH 8'								R

Chart 3. Trios à trois claviers

KEY:

1. ALTERNATIVE CHOICE
2. MINUS LARIGOT
3. NOT MENTIONED, BUT ESSENTIAL
4. FAILING FLUTE 4, USE PRESTANT
5. MINUS LARIGOT AND 2'
6. CHECK INSTRUCTIONS FOR MORE INFORMATION
L. LEFT HAND
R. RIGHT HAND
( ) OPTIONAL

Sources: LE BÈGUE 1676 · RAISON 1688 · BOYVIN 1689 · CHAUMONT 1695 · M. CORRETTE 1737 · ANON. CAEN 1746 · DOM BEDOS 1766-70

RÉCIT

Stop	Le Bègue 1676	Raison 1688	Boyvin 1689	Chaumont 1695	M. Corrette 1737	Anon. Caen 1746	Dom Bedos 1766-70
CORNET SÉPARÉ	R		R	R	L	R	R · L · R · R R¹ · R R¹ · R · L · R
TROMPETTE 8							R¹

GRAND ORGUE

Stop	Le Bègue 1676	Raison 1688	Boyvin 1689	Chaumont 1695	M. Corrette 1737	Anon. Caen 1746	Dom Bedos 1766-70
8' STOPS							
PRESTANT 4				R		R	R
GRAND JEU DE TIERCE	L		L⁵				L¹
PETITE TIERCE DU G.O.		R		L			
VOIX HUMAINE, BDN.8, FL.4	L⁴			L⁵			L
TROMPETTE 8				R	R	L⁶	L⁴ · L¹ · R¹
CLAIRON 4, BDN.16						L⁶	R¹
8, 8, 4, 2⅔		L		R			R
TREMBLANT DOUX	X	X	X	X	X	X	X

POSITIF

Stop	Le Bègue 1676	Raison 1688	Boyvin 1689	Chaumont 1695	M. Corrette 1737	Anon. Caen 1746	Dom Bedos 1766-70
BOURDON 8	R	R	L	R			L · L L · R¹
FLUTE 4			R¹	R¹			L · L L · L
PRESTANT 4	R	L	L	R			R¹ · R¹
CROMORNE 8	R	R	L	R			L · L
JEU DE TIERCE	R			R	R⁵		R² L · L · R
NAZARD 2⅔		L		L			
BOTH 8'							L
G.O. AND POS. 8'							LR

PÉD.

Stop	Le Bègue 1676	Raison 1688	Boyvin 1689	Chaumont 1695	M. Corrette 1737	Anon. Caen 1746	Dom Bedos 1766-70
FLUTES	X	X X⁶	X⁶	X³ X³ · X³ · X³	X	X	X · X · X · X · X · X · X
JEU DE TIERCE							X · X · X · X · X · X · X

RÉCIT GRAND ORGUE POSITIF PÉD.

Chart 6. Le Quatuor

Division	Stop	BOYVIN 1689		JULLIEN[2] 1690		DOM BEDOS 1766-70			
RÉCIT	CORNET SÉPARÉ		S A	S A		S	S A		S
GRAND ORGUE	TROMPETTE 8								
	OPEN 8				S B				
	BOURDON 8		B[3]		S B				
	PRESTANT 4		B[3]		S B				
	PETITE TIERCE DU G.O.	L	S B[3]				A	A	
	TROMPETTE 8								
	NAZARD 2⅔		B[3]		S B				
	QUART DE NAZARD 2				S B				
POSITIF	TREMBLANT DOUX	X			X				
	BOURDON 8	R	T A	T B	T A				
	PRESTANT 4	R	T A	T B	T A			T	T
	NAZARD 2⅔				T A[1]				
	JEU DE TIERCE DU POS.		T				T	T	T
	CROMORNE 8	R	T A	T B	T A	A T	T	T	T
PÉD.	PEDALLE DE FLUTE					B	B	B	B
	JEU DE TIERCE					B[1]	B[1]	B[1]	B[1]

Comparison chart of French classical organ tierce registrations. Top-right annotation: **(X)=OPTIONAL**. Heading over the left section: **(PETIT JEU DE TIERCE DU GRAND ORGUE)**. NIVERS row annotation: **(GROS JEU DE DIMINUTIONS)**.

GRAND ORG. (GRAND JEU DE TIERCE)

Source	BOURDON 16	MONTRE 8	BOURDON 8	PRESTANT 4	NAZARD 2⅔ (QUINTE)	DOUBLETTE 2	TIERCE 1⅗	FLUTE 4	DOUBLE TIERCE 3⅕ (GROSSE)	GROS NAZARD 5⅓	QUARTE 2	TREMBLANT DOUX	MONTRES 32,16
DOM. BEDOS 1766-70		X	X	X	X		X				X		
DOM. BEDOS 1766-70	X	X	X	X	X		X		X	X	X		X
ANON. CAEN 1746													
ANON. CAEN 1746													
ANON. CAEN 1746													
M. CORRETTE 1737													
M. CORRETTE 1737	X	X	X	X	X		X		X				
ANON. TOURS 1710													
G. CORRETTE 1703	X		X	X	X		X		X		X		
G. CORRETTE 1703		X	X	X	X		X		X		X		
CHAUMONT 1695			X	X	X		X					X	
CHAUMONT 1695	X		X	X	X		X			X			
BOYVIN 1689	X		X	X	X		X			X			
BOYVIN 1689			X	X	X	X				X			
RAISON 1688													
RAISON 1688	X		X		X		X	X	X	X			
ANON. 1678													
LE BÈGUE 1676			X	X	X		X				X		
NIVERS 1665	(X)	(X)	X	X	(X)	X	X						

POSITIF (PETITE TIERCE)

Source	BOURDON 8	PRESTANT 4 (MONTRE)	FLUTE 4	NAZARD 2⅔	QUARTE 2	DOUBLETTE 2	TIERCE 1⅗	LARIGOT 1⅓	CROMORNE 8	MONTRE 8
DOM. BEDOS 1766-70	X			X	X		X	X		X
DOM. BEDOS 1766-70	X	X		X	X		X			X
ANON. CAEN 1746		X		X		X	X		X	
ANON. CAEN 1746	X	X		X			X			
ANON. CAEN 1746	X	X		X		X	X			
M. CORRETTE 1737	X	X		X		X	X			
M. CORRETTE 1737	X	X		X			X			
ANON. TOURS 1710	X	X		X	X	X	X			
G. CORRETTE 1703	X	X		X		X	X	X		
G. CORRETTE 1703	X	X		X						
CHAUMONT 1695	X	X	X	X		X	X			
CHAUMONT 1695	X	X		X			X			
BOYVIN 1689	X	X		X			X			
BOYVIN 1689	X	X		X		X	X	X		
RAISON 1688	X	X	X	X		X	X	X		
RAISON 1688	X	X		X			X			
ANON. 1678	X	X		X		X	X			
LE BÈGUE 1676	X	X	X	X		X	X	X		
NIVERS 1665										

Chart 8. Récits (except Tierce): Grand Orgue

TABLE VIII RÉCITS (EXCEPT TIERCE): GRAND ORGUE

KEY:
S = SOPRANO
T = TENOR
B = BASS
X = RANGE NOT GIVEN
( ) = OPTIONAL
1 = CALLS FOR TWO
∅ = CHECK INSTRUCTIONS, FOR ADDITIONAL INFO.

Source	RÉCIT DE —	Bourdon 16	Bourdon 8	Prestant 4	Flûte 4	Nazard 2⅔	Trompette 8	Clairon 4	Voix Humaine 8	Cornet	Tremblant Doux	Tremblant Fort
NIVERS 1665	BASSE DE TROMPETTE	X	X	X			X	X				
NIVERS 1665	VOIX HUMAINE	X	X	X					X	X		
NIVERS 1665	↑		X	X	X		X	X				
LE BÈGUE 1676	BASSE DE TROMPETTE		B	B		B						
LE BÈGUE 1676	VOIX HUMAINE		X	X	(X)	(X)			X	X		
LE BÈGUE 1676	↑		X	X	(X)	(X)			X	X		
ANON 1678	BASSE DE TROMPETTE		B	B			B					
ANON 1678	DESSUS DE TROMPETTE		S				S					
ANON 1678	↑		S				S					
RAISON 1688	BASSE DE TROMPETTE		B	B			B					
RAISON 1688	CLAIRON EN BASSE	B						B				
RAISON 1688	VOIX HUMAINE		X			X			X	X		
BOYVIN 1689	↑		SB		SB			SB				
BOYVIN 1689	BASSE DE TROMPETTE		B		B		B					
BOYVIN 1689	↑		B	B			B	B		B		X
CHAUMONT 1695	BASSE DE TROMPETTE		B	B			B					
G. CORRETTE 1703	↑		B	B			B					
ANON. TOURS C.1710 ∅	TROMP.		X	X		X	X					
ANON. TOURS C.1710 ∅	VOIX HUM.		X	X					X			
M. CORRETTE 1737	BASSE DE TROMPETTE						B	B		B		X
M. CORRETTE 1737	DESSUS DE TROMPETTE						S	S				X
ANON. CAEN 1746	VOIX HUMAINE		X	X		X			X			
ANON. CAEN 1746	BASSE DE TROMPETTE		B				B[1]	B[1]				
D. BEDOS 1766-70	↑		B	(x)			B[1]	B[1]				
D. BEDOS 1766-70	VOIX HUMAINE		X	X	(x)	X						

Chart 9. Récits (except Tierce): Positif

Sources (columns, left to right):
NIVERS 1665 · LE BÈGUE 1676 · ANON. 1678 · RAISON 1688 · BOYVIN 1689 · CHAUMONT 1695 · G. CORRETTE 1703 · ANON. TOURS C.1710 · M. CORRETTE 1737 · DOM BEDOS ⊘ 1766-70

Stops (rows, bottom labels):
BOURDON 8 · PRESTANT 4 · FLUTE 4 · NAZARD 2⅔ · TIERCE 1⅗ · DOUBLETTE 2 · LARIGOT 1⅓ · CROMORNE 8 · TROMPETTE 8 · VOIX HUMAINE 8 · TREMBLANT DOUX · QUARTE DE NAZ.

RÉCIT DE — (right-hand descriptors)

Stop	NIVERS 1665	LE BÈGUE 1676	ANON. 1678	RAISON 1688	BOYVIN 1689	CHAUMONT 1695	G. CORRETTE 1703	ANON. TOURS C.1710	M. CORRETTE 1737	DOM BEDOS 1766-70	RÉCIT DE —
DESSUS DE CRO.		S							S	S	DESSUS DE CRO.
BASSE DE CRO.									B	B S	BASSE DE CRO.
TROMP. EN TAILLE									T (T)		TROMP. EN TAILLE
↑									T	T T	↑
CRO. EN TAILLE		T	T	B T	B		T	T	S T	T	CRO. EN TAILLE
NAZARD		S	S		S	B T	B	S	S T		NAZARD
BASSE DE CRO.							B	B S		B S	BASSE DE CRO.
NAZARD		S	S		S	B B	S	X		X	NAZARD
↑		B	B T	B T		B B	S	X (X)	X		↑
CRO.							S	X X X		X	CRO.
V. HUM.		S			S	B T	S	X		X	V. HUM.
DIALOGUE DE V. HUM.		S	S	S T	X	SB	SB		X	SB	DIALOGUE DE V. HUM.
CRO. EN TAILLE	X X	S	S			B T					CRO. EN TAILLE

Chart 10. Jeu doux

Source	Accompaniment for →	Montre 16	Bourdon 16	Montre 8	Bourdon 8	Prestant 4	Flûte 4	Flûte 8	Nazard 2⅔	Doublette 2	Larigot 1⅓	Tremblant doux	Tremblant fort
NIVERS 1665			X	X	X	X				X			
			X	X	X	X				X			
				X	X	X				X			
				X	X	X							
					X		X						
LE BÈGUE 1676	DESSUS DE CROMORNE				G	G							
	DESSUS DE						G						
	CORNET				P	P							
	BASSE DE TR.				P	P							
	BASSE DE TR., USING CRO.				G	G							
	V. HUM.				P	(P)	P					X	
	ECHO				P	P							
	ECHO						G						
	EN TAILLE	G°	G		G	G							
	CROMORNE				G	G							
	TIERCE OR				G	G							
ANON. 1678	CROMORNE				G	G							
	BASSE DE TR.				P	P	P						
	DESSUS DE TR.				P	P	P						
	CORNET				P	P	P						
	V. HUM.				P	P	P		P				
RAISON 1688	CORNET				G	(G)	G						
	BASSE DE TR. OR CRO.				X	X							
	CLAIRON + 16' EN BASSE				P	P	P						
	BASSE DE TIERCE				G	G	G						
	TIERCE EN TAILLE		G		G	G	G						
	RÉCIT DE CRO.				G	G	G						
	V. HUM.				P	P	P		P			X	
	CRO. EN TAILLE				G	G							

KEY:
G = GRAND ORGUE
P = POSITIF
( ) = FL. 4 PREFERRED
Ø = SECOND CHOICE

Chart 10—Continued

Top section spanning MONTRE 8–FLUTE 4 columns: **PLEIN JEU**

Source	MONTRE 16	BOURDON 16	MONTRE 8	BOURDON 8	PRESTANT 4	FLUTE 4	FLUTE 8	NAZARD $2\frac{2}{3}$	DOUBLETTE 2	LARIGOT $1\frac{1}{3}$	TREMBLANT DOUX	TREMBLANT FORT	ACCOMPANIMENT FOR →
													SINGING CONGREGATION
													V. HUM.
DOM BEDOS 1766-70			G	G									RÉCITS DE DESSUS, BASSE DE CRO.
													BASSE DE TR.
			G	G			G						TIERCE, CRO., AND TR. EN TAILLE
ANON. CAEN 1746			G	G		G							TIERCE·EN TAILLE
				P						P	P		BASSE DE TR.(2)
					P					P	P		BASSE DE TR.(1)
			G	G									TIERCE
			P	P									CORNET
			G	G			"+2 FLUTE ALLEMANDE"						V. HUM.
				P		P					P	X	DESSUS DE TR.
			G	G									TIERCE EN TAILLE
M. CORRETTE 1737		G	G	G									CRO. EN TAILLE
			G	G									TIERCE EN TAILLE; ALSO NAZARD
			P	(P)	P								TR.
			G	G									NAZAR
			P								P	X	BASSE DE TR.
			G										BASSE DE CRO.
ANON. TOURS C.1710 +		G	G	G									DESSUS DE CRO., NAZ., TIERCE, TR.
G. CORRETTE 1703			G		G							X	DIALOGUE DE V. HUM.
		G	G		G								TIERCE EN TAILLE
			G	G									CRO. EN TAILLE, OR EN BASSE
			P	P									BASSE DE TR.
			G	G									DESSUS DE PET. TIERCE
			G		G								NAZAR
CHAUMONT 1695			X	X		X		OR A SUITABLE					CORNET; ECHO; DESSUS ET BASSE DE V. HUM.; DESS. DE CRO.
			X	X	X			SELECTION FROM THESE					
			X	X									BASSE DE TR., OR CRO.
	(G)	G	G	G									TIERCE OR CRO. EN TAILLE
BOYVIN 1689			P								P	X	BASSE DE TR.
			P		P							X	V. HUM. OR REGALLE
		G											CROMORNE
			G	G									ALL RÉCITS EXC. CRO.

Appendix A

Texts of Sixteenth-Century Organ Contracts

Contract for the construction of an organ by Arnaud de Guyssaurret for the Church of Saint-Seurin, Bordeaux (1514). Arch. dép. Gironde, série G, 1162, f° 202 v°. (Transcribed and published by Mlle. Cluzan in *Archives historiques de la Gironde*, Tome 52, p. 57.)

. . . Premeyrament, reffara ledeit de Guyssaurret lo sommier et totz les autres faultz sommiers dudeit principau sommier, despendes et porte vens, segont l'ordre et forme et maneyra que court per lo temps present.

Item, sera tousiours lo gros corps de boucque garnyt de huict tuelz, tant principau que furniture, per marches sens les jocz de las fleustes.

Item, a promes de y far detz corps d'orgues qui se peyran jougar cascun per sin et cascun disferent en multiplicant l'armonye tousiours.

Item, fara et a promes de far lodeit de Guyssaurret jogar lo principau per sin segond son regestre.

Item, apr$_e$s a promes far jougar semblablement la double deudeit principau pe$_r$ sin et en son regestre, et sera tengut la mectre sur la monstre ayssi cum lo principau.

Item, a p omes deudeit principau ayssi medis per sin et per son regestre.

Item, et $_r$a super douzaine cum les autres et per son regestre.

Item, la ^{1}XXIIme semblablement per sin et per son regestre.

Item, la double de la sobre douzaine per sin et per son regestre.

Item, apres la XXIXme ayssi medis per son et per son regestre.

Item, la double de la XXIXme ou ben une petite fleuste et double dessus les autres doas, dessoubz nompnadas et declaradas et a la voluntat deu medis de Guyssaurret ou ben atau cum sera divisat en fasen ladeita besonhe.

Item, apres fara des jocs de fleustes de plomb en una grossa fleute de plomb de petz de long per sin et per son regestre.

Item, apres une petit fleuste double de ladeite precendente fleuste, et par aqueras doas fleustes ab las autres aqueras precendens se poyram multiplicar les jocqs deusdeits orgues en meys de seyssante maneyres toutes differentes, comme de jocs de Papegueytz petitz et grans, ensemps plusieurs jocqs de Acquebutez, jocz de cornetz, jocs de grosses fleustes d'alemans et de petit jocs de chantres, jocs de cymbales et plusieurs autres jocs qui monterant quant lodeit orgue sera prest et se poyran jugar cascun par sin ayssi cum doict es, et multiplicquera en nau vegadas nau, en toute verayre et bonne armonye.

Item, a promes et promet far lodeit organiste ung petit clavey et ung petit orgue qui sera darrey aquest qui sonnera lodeit orgue et sera de la quinzeyne deu principau deudeit orgue et furnyt de sa double et tout per cum et par aquest clavier et petit orgue plan nes cleyat et compartit ab lodeit grant orgue, tout ayssi cum deu sera lo jogador qui sonnera deusdeits orgues qui semblablement se trobera tres en grant armonye et douce melaudia en plusiors sortes de différences.

Contract between Jacques Loup and the Couvent des Frères Mineurs, Bordeaux, February 23, 1518, for the construction of an organ. Arch. dép. Gironde, 3 E 9456. (Transcribed by Paul Roudié.)

Dudit jour XXIIIe de février au couvent des Frères Mineurs.
Entre Sire Jhéronym de Campagne, marchant et bourgois de Bourdeaulx, ou nom et comme scindic du couvent ancien des Frères Mineurs de Bourdeaulx d'une part, et Jacques Loup, maistre organiste, demourant à Bourdeaulx, d'autre. Ont esté faictz et passez et accordez les marchez et appoinctemens qui sensuivent entre ledit de Campaigne audit nom et ledit Loup, présens à ce venerables et religieuses personnes frère Pierre Gorgoilhon, docteur en Théologie, gardien, Jehan de Abbacia . . . et plusiers autres, les tous religieux dudit couvent assemblez ou chappitre dudit couvent, tractans cappitulairement les affaires d'icelluy, ainsi qu'est de coustume, par lequel marché et appoinctement ledit Jacques Loup a promis et promet faire les orgues dudit couvent ainsi et en telle [?] manière qu'il sensuit: C'est assavoir qu'il sera tenu faire servir la menuiserie desdites orgues en la facon et manière qu'elle est à présent, et en oultre sera tenu faire le sommier et le clavier tout à neuf, et y faire ung soufflet de boys, si mestier est, et pourra faire servir les tueaulx qui y sont à présent et rabiller ceulx qui en auront mestier pour les faire servir. Plus sera tenu ledit maistre de faire ung jeu de fleutes de plomb d'allemant tout neuf à la mode nouvelle avec sept tirans, lesqueulx tirans se joueront en quinze ou seze façons. Et sera tenu ledit maistre fournir de toutes estouffes, comme est plomb, estaing, boys, charbon, cloux, fil d'archal, cuyr, parchemyn, colle et toutes autres choses à ce necessaires et payer les

menuisiers et tout autre manière de gens à ses propres despens ainsi que bon lui semblera. Et pour ce faire ledit de Campaigne audit nom a promis et promet bailler et payer audit Loup la somme de quatre vingtz dix livres tournois par tiers . . . Et en oultre sera tenu ledit de Campaigne oudit nom nourrir et alimenter par chascun jour ouvrier tous ceulx qui besoigneront en ladite besoigne à la requeste dudit Loup, et ledit Loup et ses serviteurs ordinaires festes et jours ouvrables, ainsi qu'il sappartiendra. A la façon de laquelle besoigne ledit maistre sera tenu commancer dedens le XIIe jour de mars prochainement venant. Et sera tenu icelle besoigne et choses susdites avoir faictes et parfaictes bien et deuement dedans quatre moys prochainement venans et à la fin d'iceulx au dit de gens de bien audit art et office entendu comme dit est . . .

Contract between Louis Gaudet and the Church of Sainte-Croix, Oloron, April 9, 1521, for the construction of an organ. Arch. dép. Gironde, 3 E 6650, fº 221 rº–222 rº. (Transcribed by Paul Roudié.)

Au jourduy neufviesme d'avril l'an mil cinq cens vingt et ung personnellement establys en droit maistre Loys Gaudet, lequel de son bon gré a promis et promect faire unes orgues de la grandeur sorte et manière de celles de l'église Sainte Eulaye de Bourdeaux et icelles mectre et pouser en l'église de Saincte Croix d'Oloron en Béarn, et est tenu fournir les barquins sive souffetz, segretz et sommier tous garnitz, et de ce faire s'est obligé envers les ouvriers de ladite église absens, maistre Bernard de Lambège présent stipulant et acceptant pour lesdits ouvriers et juralz de ladite ville, esqueulx ledit Gaudet a faict et conclud ledit marché, et sont tenuz lesdits ouvriers et juratz fournir tout l'estaing et autre estoffe nécessaire à faire et accoustrer lesdites orgues, et davantaige sont tenuz faire porter à leurs despans de ceste ville de Bourdeaux jusques audit lieu d'Oloron tout l'ouvraige nécessaire esdites orgues que ledit Gaudet fera en ceste ville, et ce moyenant le pris et somme de cent cinquante livres tournois . . . laquelle besongne d'orgues ledit Gaudet doibt avoir parachevé de faire, Dieu aydant, dans le jour de saincte Croix du moys de Septembre prochainement venant . . .

Organ contracts, December 3, 1529, Church of Saint-Eloi, Bordeaux, for the construction of an organ by Bertrand Jehan. Arch. dép. Gironde, 3 E 7143, fº 129 rº–130 rº.

Sensuyt se que je suis tenu de faire pour les orgues de Sainct Eloy Et primo hung orgue de six piés, comme il pert au fustaige vieulx qui est en l'église dudict sainct Eloy, et dans ledit fustaige et tabernaigle je suys tenu de forny les jeus qui sensuyvent: et primo hung jeu de six piés en tonnes en ton de chappelle.

Item hune octave dudict principal de six piés.

Item une quinziesme.

Item hune XIXme.

Item hune XXIIme.

Item ung jeu de simballes et le tout dessus nommés de bonn estaing.

Item j'ay encores trois jeus de plomn, le premier octave octave du gros jeu de six piés, le segonnt ser pour faire les jeus de canars, le tiers set la quinziesme de flautes qui sert d'ung petit jeu de flauioles de Poitou, et le tout de plomn, set assavoir ses troys jeus, et le tout estoit prest à monte [?] et achevé quant je fis ma protestacion et avois faict et parfaict mon dict oubraige, se que me faudra tout refaire et fis pourter mon sommier à ma maison et ung coffre plens de tueaulx et aultres besoignes apartenans audictz orgues quy me couta, hou aler et venir, plus de troys livres tournois.

Item je ne serois refaire les tueux quy se seront deruis [?] et gastés, lesqueulx estoient toutz prest, que n'y mete deux mois hou plus. Item je suppouse avoir pardu des chouses qui me porteront domaige de plus de X livres tournois. Signé: Bertrand Jehan.

Personnellement establyz maistre Jehan Thory et Bernard Constantin au nom et comme ouvriers de l'église parochialle Sainct Eloy de Bourdeaux, lesqueulx ont faict marché avecques Bertrand Jehan, maistre organiste du lieu de Marmande, à présent demorant au Mas d'Agenoys, de ce que sensuyt: c'est assavoir que ledit Jehan a promis et sera tenu faire et parfaire les orgues au dedans l'église Sainct Eloy de Bourdeaulx ainsi qu'elles sont divisées au présent fuilhet et seront assizes ou est assis le fustaige et sera tenu le tout fournir à ses despens et icelles rendre parfaictes à sonner, sauf et réservé des courtynes, icelles sera tenu avoir parfaictes dedans le jour et feste de Pasques prochainement venant et moyennant la somme de trente escuz d'or sol. dont ledit Jehan a confessé avoir receu des ouvriers qui estoyent précédemment troys escutz d'or sol., cincq escutz d'or sol. que lesdits ouvriers ont baillé et livré sur ces présentes audit Jehan, et incontinant qu'il aura ses sommiers et ce qu'il apartient à faire lesdites orgres en la présente ville de Bourdeaux seront tenuz lesdits ouvriers luy bailler une chambre bonne et suffizante, ensemble la somme de dix escuz d'or soleilh, et la fin de payement incontinant lesdites orgues parfaictes. Et pour assurance desdictes chouses a esté personnellement estably monsieur maistre Jehan de Carmantrand, greffier des présentacions, lequel de son bon gré est entré plèges pour et au nom dudict Jehan envers lesdits ouvriers pour raison des chouses susdites et ce que ledit Jehan a promis relever indampne . . . Obligent l'ung pour l'autre et l'une partie à l'autre . . . Présens sire Arnaud de Peyperoulx et Guillem Lamoureulx tesmoings.

Documents relating to the refurbishment and enlargement of an organ for the Toulouse Cathedral, 1531. Arch dép. Haute Garonne 3 E 7067. (Transcribed by Paul Roudié.)

Sansuit ce que il faust a votre [?] orgues
Et premierement

Item il faust ellarguit le fust de lorgues jusques aust fleur de lis.

Item il faust le sommier auesques VIII tirand et les couvertures.

Item deux tables en gravures qui porteront le vans ales montres.

Item il faust troys soufles tout neufs avesques VIII elles a chascund souflet et les boust qui tiendrond les bost de elle.

Item il faust faire les marches toutes neufves et les verges pour atacher les marches et souspaspes ensenbles.

Item une estoille pour outer le vens du sommier et le conduyt de boys pour conduise le vens alletoille pour la vire.

Item neuf barre de fert et unne grousse cheville de fert pour tire les jeulx a travers le barres pour tenir les barres.

Item en coille pour coiller les soufles et le sommier et et le boys et les conduyt et les soupaspes, ung quintal.

Item en peaulx de mouton pour couvrit les soufles doubles et le sommier et les conduyt, VI douzegnes.

Item en papier pour doubles les tables des soufles et le conduyt, IIII mains.

Item en filz de fert pour les pointes des marches et les bouches, I livre et demi.

Item en filz de leton pour fayres les resors et atascher les tringles au souspaspes et au clavier, IIII livres.

Item en cloux de quatre ongles pour clouver le coufres en lantour du sommier et ou se metra le vans et les couvertures du sommier et le conduyt du vans et les boustes, IIII cens.

Item en cloux d'ung dourt pour clouver les barre du boust des soufles ou seront assizes les elles et barres ou tiandront les contre poics de soufles, III XX.

Item en cloux de deux ongles, II cens.

Item en petit cloux de guingueson, IIII cens.

Item en filz de lin pour doudres les premiere peaulx de mouton pour couvrir les soufles et les bourcestes, demye livre.

Item en ficelles pour coudres et virongner [?] les premiere peaulx de mouton qui seront coillers sus les soufles.

Item il me faust de letaint pour fayre le anchestes et les cornes des resgalles, XXXV livres.

Item il me faust du plomb pour fayre les pestistes fleustes et les de . . . [?] . . . (I) . . . II cens et demi.

Item du boys et du cherbon pour fondre le plomb et presse le sommier et chaufer les soufles quant on les collera.

Sansuit les diferand des jeulx de l'orgue
Et premierement

Item le grand jeulx
Item le jeulx de papegayl
Item le jeulx des chantres
Item le jeulx des fleustes dallemans
Item le jeulx de pifres
Item le jeulx sourt
Item le jeulx de nazars petit et groulx
Item le jeulx des cornes
Item le jeulx des simballes
Item le jeulx des fleustes
Item le jeulx de petit carillons
Item le jeulx de petites orgues
Item le jeulx de petistes orgues en fleustes et le sic de aliis
Item le tabourin
Item ung jeulx de regalles
Il faust fare troy tirans de jeulx de fleustes et la soubres doxiemes
Le principal
la octave
la XVe
la XIXe
la XXIIe
les nefs [?], la grosse fleute

    les cornes
    la petite fleute
    les hautz bois

Cormier [signed]

Sachent tous, presens et advenir, que comme ainssi soyt que messieurs les bailles regens et surentendens de la table et confrairie du corps de Dieu, en leglise metropolitaine Sainct Estienne de Tholouse instituee, heussent baille a reffaire les orgues de ladicte table a maistre Jacques Cormier, maistre orgueniste de Tours, et ce a faire auxditz orgues les jeulx qui sensuyvent, ascavoir est le principal, la octave, le xvme, la xixe, la xxiie, la grosse fleute, la xiie de la fleute, la xve de la fleute, et ung jeu de regales, que montent tout neuf jeux differens, pour le prix et somme de cent quarante livres tournois . . . comme plus a plein est contenu en l'instrument sur ce passé par moy notaire subsigne. Et soyt ainssi que lesdictz messieurs les chanoynes de ladicte eglise de se pouvoir ayder desdictes orgues, pourveu que fussent tenus de iceulx tenir accordes en forme deue a leurs propres coutz et despens au temps avenir, ce que lesdicts messieurs les chanoynes avoyent accorde, ainsi que apert par instrument retenu par maistre Jehan Danyel, notaire dudict chapitre, et soyt ainssi que tant ledict Cormyer pour sa descharge que aussi lesdicts messieurs les bailles heussent convoques plusieurs maistres orguenistes pour visiter lesdites orgues, icelles faire sonner, voir si ledict Cormier auroit acompli la tenur des pactes sur ce passes, par ainssi est que, l'an que l'On conte mil Vc xxxi et le dernier jour du moys de julhet, en ladicte glise et table, personnelement constitues ascavoir est maistres Fermyn de La byardiere, de Amians en Picardie, Fortis Pujolh, de Carcassone, Nycholas Pongi de Usès, maistres orguenistes, messires Guillem Picavan, mestre des enfans de cuer, de ladicte eglise, Pierre Chevallié, chantre et contrehaute dudict cuer, lesquels tous moyenent serment par eulx preste ont reffere avoir visite lesdictes orgues ensemble les pactes passes avec ledict Cormyer et, icelles visitees, avoir trouve ledict Cormyer avoir accomp[li] le contenu ausdicts pactes et lesdictes orgues estre bien accordes, les jeulx contents en iceulx pactes avoir esté fai[cts] par le susdict Cormyer et acomplis, et iceulx orgues estre de bon accort et perfecti[on] et aussi la soufflerie estre faicte selon le contenu esdicts pactes, desquel[les] chouses dessusdictes tant ledict Cormyer pour sa descharge que aussi lesdicts messires les bailles ascavoir est messieurs Pierre Rolli [?] Arnauld de Blancons, temoins maistre Gerauld Pugarnier [?], procureur en parlement, Pierre Malhard appothicaire, ont requis a moy notaire subsigne leur retenir acte de se dessus pour leur servir en temps et lieu contre ledict chapitre entendu qu'il balhent lesdicts orgues a present accordes la[?] out[?] et que ledict chapitre, ensuy-vant sa promesse, ne vouldroit tenir accordes lesdits orgues en ensuyvant l'obligation par eulx faicte en presence de messire Pierre Calelh, docteur, messire Jehan de S . . . [?] procureur du Roy de la . . . [?] messire Dominique de Sainct Ange, messire Arnauld de Arro, bachellier, messire Pierre de Quercu, panatie [?] dudit chapitre et de moy.

Documents relating to the construction of an organ for the Church of Sainte-Eulalie, Bourdeaux, June 11, 1548. Arch. dép. Gironde 3 E 6557, fº 128 vº, and fº 129 vº.

A Bourdeaulx le unziesme jour du mois de juing l'an mil cinq cens quarante huict. Personnellement constitués Jehan Guinherie et Jehan Guirault, ouvriers de l'église parochielle de Sainct Eulaye de Bourdeaulx d'une part, et Olivier Artaud maistre menuisier de Bourdeaulx d'autre part, entre lesqueulx a esté faict le marché qui s'ensuit. Premièrement sera tenu led. Artaud faire le fust des orgues de douze piedz et sera tenu fournir le bois et de toute façon selon la devise, portraict et plate-forme du poseur d'orgues, qui sera faict et assis dedans quatre mois amprès le marché faict. Item sera tenu de faire le sommier, fornir de bois et façon selon la devise dudit faseur d'orgues, aussi des règles et tirances pour la différance des jeuz, comme il est requis. Item sera tenu faire l'établement dudit sommier pour l'asseoir dans le feust, le tout scelon la devise de l'organiste. Item sera tenu faire la brege [?] dudit sommier ensemble les tirétes, avec le clavier et chassis d'icelluy, et fornir le bois à ce requis. Item sera tenu faire les quatre souffletz et fournir le bois, tant de tables, barres, boytes, souppapes et chassis, et aussi les barres pour les souffletz avecques leur assiète[?] canons pour porter le vent au sommier et autre bois requis. Item sera tenu faire les estoilles[?] de façon porte-ventz et fourniture de bois. Item sera tenu de faire les liésons des thuieaulx, tant grands que petitz, qui sont de bois et tables scelon l'ordonnance de l'organiste. Item sera tenu de faire la façon des molles qui seront besoing à l'œuvre desdites orgues. Item sera tenu de faire la table pour fondre l'estaing et plomb pour faire les thueaulx qui fault de la longueur de seze piedz, qui sera faicte scelon l'ordonnance de l'organiste aussi les rouables et cuy . . . [?] pour gecter l'estaing et plomb. Item sera tenu de faire les acoutouers de la galerie des souffletz de montans et panneaulx tous plaintz, et portes, s'il en fault. Item sera tenu de faire le lieu pour metre les régalles, sommiers et canons porte-ventz, si mestier est, et comme il est requis. Item que tous ces

articles[?] dessus mentionnés seront faictz tout ainsi que l'organiste les demandera et à l'heure qu'il en aura mestier et sera tenu le tout fournir, réservé le grand fustaige qu'il ne sera tenu fournir, et sera tenu faire le plancher, touteffois ne sera tenu fournir les cloux [Prix 290 fr. bord] le vieux feust des orgues sera audit menuizier qu'il fera servir derrière, non davant, ni aux coustés, et sera tenu mectre le tout bon bois de chesne net pur et marchant, scelon le portraict à luy baillé et monstré . . .
Signature de Olivier Hertault.

A Bourdeaulx le unziesme jour de juing l'an mil cinq cens quarante huict. Personnellement constitué sire Jehan Guinherie et Jehan Guirault, ouvriers de l'église Saincte Aulaye de Bourdeaulx, d'une part, et frère Jehan de Cyvrac, infirmier de Sancte Croix de Bourdeaux d'autre, lesquelles parties de leur bon grés et voluntés ont [fait] . . . marché en la manière que s'ensuit. Scavoir est que ledit de Cyvrac a promis, doint et sera tenu faire leurs orgues de douze piedz à douze tirans avecques les leuz qui s'ensuyvent: Premièrement le principal, fleustre de six piedz, fleustre à neuf trous, fleustre d'allemant, flageotz, doulssannes, canardz, nazards gros, moiens nazards, petis nazards, petis cornetz, saqueboutes, voix humaines, musette, petits phiffres, gros cornetz, papegaulx, cymballes, musette grande, principal ou grand jeu fleustre. Et sera tenu fondre l'estaing et plomb et rendre le tout faict et parfaict à ses despens en fournissant par lesdits ouvriers toute estoffe, aussi fournissant peaulx, colle, ferrure cloux et toute aultre estoffe nécessaire [Prix 250 l. tourn.].

Contract for an organ, Notre-Dame, Alençon, September 17, 1537. (Text as published by G. Despierres, in *Les Orgues de Notre-Dame d'Alençon*, Argentan, 1888.)

Du X^vii j° de septembre Lan mil V°XXXVII devant les tabellions cy sobz signez A Alençon.

Furent Tous maistres Gratien de Cailly et Symon Le Vasseur organistes et faiseurs d'orgues lesquels par alleu et marche par eulx faict avecqz les trésoriers bourgeois de ce lieu d'Alençon se submisrent et obligerent faire parfaire et accomplir unes orgues en lesglise de Notre-Dame du dit lieu d'Alençon bonnes et suffisantes de douze piedz les principaulx tuyaulx et de grosseur a Lequippollent Et des tuyaulx de six piedz des orgues de Notre-Dame de Guibray Au dessus et au dessoulx a la dite equippollence Ou sensuyvront tous Les aultres tuyaulx des dites orgues Le parement desquels sera de fin estain et des aultres tuyaulx de dedans tant pour la fourniture du principal que de celle de six piedz Et aultres lieux ou il sera mestier y en faire d'estain Et le reste de tous Les tuyaulx des dites orgues sera de plomb net bon et suffisant.

Lesquelles orgues seront entonnees du ton du coeur Et esquelles y aura XIII ou XIIII differences de jeulz entiers et particuliers Grand est le dit jeu de douze piedz destain Ung aultre jeu pareillement destain de troys piedz Lesquels troys jeulz destain prennent dembas sur le hault pour myeulx fournir a la fourniture.

Item une fourniture d'huyct tuyaulx sur marche Le tout destain avec une cymballe pareillement destain qui sont cinq jeulz servant tous au principal du corps des dites orgues.

Item ung jeu de flustes entonnee de six piedz estouppee pour faire le nazard qui sera de plomb

Item une fleuste de troys piedz pareillement de plomb

Item ung aultre jeu de doubles fleustes pareillement de plomb de troys piedz

Item une aultre fleuste de plomb de pied et demy pour servir au jeu du nazard

Item une fleuste hors ton pour le nazard pareillement de plomb

Item ung aultre petit jeu de nazard

Item ung jeu tremblant qui tremblera sur lequel des jeulz quil plaira a lorganiste sans segonde personne

Item ung jeu de Rossignol ou de Bedou

Et cy au corps d'orgues y aura XIII trayantz

Item devant lesquelles orgues y aura ung positif du pourtraict qui a este baille par les sieurs Maistres aux sieurs tresoriers et bourgeoys Auquel positif y aura ung jeu de trompettes de six piedz Et cy ce sera comprins ung jeu de voix humaines et ung jeu de herpes Et seront tous les dits tuyaulx de bonne et suffisante espesses de tuyau sans y espargner estain ou plomb.

Le tout selon qu'il sera requis raisonnablement Et auxquelles orgues y aura un sommier et sommiers bons et suffisans de la forme de ceulx des orgues dArgentan qui seront de telle grandeur et spaciosité quil sera requis selon lœuvre Et auxquelles orgues y aura cinq grands soufflets emboytes pour le corps des dites orgues et deux pour le positif

Et entant que la menuiserie elle sera pour le corps dorgues depuys lassiette du sommier jusques au hault De la forme du pourtraict des orgues dArgentan Mais en oultre y seront Les quatre tourelles a rond et a pendz a cul de lampe pendant Et les lanternes de dessus jouant celles des orgues dArgentan ou de celles pourtraictes au pourtraict baillé par les sieurs organistes aux sieurs tresoriers et bourgeoys au choix diceulx bourgeoys Lesquelles Lanternes seront de telle grandeur que le cas requerra Pour lesquelles orgues faire et fournir de toutes matières et toutes choses generallement quelconques Et les rendre toutes prestes faites de telles painctures de argent et azur qu'il plaira aux sieurs bourgeois . . .

Iceulx tresoriers qui sont maistre Jehan Moynet escuïer sieur de Neauphle Cleriadus Bouvet sieur de Vendelle et Anthoine Le Lieuvre prêtre ont promis payer aux dits organistes La somme de quatorze cents livres Et aultre somme de cent livre qui demeure a l'admistion des sieurs bourgeoys Laquelle somme de cent livres ils payeront aux dits organistes au cas que les dites orgues soient parachevees et accomplyes jouant Et quant aux quatorze cents livres elles seront payeez aux dates qui ensuivent cest asscavoir dedans la toussaint prochaine deux cents livres et cent livres a Noël trois cents livres dedans paques aultre cens livres a la pentecoste et les aultres sept cents livres elles seront payeez a la mesure que la besoigne se fera . . . et accorde que dedans la nativité Saint Jehan-Baptiste prochaine les organistes rendront partie des dites orgues et l'autre partie au plustôt que faire se pourra.

Contract for rebuilding the large organ in Chartres Cathedral, November 16, 1542. Arch. dép. G 197, f 519 v°. (Text as published by Charles Métais, in *Les Orgues de la Cathédrale de Chartres,* 1918.)

Jeudi, XVIᵉ novembre 1542; vénérable maistres Jehan Nantier, chancellier, Jehan de la Croix, chanoines de Chartres, maistres et administrateurs de l'œuvre de l'Eglise de Chartres, lesquelz en ensuyvant l'ordonnance de messieurs du Chapitre de Chartres faicte le jour d'hyer, ont confessé avoir ce jourd'huy marchandé et composé avecques Robert Filleul, organiste, ad ce présent, de faire, parfaire par ledit Filleul les grosses orgues de l'église de Chartres selon et ainsi qu'il ensuyt, c'est assavoir qu'il sera tenu et a promis descendre, démolir et de assembler les grosses orgues de lad. église, les sommiers et les soufflets, refaire lesd. grosses orgues les mectre et asseoir dedans le viel fust, faire et remplir la monstre de tuyaulx convenables des jeux qui ensuyvent, savoir est vng plain jeu de seize pieds remply d'une double, de huit tuyaulx en bas de trente-deux pieds en pédalle, le clavier commencant en fa, ut; et seront les huict plus gros tuyaulx desdites orgues qui se joueront en pédalle, ledit plain jeu sera fourny de deux tuyaulx de huict piedz, sur chacune marche troys tuyaulx de quatre piez, et six autres de deux piedz, fourniture convenable pour lesd. orgues, et seront sur chacune marche douze tuyaulx sans le jeu des cornets et cymbale.

Item sera tenu mectre vng nazart double fourny de quattre tuyaulx sur chacune marche, et pour faire ledit nazart seront [mis] les deux tuyaulx de huict piedz dudict plain jeu.

Item le . . . de seize piedz se pourra jouer seul et avec les pédalles de tren . . . piedz et autres jeuz subsequens. Lesdites pédalles se pourront jouer avecques tous les jeuz desd. orgues, et avecques ledict jeude cornetz.

Item le jeu desd. deux tuyaulx d'huit piedz dud. plain jeu se pourra . . . seul et avecques vng chacun de tous les jeuz.

Item le jeu desd. trois tuyaulx de quatre piedz dud. plain jeu se jouera seul et avec tous les autres jeuz fors que avecques ledit nazart et cymbale.

Item vng jeu de fourniture desd. six tuyaulx sur marche dudit plain jeu qui ne sa pourra jouer seul sans estre associé des groz jeuz précedans.

Item vng jeu de cymbale fourny de troys tuyaulx sur marche, laquelle se jouera avecques tous les jeuz précedens fors qu'avec lesd. nazart.

Item vng jeu de cornets à anches qui sera mis et posé en vng petit fust derrière le joueur desd. orgues lequel jeu jourra seul et avecques tous lesd. jeuz fors que avecques lesd. cymbales et fourniture desd. orgues. Et aura led. jeu de cornetz souffletz, sommiers, porteventz.

Item vng jeu de tremblant. Et sera tenu led. Filleul faire six soufflets ou autre quantité bons et suffisans pour faire souffler et fournir de vent lesd. orgues, lesquelles seront mys dedans la prochaine chambre desd. orgues, et avecques ce fera trois petitz souffletz pour lesd. cornetz, les sommiers, buzes, porteventz, secretz et clavier sans abrégé. Et rendra led. Filleul lesd. orgues, savoir est le plain jeu de seize piedz sonnant et jouant dedans vng an et demy prochain venant pour servir à lad. église. Et le reste le rendra faict et parfaict en bon estat et suffisant audict de gens ad ce congnoissant, dedans deux ans prochainement venantz et sera tenu faire le calvier desd. orgues facile et doulx à jouer. Et avecques ce sera tenu et a promis led. Filleul bailler au menuysier le devys, patron et ordonnance qu'il fauldra pour enrichir bien et convenablement led. fust et au cas que led. enrichissement cousteroit plus de cent livres tant pour facon de menuysier que pour le bois, sera tenu et a promis led. Filleul que ce [sera] à ses coustz et despens, et le desduire sur la somme qui luy [est] et a esté promis pour le présent marché. Et ou il se trou[vera] quelque faulte ou défaillance desd. orgues sera tenu led. Filleul les réparer rendre et remestre en bon estat et deu à ses coustz et despens et sur peine de tous despens, dommaiges . . . Cest convention et composition faictz moiennant que lesd. Nantier et de la Croix esd. noms ont pormis et seront tenus fournir, livrer et bailler aud. Filleul, toutes les estouffes et matières comme estaux, colle, ferreure, cuyr, charbon et autres estouffes nécessaires, et faire les eschaffaux, et avecques ce moiennant la somme de treize cens livres tournois et deux muys de blé, laquelle somme de deniers lesdits

Nantier et de la Croix esd. noms ont promis et seront tenus bailler et délivrer par le clerc de l'œuvre par chacun mois aud. Filleul ainsi qu'il besongnera et fera besongner ausd. orgues et selon l'œuvre qu'il aura faicte à la discrétion desd. Nantier et de la Croix . . . et ont accordé que led. Filleul aura et luy seront baillées les chambres basses ou souloit demourer et faire residence le defunct maistre Jehan Boudet, notaire . . . Et led. Filleul sera tenu bailler pleiges et cautions Mre Robert Misery, ch^{ne} chambrier, et M. Michael de Sainte-Jame . . . tesmoings M. Jehan Fournier, organiste et curé de Chauffour, Jehan Gombault, clerc de l'œuvre et Symon Thoré, clerc, demourant à Chartres.

Inventory of pipes in the great organ in Notre-Dame, Amiens, made November 21–26, 1549. Arch. Somme, Chapit d'Am. G 1144. (As published in Georges Durand, *Les Orgues de la Cathédrale d'Amiens*, 1903.)

Primes, au grand pracqué desdites orgues estant de costé de l'église Sainct-Fremyn le Confès cotté A, ont esté levé ce quy s'ensuit.

Primes, de le furniture de le première touche dudit grant parquet, à commencher à conter prez de la tour du millieu desdites orgues, ont esté trouvés trois rengues de thueaus servans à une touche, quy sont en nombre de IIII^{xx}II thueaulx petis, dont en y a LVIII qui de sonnent poinct, et les aultres XXIIII sonnent et servent; lesdits IIII^{xx}II pour la furniture de quatre principaulx, dont en y a deux principaulx pour la devanture, qui se voyent devant, tous pollis, l'un sonnant le double en bas, et l'autre doit sonner le double en hault mais ne disoit mot et estoit bouchée par la lumière. Les deux aultres principaulx estans derrière parail à ceulx de devant, non pollis, tout en unysson, l'un sonnant le double en bas, et l'autre devoit sonner le double en hault, lequel ne disoit mot parce qu'il estoit bouché par la lumyère. Et ainsy y a quatre principaulx à tous les touches quy se déclairent cy aprez et de parail son, comme celles de cy-devant, selon les degrés du principal ton desdites orgues.

En la seconde touche en suyvant, y a III^{xx}VI thueaulx servant pour la furniture de quatre principaulx d'icelle touche, dont les XLVI ne sonnent poinct, et les aultres XL parlent et sonnent.

La troizième touche ensuyvant, y a LXXIX thueaulx, pour la furniture de quatre principaulx, deux devant et deux derrière comme dessus, servans à ladite IIIe touche, dont les XLI ne disent mot, et les aultres XXXVIII sonnent et parlent.

Le quatriesme touche ensuyvant, y a LXXIIII thueaulx pour la furniture de quatre principaulx, deux devant et deux derrière, comme dessus, servant à ladite IIIIe touche, dont les XXXIII ne disent mot avec les quatre principaulx, et le reste sonne.

La cincquiesme touche ensuyvant, y a LXXV thueaulx, pour la furniture de quatre principaulx, dont les XXX ne disent mot avec les quatre principaulx.

La sixiesme touche ensuyvant, y a LIIII thueaulx pour la furniture de quatre principaulx, dont les XLIII ne disent mot avec les quatre principaulx, les XI aultres parlent.

La VIIe touche ensuyvant, y a XLIIII thueaulx pour la furniture de quatre principaulx, dont les XXIIII ne disent mot avec les quatre principaulx, et les aultres XX parlent.

La VIIIe touche ensuyvant, y a XXXVII thueaulx, pour la furniture de quatre principaulx, dont les XXVIII ne disent mot avec les quatre principaulx et les IX aultres parlent.

La IXe touche ensuyvant, y a XXXIII thueaulx, pour la furniture de IIII principaulx, dont les XXIIII ne disent mot avec les IIII principaulx.

La Xe touche ensuyvant, y a XXXV thueaulx, pour la furniture de quatre principaulx, dont XXIIII ne disent mot avec les IIII principaulx.

La XIe touche ensuyvant, y a XLI thueaulx, pour la furniture de quatre principaulx, dont les XXVII ne disent mot avec les IIII principaulx.

La XIIe touche ensuyvant, y a XLVIII thueaulx, pour la furniture de quatre principaulx, dont les XXXIII ne disent mot.

La XIIIe ensuyvant, y a LXIII thueaulx, pour la furniture de quatre principaulx, dont les XXX ne disent mot avec les IIII principaulx.

La XIIIIe ensuyvant, y a LXX thueaulx, pour la furniture de quatre principaulx dont les XLVI ne disent mot avec les IIII principaulx.

La XVe ensuyvant, y a LXXVII thueaulx, pour la furniture de quatre principaulx, dont les XXVIII ne disent mot avec les IIII principaulx.

La XVIe ensuyvant, y a LXXIII thueaulx, pour la furniture de quatre principaulx, dont les XXIX ne disent mot avec les quatre principaulx.

La XVIIe ensuyvant, y a IIII^{xx}XI thueaulx, pour la furniture des quatre principaulx, dont les LVIII ne disent mot avec les quatre principaulx.

Au grant pracquet cotté B, du costé vers la chappelle Saint-Christofle, esté levé pour la furniture des principaulx ce quy ensuyt:

Primes, en la première touche servant pour furniture dudit parcquet, commenchant du costé de ladite chappelle Saint-Christofle prez de la tour des cincq gros tureaulx, y a IIII^{xx}VI thueaulx, dont les LV ne disent mot avec les quatre principaulx.

La deuxiesme touche ensuyvant, y a XIIII^{xx} thueaulx, pour la furniture de quatre principaulx, deux devant et deux derrière, dont les XXXII ne disent mot avec les IIII principaulx.

La IIIe touche ensuyvant, y a LXXII thueaulx, pour la furniture de quatre principaulx, dont les XXXVIII ne disent mot avec les quatre principaulx.

La IIIIe touche ensuyvant, y a LXXVII thueaulx, pour la furniture de quatre principaulx, dont les XXVI ne disent mot avec les quatre principaulx.

La cincquiesme ensuyvant, y a LV thueaulx, pour la furniture de quatre principaulx, dont les XL ne disent mot avec les quatre principaulx.

La sixiesme ensuyvant, XLIIII thueaulx, pour la furniture de quatre principaulx, dont les XXXI ne disent mot avec les quatre principaulx.

La VIIe touche ensuyvant, XXXVIII thueaulx, pour la furniture de quatre principaulx, dont les XXIII ne disent mot avec les quatre principaulx.

La VIIIe ensuyvant, XXXIIII, pour la furniture de quatre principaulx, dont les XIX ne disent mot avec les quatre principaulx.

Le IXe ensuyvant, y a XXXV thueaulx, pour la furniture de quatre principaulx, dont les XXV ne disent mot, avec les quatre principaulx.

Le Xe ensuyvant, y a XL thueaulx, pour la furniture de quatre principaulx, dont les XXV ne disent mot avec les quatre principaulx.

Le XIe ensuyvant, y a XLVIII thueaulx, pour la furniture de quatre principaulx, dont les XXI ne disent mot avec les IIII principaulx.

Le XIIe ensuyvant, y a LXII thueaulx, pour la furniture de quatre principaulx, dont les XXIII ne disent mot.

Le XIIIe touche, y a LXX thueaulx, pour la furniture de quatre principaulx, dont les XXX ne disent mot.

Le XIIII ensuyvant y a LXXVII thueaulx, pour la furniture de quatre principaulx, dont les XXXIII ne disent mot.

Le XV touche ensuyvant IIII^{xx}IIII thueaulx, pour la furniture de quatre principaulx, dont les XLVI ne disent mot avec les quatre principaulx.

Le XVI touche ensuyvant y a IIII^{xx}XI thueaulx . . . dont les LXII ne disent mot, avec les quatres principaulx.

A la tour du millieu, y a à la première touche XX thueaulx, avec deux principaulx, dont les XI ne disent mot et les aultres IX parlent.

La seconde, y a, avec les deux principaulx, XXI thueaulx pour la furniture, dont les XIIII ne disent mot et les VII parlent.

La IIIe ensuyvant, y a XXIII thueaulx avec les deux principaulx, dont l'un est fort gatté derrière, et ne sonnent poinct par faulte de touche.

En la grosse tour du costé des cloistres, avec les deux doubles principaulx, pour furniture y a XIX thueaulx servans pour la furniture d'une touche, dont les XI ne disent mot et les VIII parlent.

La IIe touche, avec les doubles principaulx, y a XIX thueaulx, dont les XV ne disent mot et les IIII parlent.

La IIIe touche, avec les principaulx, y a XIX thueaulx dont ilz ne disent mot.

La IIIIe touche, y a XXI thueaulx, avec les deux principaux, dont les XIIII ne disent mot.

La ve touche, y a XXIII thueaulx, avec les deux principaulx, dont les XIII ne disent mot.

A la tour du costé vers l'église Saint-Fremyn, avec deux principaulx, y a à la première touche XXII thueaulx, dont les XVIII ne disent mot, et les IIII parlent.

La seconde touche, avec deux principaulx, y a XXVII thueaulx, dont les XVIII ne disent mot et les IX parlent.

La IIIe touche, avec les principaulx, y a XX thueaulx dont les XII ne disent mot, et les VIII parlent.

La IIIIe toche, avec les principaulx, y a XXV thueaulx dont les XV ne disent mot, et les X parlent.

La Ve touche ensuyvant, avec les principaulx, y a XXVII thueaulx, dont les XV ne disent mot, et les XII parlent.

Somme desdictz thueaulx et principaulx, est XXIIII^c IIII^xx XV thueaulx, dont en y a XIII^c IIII^xx XV quy ne disent mot, et le XIe parlent.

Caignart [signed]

Contract for an organ to be constructed by Jean Pistre for Pierre de Labatut, January 3, 1558, Bordeaux. Arch. dép. Gironde, 3 E 11143, f° 233 r°–235 r°. (Transcribed by Paul Roudié.)

Sachent tous, a esté présent et personnellement estably messire Jehan Pistre, prestre, demourant en la paroisse Sainct Michel de Bourdeaulx, lequel de son bon gré et volonté a promis et sera tenu faire pour Pierre de Labatut, marchand, illec présent stippullant, scavoir est unes orgues à cinq tirans au grand clavyer, dont le principar sera du ton de troys piedz en flustes, le segond tirant octave du principal en flustes, le tiers tirant douziesme du principal bastard en flustes, le quart tirant quinziesme du principal taille de tuyeaulx qui ne sera du ton de flustes, le cinquiesme tirant une régalle consonant au principal, et que ung chescun desdits jeulx jouera à part sey [celui] que vouldra, et ung jeu tramblant qui sera en la forme et qualité que ledit Pistre l'entend, et toutes les flustes desdites orgues seront myses en tamys de bois sans estre atachées à fil d'archeaulx, fer, ni autrement, lesquelles flustes seront toutes d'estaing et toutes bien faictes et accordantes au dire d'organistes et chantres, et seront lesdites orgues myses dedans ung coffre de boys faict à panneaulx tout uny, et la soufflerie d'icelles sera dessoubz à troys soufflets en ung coffre faict semblablement à panneaulx tout planier, et ne paraistra tirens ni autre choze dehors, mais sera le tout enclos dans lesdits coffres fermens en clefs, le tout de bon boys de noyer bien sec . . .

Appendix B

Instructions for Registration (1504–1636), in English Translation

Appendix B contains instructions about the use of organ stops, taken from various contracts and theoretical treatises. Numbers 1–8, 11, and 12 are translated from M. A. Vente, *Die brabanter Orgel*, pp. 22, 32–33, 35–36, 37, and 160–62, and from Vente, *Proeve*, pp. 160, 182, and 184. Number 9 was kindly transmitted by Dr. Hans Klotz, Cologne. Number 10 is an excerpt from Costanzo Antegnati's treatise on organ building, first published in 1608.

1. 1498–1504. Daniel van der Distelen, St. Jan Church,'s Hertogenbosch. The Hauptwerk ("das grosse Plenum") was placed on a Blocklade. The Positiv, on two chests, the forward of which had a slider for one of its two registers, provided "four different voices," or registrations:

   a. All three registers on (i.e. "das Kleine Plenum"—fourteen ranks in all)
   b. The posterior chest off: "Zimbel 6'" (i.e. Principal 6', two to three ranks, and Grobe Zimbel, two ranks)
   c. Posterior chest and Zimbel slider off: "Doeff 6'" (i.e. Principal 6', two to three ranks)
   d. Forward chest off: "Scharfes Positiv 3'" (i.e. Octave 3' with the sharp Mixture)

   A fifth combination was, of course, provided on the Blockwerk itself.

2. 1505. Daniel van der Distelen, unfinished organ for the Liebfrauen-kapelle of the Hauptkirche, Antwerp.

Specification:

RÜCKPOSITIV
Prinzipal 4', F-f''
Flöte 4'
Mixtur
Scharf
Zink 8', f-f''
Regal 4'
Pedal: Hohlpfeife 8' [?]
Pedal: Flöte 4'

HAUPTWERK, F-f''
Prinzipal 8' (two ranks, open and
    stopped)
Oktave 4'
Flöte 4' or Oktave 2'
Mixtur, sehr stark
Scharf

POSITIF IN DER BRUST
Trompete 8', f-f''
Krummhorn 8'
Scharf or Zimbel
Pedal: Hohlpfeife 8', F-e
Pedal: Mixtur 4', F-e
Pedal: Scharf

Registrations:

HAUPTWERK
Prinzipal 8', two ranks
Flöte 4'
Prinzipal 8', Oktave 4'
Prinzipal 8', Oktave 4', Mixtur
Oktave 4', Scharf
Flöte 4', Scharf
Prinzipal 8', Oktave 4', Mixtur, Scharf: das grosse Plenum

RÜCKPOSITIV
Prinzipal 4'
Flöte 4'
Zink 8'
Regal 4'
Prinzipal 4', Flöte 4'
Prinzipal 4', Flöte 4', Mixtur
Flöte 4', Mixtur
"Principael posityff": das kleine Plenum

BRUSTWERK
Krummhorn
Trompete
Krummhorn, Zimbel
Trompete, Zimbel

Trompete, Krummhorn
Trompete, Krummhorn, Zimbel

3. 1505. Meister Johann (von Koblenz?), St. Michael Church, Zwolle.

Specification:

RÜCKPOSITIV: F-a″
Prinzipal 4′, Hohlpfeife 8′, Scharf, Zungenstimme (Harfe or Schalmei)

HAUPTWERK: Contra F-a″
Blockwerk 16′ (24′)—32 or 34 ranks

OBERWERK: c-a″
Prinzipal 8, Oktave 4, Scharfe Stimme (Oktave 2?), Grosse Zimbel (divided probably between two registers, Mixtur and Scharf)

PEDAL: F-c′, coupled to Contra F-c of the Blockwerk

Registration instructions for combinations possible within Oberwerk:

Prinzipal 8
Oktave 4
Oktave 2
Prinzipal 8, Oktave 4
Prinzipal 8, Oktave 2
Prinzipal 4, Oktave 2
Prinzipal 8, Oktave 4, Oktave 2
Prinzipal 8, Mixtur
Prinzipal 8, Oktave 2, Mixtur
Prinzipal 8, Oktave 4, Oktave 2, Mixtur
Oktave 4, Oktave 2, Scharf
Prinzipal 8, Oktave 4, Oktave 2, Mixtur, Scharf

4. 1510. St. Andreas Kirche, Worms.

Specification:

Manual:	Prinzipal (4)	Quinte ($1\frac{1}{3}$)
	Grosse Holflöte (8)	Mixtur
	Oktave (2)	Zimbel
	Kleine Holflöte (4)	Trompete (8)
		Rausswerk (Regal 8)

Pedal: Prinzipal (8)
   Oktave (4)
   Mixtur
Tremulant, Trommel, Ventil

Registration Instructions:

Das Prinzipal (4)		When an organist
Grosse Holflöte (8)	each one alone	plays on these stops,
Kleine Holflöte (4)		he should draw the
		pedal Prinzipal
Oktave		along with them.

The Prinzipal and the Oktave make a good combination and the Tremulant sounds well with it.

The Prinzipal and Grosse Flöte are also good together; the Quinte may also be drawn along with them, and the Tremulant is also good in this combination.

The Prinzipal and Kleine Holflöte sound good together.

The Grosse and Kleine Holflöte and the Quinte sound best with the Tremulant.

The Grosse Holflöte and Kleine Holflöte are successful, too, and may be used with the Prinzipal and Oktave of the pedal.

Zincken: the Rausswerk, Grosse Holflöte, Quinte; together sound like a Zink.

The Rausswerk and the Grosse Holflöte sound like a Krummhorn.

Zimbel: The Zimbel sounds nowhere so good as with the two Holflöte.

The two Mixtures in manual and pedal should never be used except with the Plenum.

The drum sounds bad if used when one is playing in the key of C.

The Tremulant should not be used with the Rausswerk.

The Busaunen should not be used alone on account of the strength of the wind supply.

The Rausswerk also should not be used alone on account of the strength of the wind supply.

Do not forget that the Ventil is used for everything.

5. 1522. Joris Buus of Bruges, for the Church of St. Denis, Veurne (West Flanders).

Specification of small organ:

Principal 4', Flute 4', Fifteenth 2', Flute 2', Mixture, Scharf II

Registration possibilities given:

Principal 4	Flute 2
Principal 4, Fifteenth	Flute 4, Flute 2
Principal, Fifteenth, Mixture	Principal, Flute, Fifteenth, Mixture
	Principal, Flute 4, Flute 2, Scharf
Principal, Fifteenth, Mixture,	Principal 4, Flute 4, Fifteenth,
Scharf	Mixture, Scharf
Flute	

6. 1563. Herman Rodensteen, for the Schlosskirche organ, Dresden.

Specification (Vente reconstruction) one manual, 13 stops plus tremulant:

1. Prinzipale 4	6. Querpfeiffe 4	11. Regal 8 or 4
2. Gedackte 8	7. Gemsenhörner 2	12. Kleine flöttlein 1
3. Quintadehne 8	8. Sufflet 1⅓	13. Tremulanten
4. Octave 2	9. Trommetten 8	14. Mixtur
5. Zimbeln (Scharf)	10. Krumphörner 8 or 4	

Registrations of Rodensteen:

a. One-stop registrations: 1, 2, 3, 6, 7, 9, 10, 11, 12

b. Two-stop registrations:

Prinzipale	with 3, 4, 5, 6, 7(& 13), 8, 9, 10, 11, 12(& 13), 13
Gedackte	with 3, 5, 6, 7(& 13), 8, 9, 10, 11, 12, 13
Quintadehne	with 4, 5, 6, 7, 8, 9, 10, 11, 12
Oktave	with 6, 9, 10, 11, 12, 12 & 13
Zimbeln	with 8, 9, 10, 11, 12
Querpfeiffe	with 8, 9, 10, 11
Gemsenhörner	with 8, 9, 10, 11, 12
Sufflet	with 10, 11, 12, 12 & 13
Trommetten	with 12
Krumphörner	with 12
Regal	with 12

c. Three-stop registrations:

Prinzipale	with 2 & 4, 2 & 5
Gedackte	with 3 & 4
Octava	with 3 & 5
Zimbeln	with 6 & 8, 9 & 12
Querpfeiffe	with 7 & 8

    d. Four-stop registrations:
      Prinzipale   with 2, 4, & 5
      Gedackte   with 3, 4, & 5
    e. Five-stop registration: 1, 2, 4, 5, 14 (Plenum)

7. Ueberwasserkirche, Münster. Organ built around 1565 by Jan Roose, who wrote instructions for the use of the organ—about 1580.

Specification:
Blockwerk 16′ (from F): Staand Principaal

Positiv (from F): Prestant 8   Mixtur or positien
              Holpype 8   Nazat ($2\frac{2}{3}$)
              Fleute 4   Schuifflet (1)
              Octava 4   Trumpet 8 (bass and descant, on
              Superoctava 2   Borstlade, but played on Positiv
                                      manual)
              Tramblant, Nachtigall, and Trummell
              Pedal coupled

"Ordonansio":

    draw the "groete Principael" and shut off the "posetyf"
    for the "cleyne principael," prestant, holpype, octave, superoctaef,
      positien [mixture]
    prestant, holpype, octave
    holpyp, prestant
    holpyp, nazaer
    holpyp, nazaer, schufelet
    flute, nazare
    holpyp, nazare, octaef
    holpyp, nazare, superoctaef
    holpype, flute
    holpyp, octaef
    holpyp schufelet
    flute alone
    flute en schufelet
    flute nazare
    holpyp positie
    flute superoctaef
    holpyp superoctaef

holpyp superoctaef, and positie [mixture]
flute with nachtergel and trommel
trompet alone
trompet descant and holpyp
holpyp, nazare, octaef, and trompet bass
trompet, prestant
trompet, nazare, octaef
trompet, superoctaef, and positie
trompet, holpyp
flute, positie
holpyp, flute, schufelet
trompet octaef
holpyp, octaef and trompet descant
holpyp nazare, and trompet descant
holpyp alone with tramblant
holpyp, octaef and superoctaef
trompet, octaef, and superoctaef
trompet, prestant, octaef, superoctaef, and positie
The tremblant should not be used alone with the Trompet,
Trommel, or "nachtergael."

8. 1589. Willem van Lare, builder of the organ for St. Jakob Church,
Antwerp. Registration instructions included in contract.

Specification:

RÜCKPOSITIV, F-a″   HAUPTWERK, F-a″

1. Flöte 4	8. Prinzipal 8	15. Grosser Scharf
2. Oktave 2	9. Hohlpfeife 8	16. Kleiner Scharf
3. Flöte 2	10. Oktave 4	17. Kornett diskant
4. Scharf	11. Flöte 4	18. Trompete 8
5. Regal 8	12. Nazat 2⅔	19. Krummhorn 8 diskant
6. Diskantregister	13. Gemshorn 2	20. Tremulant
(Regal 4?)	14. Mixtur	21. Nachtigall
7. Tremulant		22. Harfe
		23. Trommel

Registrations:

a. One-stop registrations: 8, 9
b. Two-stop registrations:
   A. (Rückpositiv) Flöte 4   with 2, 3, 4 & 7, 5, 23

    B. (Hauptwerk)   Prinzipal 8   with 10, 11, 13
                        Hohlpfeife 8   with 10, 11, 13, 17
                        Oktave 4   with 13 & 20, 19
                        Flöte 4   with 16 & 20

  c. Three-stop registrations:
    A. (Rückpositiv)   1 & 2 & 4 (Kleines Plenum)
    B. (Hauptwerk)   10, 13, 18
                       10, 17, 18
                       8, 15, or 16, 18
                       9, 10, 22 (sounds like a bagpipe)

  d. The grosse Plenum:
                       8, 10, 14, 15, 16 or
                       9, 10, 14, 15 or 16

9. Stadtkirche, Bayreuth. One manual, built in 1572 by Herman Rodensteen. Pedal added in 1596 by Timotheus Cumpenius. Advice concerning registration was written in 1597: "Ordentliche Specification unnd Verzeichnung zur Zusammen Ziehung der underschidlichen Register beim Orgelwerk zu Bayereuth/wie das Iztem zu gerichtet ist/unnd der Orgelmacher Timotheus Cumpenius dem Organisten Haubten mit seiner eigenen Hannd geschrieben und zugestellt hat."

Specification:

MANUAL		PEDAL	
Gedackt (8′)	Prinzipal (4′)	Subbass (16′)	Tremulant
Quintadena (8′)	Oktav (2′)	Prinzipal (8′)	Trommel
Koppelflöte (2′)	Mixtur	Posaune (16′)	Vogelgesang
Flachflöte (2′)	Zimbeln	Kornett	Zimbelstern
Quintflöte (1⅓)			
Sifflett (1′)	Krummhorn (8′)		

Registrations:

1. For the Plenum, draw: Prinzipal, Quintadena, Oktave, Quint, Mixtur, Zimbeln; to that, add the Subbass, Prinzipal, and Posaunen
2. Quintadena, Koppelflöten, Krummhörner, Subbass, Prinzipal
3. Gedackt, Flachflöten, Krummhörner; Subbass, Prinzipal
4. Quintadena, Prinzipal, Oktav, Quint; Posaune and Prinzipal
5. Gedackt; Subbass and Kornett

6. Quintadena, Quint; Posaune and Prinzipal
7. Gedackt, Sifflett, Tremulant; Subbass
8. Quintadena, Krummhörner; Posaune and Subbass
9. Prinzipal; Prinzipal
10. Gedackt and Krummhörner; Subbass

10. *L'arte organica*, by Costanzo Antegnati (1608), ed. Lunelli (Mainz, 1958), pp. 74–88.

Concerning the Way to Register Organs
That Is, to Arrange The Stops

First it must be warned, as already mentioned, [that it is necessary] to become acquainted with the attributes of the organ. Therefore, I shall illustrate some [organs], and first of all ours in the Cathedral, which is made up of twelve registers, mentioned here below:

The complete principal (16′)
The split principal (16′), that is divided in two parts; it is played starting with the soprano, coming down to the bass as far as the second Do sol Re, and then it is played with the pedal for the bass section, and not with the manual keys, as is done with the soprano, above
The octave (8′)
The fifteenth (4′)
The nineteenth ($2\frac{2}{3}$′)
The twenty-second (2′)
The twenty-sixth ($1\frac{1}{3}$′)
The twenty-ninth (1′)
The thirty-third ($\frac{2}{3}$′)
Another twenty-second to blend with the octave, and octave flute (8′), and nineteenth, which gives the effect of a cornet
Flute fifteenth (4′)
Flute octave (8l)

FIRST WAY

One should ordinarily play on the ripieno for intonations, introits or preludes, whatever you may call them, as it is here below, drawing these stops:

The first principal (16′);
Leaving the second off and pulling the octave (8′), the fifteenth (4′),

the nineteenth ($2\frac{2}{3}'$), the twenty-second ($2'$), the twenty-sixth ($1\frac{1}{3}'$), the twenty-ninth ($1'$), the thirty-third ($\frac{2}{3}'$);
Leaving all the other stops off.

Son. And why are the others not included, which are all of $8'$, $4'$, and $2'$ pitches?

Father. Although they are tuned with the others, they are left out because the ripieno comes out livelier and more humorous, and a gentler sound is heard.

Son. Then, when should these other stops be used?

Father. These stops are meant for playing [accompaniments] and for making different kinds of tonal effects, as I will be telling you.

Son. Please continue. I have already seen and heard the ripieno; how are the other combinations to be arranged?

Father. [For] the second way, you use the principal, octave, skipping the others, up to the twenty-ninth and thirty-third. And the octave flute, and these five stops make just about a half ripieno. [For] the third way, use as before the principal, octave and flute octave. The fourth way, the principal and octave flute. The fifth way, the octave and nineteenth, the twenty-second for the concerto style and octave flute, and these four stops together resemble the sound of cornets. The sixth way, the octave and the octave flute; and these two are excellent for "*diminuire*," and for playing "*Canzoni alla francese*." The seventh way, the same two stops with the tremolo, but without "*diminuire*."

Son. Yet, I have heard men of reputation play "Canzoni diminuite" also with the tremolo.

Father. They will certainly forgive me, even if I say that they do not understand, for it is not proper since it makes confusion; and it is a sign that they do not have good judgment about what they are doing.
The eighth way, the principal may be played alone, which is very, very delicate; I usually play this at the Elevation of the Mass.
The ninth way, both stops called principals ($16'$) may be played in unison.
The tenth way, the octave flute alone.
The eleventh way, the same flute with the split principal; this results in a bass for the pedal, and the soprano of that principal playing (in the manual). When played in the descant, this makes a kind of harmony accompanied by two registers. When only the bass range is used, one hears the canto alone (flute $8'$), which comes out answering in unison with the soprano (since the descant is sounding an octave lower), and thus one comes to make a dialogue with the help of the *contrabassi* of the pedal etc.
The twelfth way, using the flute fifteenth with the principal, which should

be played *diminuito* (with flourishes); the octave may also be added, which creates a beautiful effect.

Son. Are there other ways to register, for making other kinds of concerto effects?

Father. Yes, but it seems to me that I have ordered them and made them up in so many different ways that it is sufficient, that by playing and changing from time to time one never becomes bored. For it is a common saying that the world is beautiful for its variety, and it is also said that there is no beautiful thing which in constant repetition does not become boring; therefore, I praise changing stops from time to time, and also changing one's style of playing, playing now *"grave con legature,"* now *"con diminuzioni,"* thus responding whenever possible to the *Musica*, or *Canto fermo* always appropriately, for this is the main task of the organist.

Son. I think I have understood so far, but you have told me, too, that there are many kinds of organs, and sorts of stops.

Father. I shall come to it, and to make it clear to you that I have dealt with the disposition and quality of the Cathedral's [organ], I shall [now] speak of the organ in San Faustino and the Graces Church in this city, as it was made by the same hand as was that in the Cathedral.

Principal	Twenty-sixth
Octave	Twenty-ninth
Fifteenth	Flute fifteenth
Nineteenth	Octave flute
Twenty-second	

METHOD OF REGISTERING THE ORGAN

First, for all *intonationi* the ripieno should be used, that is:

Principal	Nineteenth
Octave	Twenty-second
Fifteenth	Twenty-sixth

Also, in finishing at the *Deo Gratias* with toccatas, and with pedal.

ANOTHER WAY

Principal	Twenty-sixth
Octave	Octave flute
Twenty-second	

This is, one might say, the half ripieno.

ANOTHER WAY	ANOTHER WAY
Principal	Principal, and
Octave, and	Octave flute
Octave flute	

For playing all kinds of things, and accompanying motets; the Principal alone when motets with a few voices are sung, and the tremolo can also be used if it is played delicately, but slowly and without flourishes.

This is how the fiffaro only with the principal must be played, with slow and legato motion.

On the contrary, when playing on the flauto in duodecima [flute $2\frac{2}{3}'$], which should be used with the principal, flourishes and rapid motion like "canzoni alla francese" are suitable and make good effect with the octave, and the octave flute, but without tremolo.

The stops that can be played alone are the principal, on all kinds of organs, and also the flute. But on large organs, such as [those] of twelve feet [16'], the octave can be used [alone], for it has the effect of a principal on a medium organ.

And he who plays, in the above manner, one stop and then another, achieves the effect of variety without becoming boring, and when he has exhausted the possibilities, he may start from the beginning again.

    Son. Then these [organs] are similar in stops.

    Father. Yes, but I have altered the flute, which was at the fifteenth, in the [organ] of Graces [Church], and have added some bass [pipes] to make it a twelfth.

    Son. And for this organ what sequence must be used for registering?

    Father. The same order as I have said, to make the ripieno starting from:

Ripieno
{
Principal
Octave
Fifteenth
Nineteenth
Twenty-second
Twenty-sixth
Twenty-ninth
}

Which are in order as they are here [above] written; then the two flute stops are applied for use, as I have already said, but the flute twelfth is not played without the principal.

    Son. These are surely easy to understand and well arranged.

Father. Don't you think our new organ just made for the Reverend Mothers of S. Grata of Bergamo is also well arranged, for whom I must write out the present rules according to their desire, and also that of the Reverend D. Giovanni, organist of the Cathedral, and their teacher?

Son. It is [your] duty.

Father. Then, it is thus:

Principal
Octave
Fifteenth
Nineteenth
Twenty-second
Twenty-sixth
Flute twelfth
Octave flute

Fiffaro, which is called by many the stop of human voices, which to tell the truth, on account of its sweet sound, may be so named; which must be played with the principal alone, nor must anything else be used with it, for everything would come out of tune; and it must be played adagio with slow tempo; and the ripieno as legato as possible, and, as I have said, it should be used at all Introiti or preludes, as well as at the ending and at the Deo Gratias; the other way, sounding like a half ripieno, will be like this:

Principal	
Octave	
Twenty-second	ANOTHER WAY
Twenty-sixth	Principal, and
Octave flute	Octave flute

ANOTHER WAY	ANOTHER WAY
Principal	Principal
Octave	Octave, and
and Octave flute	Flute twelfth

Which is excellent for playing all sorts of things, especially "Canzoni alla francese," and florid things; and they come out well also with the stops:

Octave and Octave Flute

Son. This is surely understandable and easy, and many [organs] are made like this, but tell me of the unusual ones.

Father. The one in Carmini Church in this city is unusual, and the stops are thus:

Principal
Octave
Octave flute
Twenty-ninth ⎤
Twenty-sixth ⎦ together, that is, one stop governs them both
Twenty-second
Nineteenth
Fifteenth

Son. Thus, an organist can get mixed up.

Father. This is why I told you one must get familiar with the place. There is also the one at S. Marco in Milan, modernized by me as you know, with divided stops, in this way:

Bass principal	Nineteenth
Descant principal	Twenty-second
Bass octave	Twenty-sixth
Descant octave	Twenty-ninth
Fifteenth	
Flute twelfth	
Bass octave flute	
Descant octave flute	
Fiffaro	

Descant principale grosso. The bass is played on the pedal.

Son. These appear to be fourteen stops; and why do it in this way?

Father. I did it thus on the request of those Reverend Fathers [and] also their organist, Mr. Ruggier Troffei, and Mr. Ottavio Bariola, and why? In order to play dialogues, for these stops are divided in the middle of the keyboard.

Son. There is also the organ of S. Giuseppe in this city, which has a divided principal stop, which one day I was just about to play and enjoy; but I was confused because, pulling the first stop knob and thinking of the whole rank, there was no sound or answer, but from fourteen or fifteen pipes of the bass, so that I became then aware of the split, and pulled the next stop, so that I found it all finally.

Father. And that is why I told you from the very beginning that my instructions are necessary; and none of the art, whoever he may be, must scorn them, or he will fall into a thousand errors. Further, I shall tell you that there is the organ at the Madonna de'Miracoli in this city, the specification of which is this:

Principal	Nineteenth
Fiffaro	Twenty-second
Octave	Twenty-sixth
Fifteenth	
Flute twelfth and octave flute,	

by which anyone may be tricked. The stop for the fiffaro is next to the principal in the place where the octave should be; and it [the fiffaro] is in great discordance with the others because it should not be used with any others, but only the principal. And so it is that this art, as I always said in the beginning, belongs first and foremost to God's service. Therefore we thank the Divine Majesty for the gift that he has presented to us, in making us capable of serving Him in this profession and art, and we bring to the end desired by us this present dialogue, and our little work, initiated not so much for human profit, as for divine glory, to which be addressed all of our actions and works, just as all sorts of good and grace derive from Him.

The End

11. 1613. Organ for Church of San Juan de las Abadesas, Barcelona. Portions of the contract, translated from the original Catalan by Arthur Terry, The Queen's University, Belfast. The construction of the new instrument took the following form:

1. Insofar as in the said old organ the woodwork is in order, and the pipes on the case are in their appropriate places, in the form of a flautat (principal) of 13 palms: provided these pipes are in good condition, the manufacturer undertakes to construct the remaining pipes of the flautat up to the number of 42.

2. He will make a stop, called an octave, for the said flautat, and this will be of tin, except for the first octave, which he will make of wood, if he thinks this preferable, and if not, the whole will be in tin.

3. He will make a long fifteenth, and this will also be of tin.

4. He will make a double eighteenth, and they will be in [left blank] places, at the discretion of the manufacturer, and this will also be of tin.

5. He is to make a twenty-second [left blank] with its repetitions, also of tin.

6. He is to make a cymbale of three ranks, in [left blank] places, as the said manufacturer thinks fit, and this will be of tin.

7. He will make a stop, namely a nasard twelfth, or more accurately, nineteenth, for the principal flautat, to be of tin.

8. He will make the stop of wood, to act in unison with that on the case.

9. He is to make three sets of bellows, in their appropriate places, and these will produce the effect most suited to the music.

10. He is to construct a wind chest for the said music, and in keeping with the casing of the organ, in such a way that it cannot be played from the front, but, like others, must be played in reverse. This wind chest will be constructed as seems most fitting to the manufacturer, and in it there will be 42 channels, as in a wind chest for a full cadira [Rückpositiv].

11. He will make the action of the said organ with mechanical trackers

tremulant and devices for playing the bass pipes with the feet, which pipes will correspond to the keyboard, and he will also make bass pedals (pipes).

[Instructions on the use of stops]

To play the full organ at the principal feasts, the following stops should be opened: 1, 2, 3, 4, 5, 6, 7, 8.

To make another plenum for lesser feasts, the following stops to be opened: 1, 2, 3, 4, 5, 6.

To make another plenum in the manner of a cadira [Positiv], for playing on Sundays and ordinary feast-days, the following stops are to be opened: 1, 2, 4, 6.

To make another plenum in the manner of a smaller cadira [Positiv] (which will serve for semidoubles and the Sabbath Masses of Our Lady), the following stops are to be used: 2, 3, 4, 5, 6, 7.

To play the flautats [flues]. The flautat on the case may be played on its own, with or without tremulant, that is to say, stop number 1.

Another more solemn flautat, 1, 8.

Another louder flautat, with or without tremulant, stop number 8, which is the stopped flute.

Another flute: 1, 2, 8.

Another flute: 1, 2.

Another flute: 2, 8.

Another flute: 1, 3, with tremulant.

Another flute: 3, 8.

For playing and singing with two choirs it will be sufficient to use flautat 1, that which is on the case, as this has been proved by experience.

To make other combinations on the said organ, the player may use his own discretion, save for stops 4, 5, 6, none of which may be played on its own.

Stop 8 and 7 is the nasard.

Stop 1 and 7 is another nasard.

Stop 2 and 7 is another nasard.

Stop 3 and 7, with tremulant, is delightful.

And stop 6 and 8, with tremulant, is a combination, like small bells.

The rest is left to the taste of him who best understands it.

[Final paragraph on treatment of instrument]

May all those who lay their hands on it take care of the instrument, not in regard of him who has made it, but of Him for whom it was made and whom it serves, leaving all parts of it as perfect as its makers left them; for at the present, it is as perfect as human hands could make it, both in its construction and in its fine tuning, in which not a single pipe has been overlooked; and for the rest, may interested persons take heed of it for as long as it remains in its present state. May God grant them grace to carry out their tasks and to declare His will in every thing that they perform. And we beg them to pray to God for its maker, and for the souls of all the dead, that others may in turn pray for them. Amen.

[San Juan de las Abadesas, Archivo del Monasterio. Sheaf labeled "Documents per a la historia. Varis." Copy made by José Masdeu, priest and Keeper of the Archives.]

12. 1616. St. Leonhard Church, Zoutleeuw.

Art Memorandum
(Probable specification after restoration of 1620 by J. J. van Weert)

RÜCKPOSITIV
1. Prinzipal 8'
2. Hohlpfeife 8'
3. Oktave 4'
4. Flöte 4'
5. Quintflöte $2\frac{2}{3}'$ or $1\frac{1}{3}'$
6. Superoktave 2'
7. Sifflöte 1'
8. Kornett
9. Mixtur
10. Krummhorn 8'

HAUPTWERK
Blockwerk 16' or 8'

OTHER REGISTERS:
11. Tremulant (on the whole organ)
12. Nachtigall
13. Trommel

Registrations

a. One-stop registrations: 1, 2 with or without 11
b. Two-stop registrations: Prinzipal 8' with 2, 3, 4, 6, 9 (with or without 11)
   Hohlpfeife 8' with 1, 5, 6, 9
c. Three-stop registrations: Hohlpfeife 8' with 3 & 6, 3 & 8, 3 & 9, 5 & 6
d. The tremulant must never be used when the Blockwerk is being played.

13. 1624–25. Cathedral of Lérida. The following text has been translated from the original Catalan by Arthur Terry, The Queen's University, Belfast.

Memorandum to this and coming ages on the construction of the organ situated in the cathedral church of the See of Lérida.

1° the Chapter sought the permission of P. Jover, the Provincial of Catalonia, to place at their disposal the person of Fra Antoni Llorens, priest and confessor of the Order of Saint Francis, in order to restore the organ of the said cathedral; and in view of the difficulties encountered in restoring the said organ, and with the approval of the Chapter, it was decided to build an entirely new one, which task has not been completed.

The Chapter did not wish to conclude any act, agreement or contract for the said work; rather, bearing in mind their knowledge of the person who would carry it out, and trusting him to make them an organ such as would fit their church, they gave him freedom to perform whatever God should signify to him.

In the course of the work there were a great many hindrances, both on account of its common [communal] nature [on account of the numerous people involved] and of its excellence, for all such labors are subject to misfortunes.

They began the construction of the new organ on 4th March, 1624, and completed it on 13th December, 1625. They were [what with the restoration of the old organ and the construction of the new] altogether two years and eight days.

The said priests were lodged, along with their carpenters, in the hostel of S. Salvador, where by order of the Chapter they were provided with everything necessary for their daily needs, and likewise with all that was needful for the construction of the organ.

The names of the two priests who carried out the work are Fra Antoni Llorens, unworthy priest and monk, a native of Arbeca: and his companion, Fra Juan Olius, priest, native of Espluga de Francoli.

The said priests worked in the following way:

1. they made 5 sets of bellows, as is stated in the due place.

Item: they made two wind-chests for the orgue major [great organ], each with 45 channels: in the form of an organ measuring 13 palms (8'): and since space was lacking for the bellows—which should have been six, and each one wider and longer—it was not possible to make a larger organ of 27 palms (16').

Item: they made two keyboards of ivory, one for the orgue major, with 45 keys, and another, with 42, for the cadira [positif-à-dos, or Rückpositiv].

Item: they made two ranks of regalies [reed stops], one of 27 palms (16'), the other of 13 palms (8').

Item: on the two wind-chests aforesaid they have placed 13 stops:
1. a flautat [Flute] of wood, stopped: 27 palms (16′).
2. a flautat [Principal] on the case: 13 palms (8′)
3. an octave of 7 palms (4′), of tin.
4. another octave, of tin.
5. a long twelfth, of tin.
6. an alemanna [Mixture] of six ranks, likewise of tin.
7. a fifteenth, likewise of tin.
8. a cymbale of four ranks.
9. a flautat [Flute] of wood: 13 palms (8′).
10. a stopped flautat [Flute]: 7 palms (4′), likewise of tin.
11. a nasard twelfth, of tin and lead alloy.
12. a nasard fifteenth, likewise of tin and lead.
13. a stop of three ranks, by name tolosana [Cornet].

The seven bass pipes which are there at present were made by Joseph Bordons and adapted to the new work [added in a contemporary hand: "anima ejus requiescat in pace amen"].

On the cadireta [Rückpositiv], they made a wind-chest with 42 channels in the form of the large case, and placed nine stops on it, namely:
1. a flautat [Principal] on the case: 7 palms (4′).
2. a nineteenth of two ranks.
3. a cymbale of three ranks.
4. a tolosana of three ranks.
5. a nasard fifteenth.
6. a nasard twelfth.
7. an octave.
8. a stopped flautat [Flute]: 7 palms (4′), of tin.
9. a flautat [Flute] of wood: 13 palms (8′).

Item: they made drums and a tremulant: and a ventil for opening and closing the bass pipes.

Item: they made mechanisms for the stops, both trundles [rollers?] and draw-knobs, for the orgue major, the cadira organ and the regalies.

The method to be followed in preserving the said instrument in the future, lest any mishap befall it like those seen in many places, is as follows:

1° when the organ needs to be cleaned and tuned, they shall try to ensure that the person who is to carry out the work be a person of trust; and let them be particular in this, for if the person is not skilled, he may ruin the organ with a single tuning; supposing he has the skill, the Chapter will appoint two canons or skilled workmen to accompany the person who is to tune the organ, who will inspect the instrument to see whether all the pipes are in their places; and when the work is completed, they will inspect the instrument again to see if any pipe be missing, since experience has shown how easy it is to remove a whole register of pipes and thus ruin an organ.

On the orgue major, counting the entire fluework, the seven bass pipes and the two ranks of regalies, there are pipes to the number of 1203.

On the upper wind-chest there are pipes to the number of 689.

On the lower wind-chest there are pipes to the number of 315, which, adding the two wind-chests to the case makes the aforesaid number of 1203.

On the nine stops of the cadira [Pos.] there are pipes to the number of 568.

The orgue major and the cadira [Pos.] between them have 1771 pipes.

The administrator in the present work was the Illustrious and Very Reverend Dr. Antoni Suardell, Canon of the said Cathedral, a native of the town of Joyä, in the Bishopric of Gerona.

And since it has happened in other places that the method of registration and combining has been lost, either through neglect or on purpose, on this account a copy is to be deposited in an archive, so that if need be it may be copied and the loss made up. This method is as follows:

The manner of ordering and registering the orgue major. The stops, when pulled out, are open, and, pushed in, are closed.

The Plenum of the Organ: The stops numbered 2, 4, 5, 6, 7, 8, 9; another combination, 2, 4, 5, 6, 7, 8; another, 2, 4, 6, 7, 8; another, 2, 4, 7, 8, 9; [another], 1, 2, 4, 6, 7, 8, 9, 13. The bass pipes are to go with all these combinations.

The stop for the [large] bass pipes, when pulled out, is closed, and when pressed in, is open.

Flautats: 1; another, 2; another, 9; another, 10; another, 1, 10; 1, 2; 2, 10; 1, 2, 10; another, 1, 9; 9, 10; 1, 2, 3; 1, 2, 3, 9; another, 1, 3; 2, 3; 2, 4, 9; 1, 4; another, 2, 9; and all these may be played with or without the tremulant. For playing with two choirs, stops 2, 3, 9, with the bass pipes. For playing with a single voice, or four simple voices, stops 2, 9, without the bass pipes.

Nasards: 1, 10, 11; another, 2, 3, 11; 9, 10, 11; another, 2, 10, 11; 10, 11, 12; 1, 9, 10, 11, 12; another, 2, 3, 11; 9, 10, 11, 12. All these with or without tremulant.

Mixtures: 1, 4, 6, 13; 2, 5, 12, 13; 2, 7, 11, 13; another, 2, 5, 7, 13; 3, 9, 13; 3, 6, 9, 13; another, 2, 8, with tremulant; another, 2, 6, 10; another, 2, 8, 10; 1, 3, 5, 6; 2, 4, 13; another, 4, 9, 13; 10, 13; 2, 13; another, 6, 9, 10, 13; 6, 9, 10; 1, 5, 8; another, 1, 6, 10; 9, 10, 13; 4, 6, 9.

Manner of ordering and registering the cadireta [Rückpositiv]: The stops, when pulled towards the High Altar, are open, and pulled towards the choir are closed.

Plena: The basic plenum of the cadira [Pos.] consists of the following stops: numbers 1, 2, 3, 9; alternatively, 1, 2, 3, 4, 9; another, 1, 2, 4, 9; 1, 2, 3; 1, 3, 7, 8. In all these plena, stops 2 and 9 of the orgue major will serve as bass pipes, and the [large] bass pipes if it be desired.

Flautats: 1; another, 7; another, 8; another, 9; another, 1, 7; 1, 9; 7, 9; 8, 9; another, 7, 8; 1, 7, 8, 9; 7, 8, 9; another, 1, 8; 6, 7; and all these with or without tremulant.

Nasards: 1, 5, 6; 1, 6; 6, 8, 9; another, 5, 7; 5, 6, 9; 6, 7, 8; another, 6, 8; 5, 8; 1, 5, 7; another, 2, 7, 9; all with or without tremulant.

Mixtures: 1, 4; another, 1, 4, 7; 4, 7, 8; another, 4, 7, 9; 4, 8, 9; 4, 8; another, 4, 9; 1, 2; 1, 3; 3, 8; another, 1, 2, 9; 3, 8, 9; 3, 7, 9; another, 3, 7, 8; 3, 9; 2, 7, 8; with the organ bass pipes 3, 9; without the large bass pipes.

Method of combining the orgue major with the cadireta:

Unisonus: 2 of the orgue major. 1 of the cadira: the right hand on the treble half of the orgue [major]; the left hand on the bass half of the cadireta.

Other combinations, 9, 12 of the orgue [major]; 5, 8 of the cadira. Hands on keyboards as described above. Others, 9 of the orgue major; 9 of the cadireta: hands the same as above. Others, 10 of the orgue [major]; 8 of the cadira: hands the same. Others, 9, 10 of the orgue [major]; 8, 9 of the cadira: hands the same on either keyboard. And all these unisonus with or without tremulant; but they are better with it.

Flageolets: 2 of the orgue [major]; 5, 8 of the cadira: hands on the keyboard of the orgue major; the left hand on the bass, and the right on the treble of the keyboard of the cadira. Other combinations, 2, 9 of the orgue [major]; 5, 6, 9 of the cadira: the hands in the same way. Others, 2 of the orgue [major]; 5, 9 of the cadira: the hands in the same way. Others, 2 of the orgue [major]; 6, 8 of the cadira: the hands in the same way. Others, 2, 10 of the orgue [major]; 5, 6, 8 of the cadira: the hands in the same way. Others, 2 of the orgue [major]; 6, 7, 8 of the cadira: the hands in the same way. All these Flageolets must be played without either tremulant or the stop for the bass pipes of the orgue [major].

Gaytilles [diminutive of "gaites" = "bagpipes"; Musettes?]: 2, 3 of the orgue [major]; 3, 6, 8 of the cadira; another, 2, 3, 9 of the orgue [major]; 1, 3, 6 of the cadira; another, 2, 3 of the orgue [major]; 1, 4, 8 of the cadira; another, 2, 10 of the orgue [major]; 4, 7, 8 of the cadira; another, 2 of the orgue [major]; 4, 8 of the cadira. With all these Gaytilles and Flageolets the hands may perform as the player chooses; the usual manner is: the left hand on the bass half of the orgue [major] and the right on the treble half of the cadira: and contrariwise, if the player chooses, he may change his right hand to the treble half of the orgue [major] and his left to the bass half of the cadira.

Cornetilla [= "small cornet"]: 9 of the orgue [major] with tremulant and the right hand on the orgue major, treble half; 7 of the cadira, bass half, accompanying as far as possible with the bass pedal; the large bass pedals, however, should not be sounded; another, 2 of the orgue [major]; 6, 7 of the cadira: the hands and the rest as above.

Varieties of combinations of the orgue gran with the Regalies: 2, 10 of the orgue; 1 of the regalies; another, 10, 11 of the orgue; 2 of the regalies; another, 2, 3 of the orgue; 2 of the regalies.

Method of combining the cadira with the regalies or medio registro partido [Spanish: "half register divided"]: 1, 8, 9 of the cadira: the left hand on the keyboard of the cadira: and 10, 11 of the orgue; 1 of the regalies and the right hand on the treble half of the orgue; another, 1, 8, 9 of the cadira; 10, 11, 12 of the orgue; 2 of the regalies, right hand on the bass half of the orgue: and the left hand on the treble half of the cadira. The Regalies must be tuned to the orgue [major] stop number 2.

The sum of the different combinations which may be made—solo orgue, solo cadira, orgue and cadira together, regalies with orgue and regalies with cadira—is 117. The rest is left to the will of the player.

Expenses of all those who have worked on the construction of the organ in the hostel of S. Salvador for the space of two years, [left blank] pounds [lliures].

Wages of carpenters who have worked in S. Salvador for two years at the construction of the organ, [left blank] pounds.

The case and woodwork of the organ costs, [left blank] pounds, [left blank] sous.

The entire organ costs: [left blank] pounds, [left blank] sous.

Soli deo honor et gloria, in sæcula saeculorum, amen.

[Cathedral of Lérida, Archivo Musical, document No. 1404]

14. 1624. Samuel Scheidt—Tabulatura nova, Part III, To Organists.

Every organist who has an organ with two manuals and pedal can play these Magnificats and Hymns, as well as some of the Psalms found in parts I and II; the chorale melody might be played with a penetrating stop on the Rückpositiv (in order to bring it more clearly into relief), particularly when it appears in the soprano or tenor. When it is a Bicinium, and the chorale is in the soprano, the chorale is played on the upper manual or Werck with the right hand, and the second part with the left hand on the Rückpositiv. If the chorale is in the soprano of a four part verse, it is then played on the Rückpositiv with the right hand, the alto and tenor with the left hand on the upper manual or Werck, and the bass on the pedal. If the chorale is in the tenor, the chorale is played with the left hand on the Rückpositiv and the other parts with the right hand on the upper manual or Werck, the bass on the pedal.

In a four-part verse the alto may also be played specifically on the Rückpositiv, but the soprano must be played with the right hand on the upper keyboard, with both the tenor and bass voices together on the pedal; it must be specially composed, however, so that the tenor is no higher than C, since one seldom finds D in the pedals, and also so that these parts are not spaced too widely apart, only an octave, fifth, or third, since one cannot span a larger distance well with the feet.

But the following approach [see Example 1] is the most beautiful and

Ex. 1. A chorale to be played on the pedale, from Samuel Scheidt, *Tabulatura nova* (1624), Part III

far more comfortable, namely, to play the alto on the pedal. But the advantage of this way depends upon the stops and particular voices in the organ, which must have been disposed knowledgeably in terms of 4′ and 8′ pitch levels. The Positiv must always be based on 8′ pitch; and the pedal on 4′ pitch. Soprano, alto, and tenor should be played on the Rückpositiv on an 8′ stop. The alto will be played on the pedal with a 4′ stop. Voices of a sharp 4′ tone in the pedal: 4′ Octave plus Zimmel, 4′ Gedackt + Zimmel, Cornet bass, 4′, and so on. When such 4′ stops are drawn the alto sounds in the correct pitch relationship [see Example 2].

Ex. 2. From Samuel Scheidt, *Tabulatura nova* (1624), Part III

Certain registers or stop divisions to draw when one will play a chorale on two manuals and hear it clearly:

On the Hauptwerk

Grob Gedackt, 8'⎫
Klein Gedackt, 4'⎭ drawn together

or

Principal 8' alone and other stops according to preference

Sharp stops on the Rückpositiv to hear the chorale clearly: Quintadena or Gedackt 8' plus the klein Gedackt or Principal 4', with the Mixture or Zimmel or Superoctave; these stops together or others according to preference.

To hear the chorale clearly on the pedal: Untersatz 16', Posaune 8 or 16', Dulzian 8 or 16', Shalmei, Trompete, Bauerflöte, Cornet, and others which are found often enough in small and large organs.

The previous I would nevertheless only prescribe to those who don't yet know the style and who would like to do it properly. Other distinguished persons and sensible organists, however, will be left to direct such things after their own inclination.

15. Marin Mersenne, *Harmonie universelle* (1636), "Sixth Book of the Organ."

Proposition III

To determine in how many ways all the stops of the organ can be combined, and how some jeux composez are made up.

I have shown in the book on singing how each number of things can be varied, taking them in twos, threes, fours, etc., or taking them all together; therefore, it is easy to conclude that the twenty-two stops of the organ can be varied in 231 ways, by joining them only in pairs: in 1540 ways by joining them in threes, and 26334 ways by joining them in fives, that is to say, if five are used together as in making up the plain jeu. But, one can see the table of the aforementioned book on singing, which shows the number of all the stop combinations from simple to those composed of twenty-two stops. So, it suffices here to explain those which are in general use, because among the many possible combinations are several which are disagreeable, and which have bad effect, and because it is easy to invent several others by experimenting at the keyboard, or by considering all those which sound good together.

Now, the most important of the jeux composez is called the plain jeu, which is made up of seven or eight simple stops, namely, the Monstre, Bourdon 16' and 8', the open 8', Prestant, Doublette, Fourniture, Cymbale, and Tierce. But, the table which follows will better explain all the jeux composez than a long discussion, for the first column contains the simple stops, which are marked by the letters of the alphabet, signifying in the second list how these simple stops are combined into each jeu composé. For example, the seven letters A, B, C, D, E, F, G, which are opposite the plain jeu, signify that it is made up of the seven stops of which I have just spoken. But, because each jeu composé is varied in several ways, I have taken only the most common opposite each jeu composé, according to the style used by Monsieur Raquette, organist of *Nostre Dame de Paris*, who is one of the most accomplished in France.

Table of the Stops of the Organ
Ieux Simples

A Monstre 16', of fine tin
B Bourdon 8' stopped, or 16' open, of wood
C 8' open, half of wood, half of tin
D Bourdon 4' stopped, of wood*
E Prestant, or 4' open, of tin
F Doublette, the feet of lead, and the bodies of tin
G Fourniture, of the same material; it repeats from octave to octave, and
    has 5, 6, 7, 8 or 9 pipes for each key, and is pitched at 1' open
H Cymbale, same material, and starts at $\frac{1}{4}$', of tin
I Flageollet 1$\frac{1}{2}$'
K Tierce, the same
L Nazart à cheminée, or conical
M Fluste 2' stopped of tin, à cheminée
N Fluste douce, or à neuf trous 1'
O Flageollet 1'
P Cornet five ranks 1'
Q Trompette of tin 8'
R Cleron of tin 4'
S Voix humaine, of tin
T Cromorne of tin, 4'
U Pédale d'anche, of tin, 8'
X Pédale de fluste, of wood, 8'

  * Speaking pitch: 8'.

Ieux Composez

Plain jeu	A B C D E F G & K
Jeu musical	C D E
	D E
Doublette	D F
Gros Bourdon	B E
	B C E
Gros Cornet	D K L
	B I
	B E K
Cymbale	D H
	H L M
Nazard	D L M N
	D L
	D L N
	L M N
Flageollet	D O
	D L O
Cornet	D E L P
	D E P
Trompette & Cleron	D E G
	E G
	D E G R
Cleron	B R
	L M R
	D R
Voix Humaine	D E S
	D S
	D L R S
	D L S
Cromorne	D E T
	D L T
	D L N T
Pedale de Fluste	D M X
	D L X
Pedale d'Anche	C D E T V
	C D E M B

I shall be giving still other sorts of registrations, both simple and compound, after having explained everything pertaining to the pipes and the reeds.

Proposition XXXI

To explain all the registrations both simple and compound for the most advanced and largest organs being made today.

Although I have already spoken of the different stops of the organ, this Proposition will nevertheless supply what can have been omitted, for it contains the greatest number of combinations which are provided by the most excellent builders in the largest organs in Europe, though the centuries to come could still add others, since man's imagination has not yet reached its limits on this subject.

Now, I am marking each stop with the letters of the alphabet, so that they can serve toward understanding the jeux composez which follow the jeux simples, of which the first, which belongs to the grand jeu, which is mentioned first, is called the Montre.

Table of Single Stops on the Grand Orgue

A   The Montre, the longest pipe of which is sixteen feet open, and the last, consequently, sounding the interval of twenty-ninth above the first, is only one foot long. They are all made of tin.

B   The Bourdon is a stopped eight foot, of wood or étoffe; it sounds the unison with the Montre, but is softer, because it is stopped.

C   The other Bourdon is four feet stopped, or eight feet open in the fashion of a fleute; it is at the octave of the preceding stop, and may be of tin or of wood.

D   The Prestant is four feet open, at the fifteenth of the Montre, or two feet stopped; and it is so named, because it is used to set the tone of the organ, for the reason that it is proportioned to the human voice.

E   The Doublette is two feet open, at the twenty-second from the Montre.

F   The Flajollet is one foot open, and is at the twenty-ninth from the Montre; it should be played all alone with the four foot stopped.

G   The Nazard is about $5\frac{3}{4}'$ long, and is stopped or à cheminée; it is at the twelfth from the Montre, and of lead.

H   Another Nazard at the octave from the preceding one, around $2\frac{3}{4}'$ long, stopped or à cheminée.

I   The Fleute d'Allemand 4′ is à cheminée, that is to say that its body has two diameters [grosseurs], of which the first starts at the pipe's mouth and ends at a third of the [normal] length, up to which point it has the diameter of a stopped pipe of the same length; and the chimney extends the other two thirds in length, with the diameter of an open 2′. Thus, if this Fleute were made four feet long, a third of its body would be four inches in diameter, and the other two thirds, made en cheminée, would be two inches in diameter.

L The Tierce is about one foot, seven inches open, and sounds a third from C sol, or two foot open.

M The Fourniture has four pipes per key, of which the first is almost a foot and a half open, the second is one foot on C sol, the third eight and a half inches on G re sol, and the fourth a half foot on C sol. And if six ranks are preferred, the C sol is adjusted to two feet, and the G re sol to four inches.

N The grosse Cymbale has three pipes per key, of which the first is 1' open on C sol ut, the second eight and a half inches on G re, and the third $\frac{1}{2}'$ on C sol.

O The other Cymbale has two pipes per key, of which the first is two foot open on C sol, and the second is $\frac{1}{3}'$ on G re.

P The Cornet commences at the middle of the keyboard on C sol; it is 1' stopped à cheminée, and has five pipes per key, of which the first is just named; the second is 1' open; the third is about $8\frac{1}{2}$ inches on G re; the fourth is five inches open on E mi; now, they are all very large [scale]; and if the Bourdon and Prestant are included, as they customarily accompany the Cornet, it has seven ranks.

Q The Larigot is one foot five inches open, and starts on G re sol.

R The Trompette is eight feet long, flared at the top, like the broad end of military trumpets, and speaks at the octave of the Montre. It is about a half foot in diameter at the top, and one and a half inches at the bottom, for the pipe eight feet in length.

S The Cleron is 4', at the octave of the Trompette, and is flared in the same way.

T The Cromhorne is four feet, but at the unison with the Trompette. It measures four feet from the block to the end, and the first five inches of its length are flared, while the rest is cylindrical, with a diameter of one and a half inches.

V The Voix humaine is $\frac{1}{2}'$, at the unison with the Trompette.

X The Pedale is 8' stopped.

Y The Trompette de Pedale is 8'.

Z The Fleute en Pedale is 4' stopped.

Combinations Made Up from the Preceding Stops

I   The Plain jeu A C D E M N O

II   Another excellent [combination] with or without the Tremblant C D E H L R

III The Nazard B C D G

IV   Another Nazard C D E H

V   C D E F H with the tremblant

VI   A C, and very pleasing combination

VII   B C I, a very soft combination with tremblant, which is the
        fleute d'Allemand

VIII   The Trompette A C D R

IX   The Cornet B C D E P

X   The Cromhorne B C D T

XI   The Cleron B C D H S, with or without the tremblant

XII   A very sharp combination A D C E L

XIII   The Flajolet B C F

XIV   Another B C F H, with the tremblant

XV   Another B C D F H T, with the tremblant

XVI   The Larigot B C Q, with or without the tremblant

XVII   Another one quite strong A C D E

XVIII   Another B C O, with the tremblant

XIX   The Voix humaine B C D V

XX   The Trompette and the Cleron A C D E R S

XXI   A very melodious combination B C with the tremblant

XXII   A sharp combination A D F

XXIII   Very strong Nazard B C D E H Q

XXIV   The Cornet over the whole keyboard B C D E H L Q

Simple Stops on the Positif

The small organ which is usually placed below the grand [orgue], and which is behind the organist when he plays or faces the keyboard of the grand jeu, is ordinarily called the Positif. The same bellows serve it, the same wind supply and the same clavier [console]. In large churches, it is made up of the following stops:

A   The Montre 8', or 4' open, of tin

B   The Bourdon 4' stopped

C   The Prestant 4' open

D   The Doublette 2' open

E   The Flajolet 1' open

F   The Fleute d'Allemand 2', à cheminée

G   The Fourniture of three ranks, of which the first is 1' open on C sol, the second eight and a half inches on G re, and the third a half foot on C sol

H   The petite Cymbale has two pipes per key, of which the first is a half foot on C sol, and the second four inches on G re

I   The Tiercette of ten inches commences on E mi la

L The Nazard of seventeen inches stopped, à cheminée

M The petit Cromorne has a body four feet long, and its shallot [anche] is at the octave of the Bourdon 4′ stopped, and at the unison with the Prestant

N The petit Nazard 1½′ open on G re sol

Mixed, or Compound Combinations for the Positif

1. The plain jeu A C D G H
2. The petit Cornet for playing on two manuals B C D N E I
3. The Fleute d'Allemand B F, with the tremblant
4. Ieu harmonieux A C F
5. Another strong one A B C D
6. The Nazard B C L, with or without the tremblant
7. Another excellent combination B E L, with the tremblant
8. The Flajolet alone B E
9. Another with the tremblant B F H
10. The Doublette alone B D
11. The upside-down combination [*Ieu renversé*], or strong Nazard D L, for playing some sort of fantasie in the style of a Cornet on two manuals
12. Strong Nazard B C D L N
13. A very beautiful combination [*Ieu fort melodieux*] A B, with or without the tremblant

Corollary

It should be mentioned that the tremblant is not really a stop, but that it is nothing more than a movable board which is attached in the wind conduit so that it is raised when the speech of the pipes should not fluctuate, and lowered when the wind should be made to tremble. This is easily understood by flapping the lips with the hand, while pronouncing some vowel, for example a or o. But many people reject this fluctuation as a disagreeable noise, and I shall say more about it later.

As to the single stops, for which I have not mentioned the material, they can be made of lead, tin, or wood. Now I do not think that the Ancients could have had musical instruments so large, so diverse in their registration and so perfect as are our organs, which are continually being increased by inventions, by adding new stops to imitate the nightingale and other birds. And some are seeking a way of adding a violin stop by means of several unisons. But it may be more fitting to add the spinet stop as do those who make small cabinets in which the same keyboard sounds the pipes and strings simultaneously in unison, or at the octave. This produces a very sweeping effect, because the pipes are very soft and are blended so perfectly with the brass or gut strings that one has trouble in distinguishing them. If the violin stop is added, as many are trying to carry over to the spinet, it seems that there will be nothing more to desire in the organ, unless it be that the pipes should sound the vowels and syllables. This it seems must not be hoped for because of the great difficulty encountered.

Proposition XXXII, Corollary II

. . . I should still add that what makes the Cornet different from other stops depends particularly on the seventeenth, which makes a rather sharp sound, imitative of the *Cornet de Musique* [the musical instrument], of which I spoke in the fifth book of instruments; for the other four ranks, sounding the unison, octave, twelfth, and fifteenth, and even those sounding the third and major tenth, cannot perfectly imitate the Cornet, when the seventeenth is absent.

The Larigot is made particularly to sound the nineteenth, the Fleute the octave, the Doublette the fifteenth, and the Flaiolet the twenty-second. When the Cornet stop, which is made continuous without breaks (when there are two manuals on the organ), is combined with the Tremblant and the Cleron, this makes an excellent combination, which imitates the Hauts-bois even more than the Cornet à bouquin. The Cromhorne, added to the Nazard is a perfect imitation of the Musette. I am omitting all mention of all the other combinations which can be drawn from the stops of the organ, because that would fill an entire volume.

Proposition XXXV

The Tremblant belongs to the wind conduit, in which it is enclosed; that is why it is called the *Tremblant à vent clos*, in use today, because it is more agreeable, and doesn't cause such rude fluctuations of air, nor as fast as the one with exposed wind [*à vent ouvert, ou perdu*]; this was used formerly, and is still seen in old organs.

Now, the *Tremblant à vent clos* is nothing other than a valve lined with three or four pieces of leather, which is suspended a little on the incline, and carried on a little square of wood, hollowed at the middle, and only a half inch high all around. The edges of this square are also lined with leather, lest the beating of the valve above should make too much noise, and beat too hard. But the valve is attached only at the top to this square, so that it might open and close freely. This square must also be placed at an incline, in such a way that its base is toward the outside, and the top toward the bellows, so that the wind might have freer passage at its entrance to the conduit; for if the square should be perpendicular to the conduit, the wind would be interrupted by the valve attached there, and would be unable to supply enough to the organ stops one wished to play: this will be avoided by giving a slope of one and a half inches to the square, sometimes called "lunette"; now an iron or brass wire curved like the handle of a cabinet must be attached to the Tremblant, its two ends being so attached on the top of the valve that the handle might extend the whole length, and that it might be drawn up and curved two inches higher than the bottom of the valve, so that the lead weight for the Tremblant might be so attached at the end of the handle or ring, that it is suspended in the air. But it should be remarked that it is made to beat more or less rapidly according to the weight attached to it, for it beats faster when it is heavier, and slower when it is lighter. The job of the builder consists in balancing it in such a way that it beats neither too fast nor too slowly; for if it is too slow, it will have no more effect when several keys are played with three or four stops drawn: thus it is beating correctly when it beats eight times in the space of a measure lasting two seconds.

As to the size of the Tremblant, there is no fast rule, although it will have more success when it is large, and since the wind conduits customarily are a little too flat for attaching them, a little trunk [*quaisse*] is added extending outside the conduit where the Tremblant is. This is made so that it is longer than the height of the conduit, and with a width of four or five inches; it is good for the Tremblant to be three and a half or four inches wide and a half foot long. It should be further remarked that two grooves might appropriately be made on the two sides of this square, which has been added to the conduit, in order to have a grooved board or tail board, which would be lined with leather, and joined to the square, also lined with leather, closing the wind, and provides a way of looking at the Tremblant, when it might be necessary to touch it.

If the wind conduit is a half foot wide, the Tremblant should be five inches wide, and seven or eight long, so that it will always be around a third longer than wide. The other kind of Tremblant differs from the preceding only in that it is attached outside the wind conduit on a "lunette," or straight window, or which is inclined like the preceding: but another valve must be put in the conduit, so that it might prevent the wind from going to the Tremblant when closed, only when it is opened.

Now this Tremblant beats more firmly than the other, and also beats as fast for several stops as for one, so it should be included in the organ if we wish to hear all the various effects that grow out of different Tremblants (although this one is certainly not as agreeable as the other one), since pleasure in music consists especially in variety, which allows for dissonance as well as consonance. It might finally be said that we would have a perfect Tremblant if it did not alter the sound of the pipes too much (as occurs when it doesn't have enough of an opening, or when wind is lost in some other place), and if it beats in such a way that it imitates the vibrato of human voices in the stops of the organ: thus it is worth more if it is close to the chest where the wind does not vibrate too fast.

Appendix C

Instructions for Registration (1636–1770), in English Translation

Premier Livre d'orgue
by Guillaume-Gabriel Nivers (1665)

THE STOP COMBINATIONS

The PLEIN JEU consists of the Prestant, Bourdon, Doublette, Cymbale, and the Fourniture. When there are 8′ [Montre] and 16′, they are added; if there is no Prestant, the Flutte is used instead.

The JEU DE TIERCE, which is also called the GROS JEU DE DIMINUTIONS, is made up of the Prestant, Bourdon, Tierce, and Quinte. To these may also be added, if desired, the Doublette, and also the 8′, or even the 16′, if there is one.

The JEU DOUX is composed of the Bourdon and Flutte, or of the Bourdon and the 8′. A little stronger is the combination of the Bourdon and the Prestant, and still stronger the addition of the Doublette, or the 8′ as well, or even the 16′.

Against the Cornet, a JEU DOUX is used for the bass.

To reed stops, usually only the Bourdon is added; but the Cromorne can be played alone. To the Trompette, the Bourdon and Prestant should be combined, and the Clairon, if desired—sometimes also the Cornet.

To the VOIX HUMAINE and Bourdon, the Flutte and the Tremblant à vent lent may be added.

With the Flageollet or Larigot, only the Bourdon is used.

The GRAND JEU is composed of the JEU DE TIERCE—using the entire series of options—to which are added the Trompette, Clairon, Cromhorne, Cornet, and Tremblant à vent perdu, if there is one. The rest of this combination is left to the discretion of the performer.

PRELUDES and PLEINS JEUX are played on the Plein Jeu.

FUGUES GRAVES on the Gros Jeu de Tierce with the Tremblant, or on the Trompette without Tremblant.

PRELUDES and PLEINS JEUX are also played on the Plein Jeu de Tierce.*

DUOS are played on the treble of the Petite Tierce and the bass of the Grosse Tierce; or, on the Cornet and Trompette.

RECITS, DIMINUTIONS, BASSES, CORNETS, ECHOS, GRANDS JEUX, etc. are individually marked as to registration; but, nevertheless, they can all be changed and played on other combinations at one's discretion, and according to the specification of the organ.

Premier Livre d'orgue
by Nicolas LeBègue (1676)

PREFACE

My purpose in this work is to give the public some knowledge of the way the organ is currently being played in Paris. I have chosen Songs and Movements which I thought most practical and appropriate to the sentiment and spirit of the Church, and have tried as far as I can to bring about a beautiful effect. I have also avoided, insofar as possible, whatever would be hard to the ear or difficult in execution. These pieces (if I am not mistaken) will also be of some use to organists who cannot come great distances to hear the numerous and diverse types of stops which have recently been in use here. The Verses in this book can be played to all the Psalms and Canticles on all the tones, even to Elevations of the Mass, and to Offertories. The latter requires only taking the longest pieces, or playing two together on the same tone. The book contains almost all the types of pieces in use today in the principal churches of Paris. Connoisseurs will discover some liberties, which I believe to be justifiable for this admirable instrument. I hope particularly that all those who do me the honor of playing these pieces will want to play them according to my intentions, that is to say, with the correct combinations of stops and the proper tempo for each piece; and particularly to practice them, so that they will know them well enough to play them, for the music will then show to greater advantage and have infinitely more grace.

There are several pieces in this book which are not useful to organists whose instruments lack the stops necessary for their execution. Such are those for the Tierce or Cromorne en taille, the Trios with pedal, and the Récits au dessus and à la basse de Voix Humaine. But there is a sufficient

---

* This sentence is from the Livre of 1675.

number for all the tones, because all the other pieces can be played on all
sorts of organs.

Here is a little advice for the combinations of stops, as well as the style
[mouvement] of playing each kind of piece:

The PRELUDE and PLEIN JEU should be played slowly, and the
PLEIN JEU DU POSITIF lightly.

The DUO very boldly and lightly. On large organs, the dessus on the
Positif Tierce, and the bass on the Grosse Tierce along with the Bourdon
16'. On medium sized and small organs on the Tierce, or the Trompette
and the Cornet.

The DESSUS DE CROMHORNE sweetly and agreeably, imitating a
singing style. The bass on the Petit Bourdon [8'] and the Prestant [4'] of
the Grand Orgue, or the 8' [open] alone, and the Cromhorne alone, or
with the Bourdon [8'], or with the Positif Flutte [4'].

The CORNET very audaciously and gaily, the bass on the Positif
Bourdon [8'] and the Montre [4'].

The BASSE DE TROMPETTE heartily; the accompaniment of the
Positif Bourdon [8'] and Montre [4'], and on the Grand Orgue the Petit
Bourdon [8'], and Prestant along with the Trompette. Or, equally as good,
the bass on the Positif Cromhorne with the Montre, Nazard, and Tierce,
with the Petit Bourdon [8'] and the Prestant of the Grand Orgue as
accompaniment.

The VOIX HUMAINE a bit slowly, also reflecting the singing style;
the accompaniment on the Positif Bourdon, the Fluste, or the Montre. On
the Grand Orgue, the Petit Bourdon, the Prestant or the Fluste 4', the
Voix Humaine and the Tremblant doux, with the Nazard if it is felt
necessary.

The ECHO vigorously and fast, with the accompaniment on the Positif
Bourdon and Montre. On the Grand Orgue, the Cornet, the Petit
Bourdon, and the Prestant, or the Cornet alone, if it is strong enough; the
Répétitions on the Echo Cornet. The accompaniment may also be played
on the Grand Orgue 8' alone. The second Répétition on the Positif Flûte
alone.

The TRIO à DEUX DESSUS, the bass on the Grand Orgue Tierce,
along with the Petit Bourdon, the Prestant, Nazard, Quarte de Nazard,
and the Tremblant doux. On the Positif, the Cromhorne alone, or if it is
not strong enough, add the Bourdon, or the Fluste, or the Montre. Another
combination for the TRIO à DEUX DESSUS: the bass on the Grand
Orgue Trompette alone. The dessus on the Positif Montre, Bourdon,
Nazard, and Tierce. On small organs, the whole thing should be played

on the Tierce. On medium sized organs, simply with the Trompette and the Cornet.

The TRIO A TROIS CLAVIERS, the first dessus on the Positif Cromhorne, Bourdon, and Prestant. The other [manual] part on the Grand Orgue Tierce, Petit Bourdon, Prestant, Nazard, Quarte de Nazard, and Tremblant doux; with the Pedalle de Fluste. Or, also, the first dessus on the Tierce de Positif, and the other part on the Grand Orgue Voix Humaine, Petit Bourdon, Prestant, and the Tremblant doux; with the Pedalle de Fluste. Or, also, the first dessus on the Cornet, and the other part on the Positif Cromhorne, Bourdon and Prestant; with the Pedalle de Fluste. Or, also, the first dessus on the Trompette, the second dessus on the Tierce du Positif; with the Pedalle.

The TIERCE or CROMHORNE EN TAILLE seriously. The accompaniment should be played on the Grand Orgue Petit Bourdon, Prestant and Bourdon or Montre 16′. On the Positif, the Tierce, Bourdon, Montre, Fluste, Doublette, Nazard, and Larigot; and Pedalle. Or, on the Positif [for the Cromhorne en Taille], the Cromhorne, Montre, Bourdon, and Nazard. Other possible accompaniments: on the Grand Orgue, the Petit Bourdon, Prestant, and 8′; or, the Petit Bourdon and Prestant; or the Petit Bourdon and 8′—whichever seems to be the most effective. To my mind, this type of Verset is the most beautiful and distinctive of all organ pieces.

FUGUE GRAVE: on the Grand Orgue, the Bourdon, Prestant, Trompette, and Clairon. On small organs, the Bourdon de 4 pieds [speaking 8′ pitch] and the Cromhorne.

DIALOGUE: For the Grand Jeu, the Petit Bourdon, Prestant, Trompette, and Cornet. For the Petit Jeu, the Bourdon, Montre, and Cromhorne [Pos.]. Another Grand Jeu: Petit Bourdon, Prestant, Trompette, and Clairon. Another: Petit Bourdon, Prestant, Doublette, Nazard, Quarte de Nazard, Grosse Tierce, Trompette, Clairon, Cornet, and Tremblant à vent perdu; Petit Jeu: the Montre, Bourdon, Nazard, Tierce, and Cromhorne.

I have used two Final Cadences in the seventh Tone, which may be used at will, because in that mode they are both essentially the same.

Those who have trouble executing certain ornaments, where they are found too difficult to play, are advised to pass them by, for it is essential that the hands remain relaxed. But, special care should be directed toward observing the tempos very exactly.

Those who wish to shorten the pieces have only to begin where there is a little star (+). [Example 3 gives explanations for the ornaments found in the pieces.]

Ex. 3. Explanation of ornaments, from Nicolas LeBègue, *Premier Livre d'orgue* (1676)

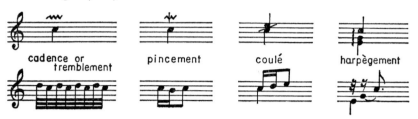

cadence or tremblement   pincement   coulé   harpègement

Anonymous Text from *Livre d'orgue II*
Nicolas LeBègue (1678)

REGISTRATION INSTRUCTIONS, IN ORDER BETTER TO KNOW
HOW TO COMBINE THE STOPS

For a PLAIN JEU, draw the Bourdon, Montre, Prestant, Doublette, Fourniture, and Cimbale; on large organs, add the Bourdon 8′ [speaking 16′ pitch].

For the CROMHORNE, the bass is played on the Grand Orgue Bourdon and Prestant, and the dessus on the Positif Cromhorne, along with the Bourdon.

The JEU DE TIERCE, for Duos and Trios, requires the Bourdon, Prestant, Doublette, Nazard, and Tierce.

For a BASSE DE TROMPETTE, the dessus is played on the Positif Bourdon and Montre, and the bass on the Trompette, along with the Bourdon and Prestant; a FUGUE GRAVE is played on the Trompette en Tierce.

For a DESSUS DE TROMPETTE, the jeu doux is played with the left hand on the Positif Bourdon and Montre, and the dessus on the Trompette alone, or together with the Bourdon.

A CORNET requires the bass as in the article above, and the Cornet on the Grand Orgue.

For a VOIX HUMAINE, if it is in the bass, then the dessus should be played on the Positif jeu doux; if it is in the dessus, the bass must be played on the Cornet . . . —for a jeu doux, Bourdon, Montre . . . and Nazard . . . —.

For a GRAND JEU, draw the Bourdon, Montre . . . Prestant, Doublette, Nazard, Tierce, Cornet, Trompette . . . on the Grand Orgue; and on the Positif, the Bourdon, Montre, Doublette, Nazard, Tierce, Cromhorne. On the Echo the Bourdon, Prestant, Doublette,

Nazard, Tierce and for a Voix Humaine Cromhorne and the Tremblant à vent perdu.

Livre de musique pour l'orgue
by Nicolas Gigault (1685)

TO THE READER

The pieces marked for two, three, or four ensembles can be played on one or two manuals. The notes for an Escho marked for the first manual could be repeated on the others. For the Trios à deux dessus, the first dessus can be played on the Grand Orgue, the second on the Positif Cromorne with the thumb of the right hand, and the bass on the Grand Orgue Tierce; or, the two dessus on the Cromorne, and the bass on the Tierce. Preludes are played on the Plains Jeux, or on the Grands Jeux d'Anches, with the Grand Tremblant. Fugues Graves are played on the Trompette, and Duos, Récits, Dialogues, and other pieces on their usual combinations.

Livre d'orgue
by André Raison (1688)

TO THE READER

As I vary the choice of stops and manuals a great deal, it is not necessary that all my pieces be played exactly as marked. Thus, what is designated as a Basse de Trompette can also be played on a Cromorne or Clairon, or on the Jeu de Tierce; what is played as a Récit de Cornet can be done on the Tierce. The Récit de Cromorne can be likewise alternated with a Voix Humaine or a Trompette without foundations, and so on, according to the specifications of the organ. Also, the manuals themselves may be treated flexibly. What is played on the Grand Clavier could also be played on the Petit [Positif], except that this must then be played in a lighter style; and the contrary is true in substituting the Grand for the Petit. The Récit de Cromorne avec Cornet Séparé or Echo can be played all on the same keyboard. The Trio à 3 Claviers and the Cromorne or Tierce en Taille can be executed with a friend playing the Pedalle de Flutte with the right hand on a soft stop of the Grand Orgue, all of which I suggest only to facilitate the pieces as much as possible.

HOW THE STOP COMBINATIONS SHOULD BE MADE UP

The PLEIN JEU for a 4′ organ is composed of the Montre [4′], the Bourdon [8′], the Doublette, the Cimbale, and Fourniture. If there are 8′

and 16′ on the Grand Orgue, they should be added; the PETIT PLEIN JEU would then be made up the same as for the 4′ organ.

The DUO is played on the two Tierces: the right hand on the Positif with the Bourdon, Montre, Tierce, and Nazard; the left hand on the Grand Orgue with the Bourdons 8′ and 16′, Flutte, Tierce, Nazard, and Gros Nazard, with the Double Tierce if there is one. It can also be played with the Cornet séparé or the Jeu de Tierce du Positif against the Grand Orgue Trompette with its foundation. If the Cornet is played with the right hand, it could be accompanied with the Petit Bourdon and the Flutte or the 4′ [Prestant].

The TRIO is played with the right hand on the Cromorne sans fond [alone], and the left on the Bourdon, the 4′ and the Flute, Nazard, Tierce, and Tremblant doux. It is also suitable with the combinations for the DUO, above. Or, possibly, with the left hand on the Grand Orgue, using the Voix Humaine, Bourdon, and Flute, and the right hand the Bourdon, Flute, and Nazard, with the Tremblant doux.

For the BASSE DE TROMPETTE or the BASSE DE CROMORNE, the appropriate reed is combined with the Bourdon and 4′ for the left hand, while the right hand goes to the Bourdon and 4′ of the correspondingly suitable manual. The Clairon, combined only with the Bourdon 16′, may also be used en basse, with the Positif Bourdon and Flute as accompaniment.

The BASSE DE TIERCE is played with the left hand on the Positif. It is composed of the Montre, Bourdon, Doublette, Flute, Nazard, Tierce, and Larigot, if there is one. The right hand then plays on the Grand Orgue Bourdon and 4′. This registration is also fitting for the TIERCE EN TAILLE, excepting that the Bourdon 16′ must be added to the Grand Orgue, plus the Pedale de Flute.

The RECIT DE CROMORNE is played with the Cromorne alone in the right hand, and the Grand Orgue Bourdon and Flute in the left.

The VOIX HUMAINE has for its companions the Bourdon and the Flute, or 4′ with the Tremblant doux. When it is played en Récit, the Positif must be used with the Bourdon, Flute, and Nazard.

The DIALOGUE is played on all the keyboards; on the Grand Orgue, the Bourdon, 4′, Tierce, Nazard, Cornet, Trompette, Clairon, and the Tremblant à vent perdu; on the Positif, the Bourdon, Montre, Nazard, Tierce, and Cromorne. The Cornet séparé and Eco are used when there are four manuals. If there are only three, the repetitions are taken on the third manual. The DIALOGUE can even be played on two manuals, for then one has only to cut off the Tierces and Nazards on the Grand and Petit Orgue, with the Tremblant.

Ex. 4. Table of ornaments, from André Raison, *Livre d'orgue* (1688)

For the CROMORNE EN TAILLE, use the same combination as for the BASSE DE CROMORNE, adding the Pedalle de Flute.

The TRIO A TROIS CLAVIERS is registered like the other Trios, adding the Pedalle de Flute.

HOW GRACE AND MELODIC CHARM ARE GIVEN TO ALL THESE PIECES

A GRAND PLEIN JEU is played very slowly. The chords should be quite legato one to the other, taking pains not to raise one finger until the other has pressed down; and the last measure should be much prolonged. The PETIT PLEIN JEU is played lightly and fluently.

The DUO, a free and easy style of piece, is played rapidly and pointedly when written in quavers (8ths).

The RECIT DE CROMORNE, or DE TIERCE is played very tenderly. Accentuate cadences in important keys, particularly the last one.

The CORNET is played with celerity, animation, and fluidity; and the chief cadences should be lengthened, especially the last.

The BASSE DE TROMPETTE, CROMORNE, and TIERCE are played boldly and neatly, with vitality and spark.

The CROMORNE EN TAILLE is played very tenderly.

The TIERCE EN TAILLE is played straightforwardly and fluently.

The VOIX HUMAINE is played compassionately and very legato.

The DIALOGUE on two, three, and four manuals is played according to the indicated tempo.

[Raison's table of ornaments is given in Example 4.]

Premier Livre d'orgue
by Jacques Boyvin (1689)

ADVICE TO THE PUBLIC, CONCERNING COMBINATIONS OF STOPS, TEMPOS, ORNAMENTS, AND HOW TO PLAY THEM

In presenting my works to the public, I have thought it appropriate to speak about the way in which they should be played. One of the most beautiful ornaments of the organ comes from knowing how to combine stops. The general manner is known, and I have no doubt that most of my readers are already acquainted with this style. However, as my book could fall into the hands of foreign musicians, it will be useful to them to find here some instruction about registration; and also some combinations have recently been discovered which seem very beautiful, and which have not, up to the present, been in use. I also believe it will be good to speak of performance, of tempos and ornaments, and of cadences and trills, mordents, arpeggios, port de voix, coulez, and others, and to give demonstrations of these, toward greater facility.

LET US SPEAK OF THE STOPS

For the PLEIN JEU in organs sizable enough to have a Positif, the keyboards are coupled, and on the Positif is drawn the Montre, which is either 8' or 4'—if it is 4', it will be called Prestant, and if it is 8', the Prestant should be drawn separately. Along with this, the Bourdon, Doublette, Fourniture, and Cymballe should be added. On the Grand Corps the same stops are used, plus the 8' open, the Bourdon 16', and the Montre 16', if there is one.

FUGUES GRAVES are played on the Trompette with its foundation, which consists of the Bourdon and Prestant, and on the Positif the Cromhorne alone. The keyboards are coupled. Or, they can be played on the

Positif only, using the Cromhorne with its foundation, which consists of the Bourdon and the 4'.

The QUATUOR is a Fugue de Mouvement whose parts are more active and more lyrical than those of a Fugue. The left hand is played on the Grand Orgue, on which is drawn the Jeu de Tierce, i.e. the Bourdon, Prestant, Nazard, Quarte, and Tierce. The right hand on the Positif, with the Cromhorne and its foundation, as above, and the Tremblant doux. Or, also, the Quatuor can be played thus: the bass and the dessus on the Tierce of the Grand Orgue, constituted as usual, and the middle parts, which are called the taille and the haute-contre, on the Positif Cromhorne with its foundation. This way is not only more beautiful but more difficult, unless one is assisted by a Tirasse or Marche Pieds.

The QUATUOR can also be performed in the following manner: assuming there is a Tirasse, the Bourdon 8', Prestant, and Nazar are drawn on the Grand Corps; on the Positif, the Tierce en Taille, that is, the Bourdon, Prestant, Nazar, Doublette, Tierce, and Larigot; and the two other parts are for the right hand on the Récit Trompette. Naturally, for this way of doing a Quatuor, four keyboards are necessary [i.e. including the pedal board]. It is essential that all parts sing equally well, particularly the Taille, sounding on the Positif Tierce, which is more penetrating and striking to the ear. Indeed, those who are capable of composing this kind of piece are almost the only ones who can play them. Thus, I have included very few in this volume, as is the case with the Dialogues de Récit, of which we shall speak later.

The DUO is played on the two Tierces: for the Petite Tierce, use the Bourdon, Prestant, Nazar, and Tierce. On the Grand Corps, the same thing is appropriate, with the addition of the Bourdon 16' and the Quarte de Nazar. Lacking a Quarte de Nazar, substitute the Doublette.

RECITS are played in sundry ways, the accompaniment always being on the Grand Corps Bourdon and Prestant, but for the Cromhorne, for which the accompaniment would be the Grand Corps 8' open alone. The Récits, themselves, are registered with the Petite Tierce, as for the Duo, or on the Nazar without the Tierce, along with its foundation; or on the Récit Trompette; or the Cromhorne alone, or Cornet séparé.

For the CONCERT DE FLUSTE, the keyboards are coupled, drawing on the Grand Corps the 8' Bourdon and Fluste, and on the Positif the Bourdon and Fluste, with the Tremblant doux.

For TRIOS A DEUX DESSUS, use the Grosse Tierce, as for the DUO, for the top part, but without the 16'; on the Positif, the Cromhorne alone, with the Tremblant doux. Other TRIOS are played on the Cromhorne with its foundation, the Cornet Séparé, and the Pedalle de Flustes. Or, instead of the Pedalle de Flustes, the Marche Pieds, or Tirasses, may be employed, using the Grand Corps Bourdon, Prestant, and Nazar.

With the VOIX HUMAINE or REGALLE, only the Bourdon and the Fluste are needed, both in the treble and in the bass; and the Tremblant doux. BASSES are played more frequently on the Positif Cromhorne than on the Trompette. Along with it go the Prestant or Montre, the Nazar, Doublette, Tierce, and Larigot, just as for the Tierce en Taille. The Bourdon is excluded because, being at the unison with the Cromhorne, it would slow it down, with the result that fast passages would not come through as neatly.

For playing BASSES on the Trompette, the Prestant and Nazar should be added. There are those who use the Bourdon in place of the Nazar, but this results in sluggish speech. BASSES DE TROMPETTE are also played with the Tremblant à vent perdu, for then other stops are used with it, as in the DIALOGUE, mentioned below. Note that the keyboards are not coupled, and the accompaniment is played on the Positif Bourdon and Larigot.

For PETITS DIALOGUES, use the Positif Cromhorne with its foundation, as above; on the Grand Corps, the Trompette, Clairon, and Cornet with foundation. The keyboards are coupled, but the Tremblant is not used.

For GRANDS DIALOGUES, the same thing as above, with the addition on the Grand Corps of the Nazar, Quarte, and Tierce, and even the Cromhorne, if there is one; and on the Positif, with the addition of the Nazar. Some even add the Tierce, as well. These pieces are performed on four ensembles, the third being the Cornet Séparé, and the fourth the Cornet d'Echo.

DIALOGUES DE RECIT may even be played on two manual organs, although they customarily require three. On a two manual instrument, the accompaniment is played on the Grand Corps, using the ordinary foundations, and proceeding directly without changing manuals on the Cromhorne or the Petite Tierce. In a trio texture, where the two upper parts are of equal importance, these are done on the same combination, the bass using the Tirasse, or the Pedalle de Flûte. On one manual organs, the same sort of thing should be done, because mutations, such as the Tierce and Nazar, and reeds, such as the Trompette and Voix Humaine, and others, are divided stops [i.e. drawn separately for bass and treble]. All sorts of Dialogues can be played even on one manual, because the melody progresses uninterruptedly, and sustains itself sufficiently alone.

Ex. 5. Table of ornaments, from Jacques Boyvin, *Premier Livre d'orgue* (1689)

"Demonstration"

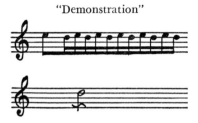

ON ORNAMENTS

The Cadence, or Tremblement, must be long, according to the note and the tempo where it is applied; it is played ordinarily in descending, and is begun on the note above [see Example 5].

The mordent [pincement] is played short, ordinarily in ascending, and commences on the note below; it must be "affected," that is to say, prepared. To slow down the note below adds much to the charm of the melody; the note below which precedes it must occupy half of the value on which it falls, and that note, although dissonant, must sound against the bass. [See Example 6. For the Coulez, see Example 7.]

The port de voix is marked thus: +; the note where it is desired must

Ex. 6. Table of ornaments, from Jacques Boyvin, *Premier Livre d'orgue* (1689)

Ex. 7. Table of ornaments, from Jacques Boyvin, *Premier Livre d'orgue* (1689)

"Coulez"

"Signifies when it is rising from the preceding note"

Ex. 8. Table of ornaments, from Jacques Boyvin, *Premier Livre d'orgue* (1689)

Ex. 9. Table of ornaments, from Jacques Boyvin, *Premier Livre d'orgue* (1689)

be struck a little, ordinarily in descending; this note must be stifled, that is to say, scarcely held, but it must be struck directly against the bass [see Example 8].

On the organ arpeggios are scarcely ever played; rather, a little tremblement on the note below [see Example 9].

Livre d'orgue
by Gilles Jullien (1690)

ADVIS

Having resolved to present this first work to the public, I have tried to avoid anything which failed to conform to the modulations and tones of the Church, in order in a more particular manner to dedicate the whole to God. I hope with all my heart that those into whose hands it falls will agree to use it in the same spirit. Pieces of different types, on all the tones, will be found here, namely, Preludes, Duos, Trios of all kinds, such as Trio à deux dessus with a bass, Trio à deux claviers and Pedalle de fluste, slow Trios to be played at the elevation of the Mass, Fugues, Cromhorne and Tierce en taille, Basse de Trompette, Récits de Voix Humaine, Cromhorne, and Cornet, Echo, Dialogues, and several other pieces. I am sure that the notation is very easy, and hope that the chants will seem quite simple, natural, agreeable, and sufficiently varied. I have put points after the first eighth notes of the piece in folio 51, to serve as an example. The others are to be treated in a like manner, more or less lightly, according to the tempo indicated. Although I have allowed myself some freedom and license, scholars will notice readily that I have not drawn far away from the rules of conservative composition, but, rather, that I have diverged from the use of ordinary chords. In each piece I have indicated the manner of performance and, as well, the agréments (or pincements), cadences (or tremblements), coulés, and harpègements, in the following manner [see Example 10].

Ex. 10. Table of ornaments, from Gilles Jullien, *Livre d'orgue* (1690)

As I do not doubt that those who play these pieces will already know the usual combinations of stops for them, this subject having been so often discussed and reiterated, it would be pointless to speak further of it here.

Nevertheless, it should be called to mind that Fugues in 4 Parts, which are ordinarily played on the Trompette or Cromhorne, can also be done, on large organs, on two keyboards en quatuor. I have written them with this intention (at least most of them), having maintained a satisfactory melodic interest among the equally imitative parts. This applies not only to Fugues and Contre Fugues, but to those pieces that move continuously in imitation, including the chromatic pieces on the first tone, all of which should be registered in the following manner: the Soprano and bass on the Grand Orgue, with the Bourdon, Prestant, 8', Nazard, and Quarte de Nazard; the alto and tenor on the Positif Cromhorne, with the Bourdon and Prestant, possibly adding Nazard, that the Cromhorne might sound fuller in texture. Use the Tremblant doux, provided that it beats regularly, or, failing that, the Tremblant à vent perdu. The Grosse Tierce is excluded from the Grand Orgue combination, lest it cause the soprano and bass to predominate over tenor and alto, which are being played on the Cromhorne.

The QUATUOR can be played in a much simpler way, to wit, the soprano and alto on the Cornet séparé, and the bass and tenor on the Cromhorne, Bourdon, and Prestant.

And for organs with only one manual, but whose stops are divided, use the Bourdon and Prestant, plus the Dessus de Tierce and Nazard, and the Basse de Cromhorne or Voix Humaine.

It is obvious that QUATUORS could be played in many other ways on large and small organs, but, as stops are not always of the same tonal character on different instruments, organists must adjust the combinations as seems best to them.

I would like to endow the organ, which is beyond contradiction the most perfect of instruments, with a new invention, for playing five-part pieces in a way which has not previously been practiced. Upon examination, connoisseurs will discover these works to be very effective in performance. While four parts are closely integrated, the fifth functions in contrast, as a Récit de Trompette. A little preparation is required, for this sort of composition is difficult to perform. The first five-part piece is the Prelude du 2ᵉ Ton, which is played slowly on the Grand Plain Jeu; the Fugue Renversée à Cinq, on the same tone, is played on a Quatuor combination, indicated above in various ways, and the fifth part, a special sort of tenor, will be done on the Pedalles de Fluste. The other PLAINS JEUX, on the third, fifth, and eighth tones, are played on the Grand Orgue, with the fifth part in the tenor range on the Pedalle de Trompette. For a fine performance of these pieces, those who honor me thus should know the tenor part from memory, so that it might sound absolutely clear and without confusion.

Foreign musicians will perhaps have difficulty determining the correct tempo for certain pieces in this book. But the problem will be simplified by noticing that the 6/8 measure can be counted in two, that is, one beat for three eighth notes. Those who are unaccustomed to such a measure should consider that these eighths are equivalent to the quarters in a simple triple meter.

I believe it not inappropriate to add to this volume of my works a three-voice Motet, with a Simphonie with two obbligato violin parts, to the praise of our patron Saint. If I am fortunate enough to have created something tasteful, meriting the public approval, then I shall willingly continue by publishing a second volume, which is already written.

Livre d'orgue
by Lambert Chaumont (1695)

ON REGISTRATION AND THE PERFORMANCE STYLE
APPROPRIATE TO EACH VERSET

The PRELUDE and PLEIN JEU, majestically on the Grand Orgue, and more lightly on the Positif.

The FUGUE GAYE on a brilliant combination, such as the Pettite Tierce, Bourdon, Montre, Nazard, etc.

The FUGUE GRAVE on the Bourdon, Prestant, and the Trompette, Clairon, and Nazard; on small organs, on the Cromhorne and the Bourdon.

The DUO boldly and lightly. On the Grand Orgue: the bass part on the Grosse Tierce, Bourdon and Prestant, Nazard, Quarte de Nazard, and Bourdon 16′. On the Positif: the dessus on the Petitte Tierce, etc. Or, the bass on the Trompette, and the dessus on the Cornet.

The TRIO A DEUX DESSUS, on the Grand Orgue the bass part on the Trompette, and on the Positif the dessus on the Montre, Bourdon, Tierce, and Nazard. Or, on the Grand Orgue the Petit Bourdon, Prestant, Nazard, Quarte de Nazard, Tierce, and Tremblant doux, and on the Positif the Cromhorne, Bourdon, and Flute.

The BASSE DE TROMPETTE and CROMHORNE, very boldly, with the Grand Orgue Petit Bourdon and Prestant, and the Positif Montre and Bourdon. But, for a Basse de Cromhorne, the Montre, Tierce, and Nazard must be added.

The CORNET and the ECHO with gaiety. The DESSUS and BASSE DE VOIX HUMAINE slowly. The DESSUS DE CROMHORNE sympathetically, imitating the cantabile style. All these stops are accompanied in similar manner, by a combination of the Bourdon, the Montre, or Prestant, Flutte, or Nazard, whichever contributes to the best effect.

For DIALOGUE, on the Grand Jeu, the Petit Bourdon, Prestant, Trompette, and Cornet, or Trompette and Clairon. Or the Petit Bourdon, Prestant, Doublet, Nazard, Quarte de Nazard, Tierce, Trompette, Clairon, Cornet, and Tremblant à vent perdu; for the Petit Jeu, the Montre, Bourdon, Nazard, Tierce, and Cromhorne.

The TRIO A TROIS CLAVIERS, the first dessus on the Bourdon, Prestant or Flutte, and Cromhorne; the second dessus on the Grand Orgue Petit Bourdon, Prestant, Tierce, Nazard, and Tremblant doux. Or, the first dessus on the Tierce, and the second on the Voix Humaine. Or, the first dessus on the Cornet, the second on the Cromhorne. Or, the first dessus on the Trompette, and the second on the Tierce.

The TIERCE or CROMHORNE EN TAILLE slowly, on the Grand Orgue the dessus on the Petit Bourdon, Prestant, Bourdon or Montre 16′; on the Positif the taille on the Bourdon, Montre, Flutte, Tierce, Nazard, Doublet, and Larigot; or the Bourdon, Montre, Nazard, and Cromhorne; for the bass, the Pedale de Flutte.

[Chaumont's explanation of symbols for ornamentation is given in Example 11.]

Ex. 11. Explanation of symbols for ornamentation, from Lambert Chaumont, *Livre d'orgue* (1695)

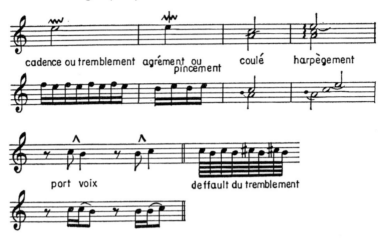

Messe du 8ᵉ ton
by Gaspard Corrette (1703)

REGISTRATION FOR THE PIECES CONTAINED IN THIS VOLUME

For the PLEIN JEU, couple the manuals. On the Grand Jeu [sic], the Bourdon 16', Bourdon, Montre, Prestant, Doublette, Fourniture, and Cymballe. On the Positif, the Bourdon, Montre, Prestant, Doublette, Fourniture, and Cymballe.

For the FUGUE, couple the manuals. On the Grand Jeu, the Bourdon, Prestant, and Trompette. On the Positif, the Bourdon, Prestant or Montre, and the Cromhorne.

For the TRIO A DEUX DESSUS, the manuals are uncoupled; the right hand playing on the Positif, and the left on the Grand Jeu. On the Grand Jeu, the Bourdon, Prestant, Montre, Tierce, Grosse Tierce, Nazar, and Quarte de Nazar. On the Positif, the Bourdon, Prestant or Montre, Cromhorne, and Tremblant doux.

The DUO is played with the manuals uncoupled, the right hand on the Positif, and the left on the Grand Jeu. On the Grand Jeu, the Bourdon 16', Bourdon, Prestant, Tierce, Grosse Tierce, Nazar, and Quarte de Nazar. On the Positif, the Bourdon, Prestant or Montre, Tierce and Nazar.

The RECIT DE NAZAR is played on the Positif, with the accompaniment on the Grand Jeu. On the Grand Jeu, the Bourdon and Montre 4'. On the Positif, the Bourdon, Prestant or Montre, and the Nazar.

The DESSUS DE PETITE TIERCE is played on the Positif, with the accompaniment on the Grand Jeu. On the Grand Jeu, the Bourdon and Prestant. On the Positif, the Bourdon, Prestant or Montre, Tierce, and Nazar.

For the BASSE DE TROMPETTE, the manuals are uncoupled. On the Grand Jeu, the Bourdon, Prestant, and Trompette. On the Positif, the Bourdon, and Prestant or Montre.

For the BASSE DE CROMHORNE, the manuals are uncoupled. On the Grand Jeu, the Montre and Bourdon. On the Positif, the Prestant or Montre, Nazar, Tierce, Doublette, Larigot, and the Cromhorne—not the Bourdon.

For the CROMHORNE EN TAILLE, on the Grand Jeu, the Montre, Bourdon, and the Pedalle de Flute. On the Positif, the Bourdon, Prestant or Montre, and the Cromhorne.

For the TIERCE EN TAILLE, on the Grand Jeu, the Bourdon 16', Montre, and Prestant, and the Pedalle de Flûte. On the Positif, the Bourdon, Prestant or Montre, Nazar, Tierce, Doublette, and Larigot.

For the FOND D'ORGUE, the manuals are coupled. On the Grand Jeu, the Bourdon 16', Bourdon, Prestant, and Montre. On the Positif, the Bourdon and the Prestant or Montre.

For the CONCERT DE FLUTE, the manuals are coupled. On the Grand Jeu, the Bourdon and Flûte. On the Positif, the Bourdon, Flûte, and the Tremblant doux.

For the DIALOGUE DE VOIX HUMAINE, the manuals are not coupled. On the Grand Jeu, the Bourdon and Flûte. On the Positif, the Bourdon, Flûte, the Voix Humaine, and the Tremblant doux.

For the DIALOGUE A DEUX CHŒURS, the manuals are coupled. On the Grand Jeu, the Bourdon, Prestant, Trompette, Clairon, and Cornet. On the Positif, the Bourdon, Prestant or Montre, and the Cromhorne.

For the DIALOGUE A TROIS CHŒURS, the manuals are coupled. On the Grand Jeu, the Bourdon, Prestant, Trompette, Clairon, Cornet, Nazar, Quarte de Nazar, and Tierce. On the Positif, the Bourdon, Prestant or Montre, Cromhorne, Tierce, and Nazar. The third Chœur is played on the Claviers d'Echo, and the Tremblant à vent perdu is used.

COMMENTS ON PERFORMANCE, AND ON THE CHARACTER OF EACH PIECE

The PLEIN JEU DE POSITIF should be played with vitality, and with care in forming and outlining trills, and cadences. In rapid passages, the fingers must be picked up and the touch almost as light as for the harpsichord, taking special care that one hand is always in contact with the keys, in order to avoid empty spots.

But, the GRAND PLEIN JEU must be played unpretentiously and with a full effect, provided that one knows how to provide a full texture for fast passages; and practically no trills, especially on 16′ organs.

The FUGUE should be slow, with great attention to detail.

The TRIO demands strict adherence to the meter, and "légèreté" within the tempo.

The DUO is lively and very gay, performed within the tempo.

The RECIT is played tenderly and neatly, imitating the singing voice as far as possible.

The BASSE DE TROMPETTE is performed daringly, imitating a fanfare.

The BASSE DE CROMHORNE imitates the bowings, nuances, arpeggios, and passage work of the Basse de Violle.

The CROMHORNE EN TAILLE is played very tenderly, in a cantabile style.

The TIERCE EN TAILLE demands languidness and nuance, then sweeping passages, full of movement.

The FOND D'ORGUE must be played tenderly, in a cantabile style.

The CONCERT DE FLUTE and the VOIX HUMAINE are played slowly, and even in the most active sections, they should never move fast, because of the Tremblant.

The DIALOGUE is played very boldly, ranging among all sorts of moods, from gaiety to languor.

EXPLANATION OF THE ORNAMENTS

The Cadance [sic] or Tremblement always starts on the note above, and it must be played rapidly and as evenly as possible, according to the value of the note over which it is placed [see Example 12].

Ex. 12. Explanation of the Cadence, from Gaspard Corrette, *Messe du 8e ton* (1703)

The Pincé is done ordinarily in ascending by conjunct degree, and by interval, sometimes in descending. But, when the Pincé goes by interval, it must commence directly on the note upon which it is placed [see Example 13].

Ex. 13. Explanation of the Pincé, from Gaspard Corrette, *Messe du 8ᵉ ton* (1703)

The Petite Virgule is indicated thus: ' or a little note, which is performed by ascending by conjunct degree, which makes a port de voix. The Petite Virgule, or little note, is struck precisely against the bass or the accompaniment [see Example 14].

Ex. 14. Explanation of the Petite Virgule, from Gaspard Corrette, *Messe du 8ᵉ ton* (1703)

The PETITE CROIX indicates a coulé, or a note which is added when descending in thirds. It is marked +, and should be struck directly against the bass [see Example 15].

Ex. 15. Explanation of the Petite Croix, from Gaspard Corrette, *Messe du 8ᵉ ton* (1703)

The Coulé is indicated by a little line, which passes in the midst of a third [see Example 16].

Ex. 16. Explanation of the Coulé, from Gaspard Corrette, *Messe du 8ᵉ ton* (1703)

The slur placed over several notes means that the fingers should not be picked up off the keys [see Example 17].

Ex. 17. Explanation of the liaison, from Gaspard Corrette, *Messe du 8ᵉ ton* (1703)

Eighth notes are ordinarily dotted, that is to say, the first one is longer than the second [see Example 18].

Ex. 18. Explanation of eighth notes, from Gaspard Corrette, *Messe du 8ᵉ ton* (1703)

The Double Cadence is marked ~ on an eighth note [see Example 19].
A little star indicates a good spot to terminate, when a piece is too long, and it is marked *.

Ex. 19. Explanation of the Double Cadence, from Gaspard Corrette, *Messe du 8ᵉ ton* (1703)

At the end of the book, I have added an Elevation and a Basse de Cromhorne for the Gradual, to provide one or two pieces for variety.

Manuscript: "Anonyme de Tours"*
(1710–20?)

GRAND JEU: Nasard, Cornet, Bourdon, Prestant, Montre, Quarte de Nasard, Trompette. Or: the fonds, Doublette, Nasard, and Tierce, dessus and bass of the Cromorne, Cornet, if there is one, and Tremblant.

PLEIN JEU: Fourniture, Bourdon, Montre, Prestant, Cimballe, Pédale.

DUO: Nasard, Bourdon, Montre, Tierce and Prestant, Tierce, Nasard. Or: Nasard, Bourdon, Montre, Tierce, Prestant, Doublette; Basse de Cromorne for variety.

TROMPETTE: Nasard, Bourdon, Trompette, and Prestant, Flute, jeu doux.

VOIX HUMAINE: Nasard, Bourdon, Voix Humaine, and Quarte (Doublette), Cromorne, Bourdon.

FUGUE: the fonds, with dessus and bass of the Cromorne.

RECIT: Cromorne, Bourdon, Flute. Or: Bourdon, Prestant and Montre and dessus de Cromorne en récit, or de Nasard, or de Tierce, or de Trompette alone. Or: for a dessus de Cornet, the fonds, Nasard and Tierce for the récit.

MUTATIONS DE JEUX: Bourdon, Montre, Fond d'Orgue dont Prestant, basse de Cromorne, Prestant, Quatre 4′ pied, Bourdon 8′, Bourdon 16′, Doublette, Montre, Fourniture and Cimbale.

TROMPETTE: Bourdon, Prestant, Trompette and Clairon. Or: basse de Cromorne, only for the bass, the 3 fonds, Nasard and Tierce.

CROMORNE: Bourdon and Cromorne.

* Translated from N. Gravet, "La Registration," L'Orgue, No. 100.

VOIX HUMAINE: Bourdon, Prestant, Voix Humaine.

NASARD: Nasard, Quarte de Nasard, Bourdon, Prestant, Doublette.

TIERCE: Tierce, Nasard, Quarte de Nasard, Prestant, Bourdon, Doublette.

CORNET: Prestant, Cornet, Quarte de Nasard.

FLAGEOLLET: Bourdon, Flageollet.

FLUTE: Fluste, Prestant or Bourdon alone. Or, Montre alone on a small organ.

VIOLON: Prestant, Flûte, and Clairon.

BOMBARDE: Montre, Flûte, Nasard, Trompette, and Bourdon.

LE MARCOU: Flute, Nasard, Doublette, Bourdon, Quarte de Nasard.

MUSETTE: Tierce, Nasard, Larigot, Montre, Doublette.

VIDE: Plain-jeu, Tierce, Bourdon, and Flûte.

Premier Livre d' orgue
by Michel Corrette (1737)

COMBINATIONS OF ORGAN STOPS

For the PLEIN JEU: manuals are coupled. On the Grand Jeu, the Bourdon, Bourdon 16', Montre, Prestant, Doublette, Fourniture, and Cymballe. On the Positif, the Bourdon, Montre, Prestant, Doublette, Fourniture, and Cymballe.

For the DUOS on pages 2 and 28, the dessus on the Cornet de Récit; the bass on the Positif Cromorne and Nazar alone. Another DUO combination, on page 10: the dessus on the Cornet de Récit, and the bass on the Positif Bourdon, Prestant, Tierce, and Nazar. Another combination, for the DUO on page 20: manuals coupled, on the Grand Jeu, the Trompette and Clairon; on the Positif, the Cromhorne alone.

For the TRIO on page 7: the manuals uncoupled, on the Grand Jeu, the Bourdon, Bourdon 16', Prestant, Montre, Tierce, Grosse Tierce, Nazar, and Quarte de Nazar; on the Positif, the Bourdon, Prestant, and Cromhorne. Another combination, for the TRIO on page 29: the manuals uncoupled, on the Grand Jeu, the Bourdon, Prestant, Bourdon 16', and Clairon; on the Positif, the Bourdon, Prestant, and Nazar.

For the TRIO A 3 CLAVIERS . . . page 12; the first dessus on the Positif Bourdon, Prestant, Tierce, and Nazar; the second dessus on the Cornet de Récit; the bass on the Pedalles de Flute, and the Tremblant doux.

For the MUSETTE, page 15 and 31: on the Positif, the Cromhorne alone and the Pedalles de Flutes.

BASSE DE CROMHORNE, page 6: manuals uncoupled, on the Grand Jeu, the Bourdon alone; on the Positif, the Cromhorne and Nazar alone.

BASSE DE TROMPETTE, page 13: manuals uncoupled, on the Grand Jeu, the Trompette, Clairon, and Grand Cornet; on the Positif, the Bourdon and Larigot, with the Tremblant à vent perdu.

RECIT DE NAZAR, page 19: manuals uncoupled, on the Grand Jeu the Bourdon, and Prestant or Montre; on the Positif, the Bourdon, Prestant, and Nazar.

RECIT DE TROMPETTE, page 30: the dessus on the Petite Trompette de Récit, and the accompaniment on the Positif Bourdon and Flûte or Montre.

TIERCE EN TAILLE, page 4: manuals uncoupled, on the Grand Jeu the Bourdon, and the Prestant or Montre; on the Positif, the Bourdon, Prestant, Tierce, Nazar, Doublette, and Larigot; the Pedalles de Flûtes.

CROMHORNE EN TAILLE, page 22: manuals uncoupled, on the Grand Jeu, the Bourdon, Prestant, and Bourdon 16′; on the Positif, the Bourdon, Prestant, and Cromhorne; and the Pedalles de Flûtes.

For the FLUTES, page 21; manuals coupled, on the Grand Jeu, the Bourdon and Montre; on the Positif, the Bourdon alone, and the Tremblant doux; and the Pedalles de Flûtes.

For the GRAND JEU, pages 8, 16, 24, 32; on the Grand Jeu, the Bourdon, Prestant, Trompette, Clairon, Grand Cornet, Tierce, Nazar, and Quarte de Nazar; on the Positif, the Bourdon, Prestant, Cromhorne, Tierce, and Nazar, with the Tremblant à vent perdu (the Bourdons can be omitted).

EXPLANATION OF ITALIAN TERMS USED IN THIS BOOK

Adagio means very slowly.
Affettuoso means tenderly.
Allegro means lightly, but with moderate movement.
Da Capo means to repeat the beginning.
Fuga doppia means a fugue with two subjects.
Gracioso means with a gracious and comfortable measure.
Largo means slowly, with taste.
Preludio means Prelude.
Presto means fast, with great celerity.
Vivace means rapidly, but more moderately than Allegro.

La Manière très facile pour apprendre la facture d'orgue
(Anonymous Manuscript from Caen, 1746)

THE STOP COMBINATIONS WHICH ARE PLAYED TOGETHER

For a PLAIN JEU, Grand Orgue: Cimballe, the two Fournitures,

Montre, Prestant, 16′, Bourdon 8′, Doublette, with the Trompette and Cleron from the Pedalle reeds.

For Playing LES FLUTE, Flute, two Flute Almande, Montre, Bourdon 4′. Nothing else. The Tremblant doux. In the Pedalle, two flutes and Bourdons.

For Playing a TIERCE EN TAILLE, Grand Orgue: Bourdon 4′, Montre. Positif: Bourdon 4′, Prestant, Petite Tierce, Nazart, Larigot. Pedalle: Bourdon 16′, two flutes.

GRAND JEUX, Trompette, Clerons, Prestant, Gros Cornet, Nazart, Petite Tierce, the same thing on the Positif. All the Trompettes of the Pedalle. Tremblant fort.

For Playing a DESSUS DE TROMPETTE, Grand Orgue: Trompette and Clerons. Positif: Bourdon 4′, Bourdon 8′, Larigot, and then the Cornet de Recit, with the Tremblant fort.

For the VOIX HUMAINE, it is used with the Nazart, Bourdon 4′ and Prestant. Grand Orgue: the two flute Allemande, with the Bourdon 4′ and the Montre. Pedalle, the two flute and Bourdon.

JEU DE FON, the Montre, the Bourdon 8′ and 4′, 16′ and Prestant. "Voyez à la fin du Livre (B)"

For a GRAND JEU, on the Pedalle, the Trompette, Bombarde, Cléron. Grand Orgue: Prestant, Petite Tierce, Nasard, Gros Cornet, Trompette and Clérons. Positiffe: everything like the Grand Orgue, plus the Cromorne.

For a PLAIN JEU, on the Pedalle, the Trompette, Bombarde, Clérons. Grand Orgue: the Fournitures, Doublette, Prestant, Montre, Bourdon 8′ and 4′, Cimballe, the 16′. On the Positiffe, the same.

For a DUO, Grand Orgue: the Cornet de Recit. Positiffe: the Chromorne and the Bourdon 4′, Prestant.

RECIT DE CORNET, the dessus on the Grand Orgue Cornet alone. On the Positif, the Bourdon 4′ and the Montre. Another DUO, the dessus on the Grand Orgue, Bourdon 4′, Montre, Prestant, Tierce and Nasard. Positif: Bourdon 4′, Montre Tierce, Nasard.

RECIT DE TIERCE, the dessus on the Positif, Bourdon 4′, Montre, Tierce, Nasard. Grand Orgue: Bourdon 4′ and Montre.

BASSE DE TROMPETTE, Grand Orgue: the two Trompettes, two Clérons, Prestant. Positif: Prestant, Doublette, Larigot.

JEU DE FLUTTE, TRIO, Grand Orgue: the two Flutte Almande, Bourdon 4′, Montre. On the Positiffe the same. Pedalle, the Flutte and the Bourdon. Tremblant doux.

BASSE DE TROMPETTE, Grand Orgue: Trompette and Cléron, Prestant. Positiffe: Larigot and the Bourdon 4'.

JEUX DE FOND, the Montres, Bourdons 8' and 4', the 16', Prestant.

PRELUDE, all the Bourdons, Montre, Fourniture, Cimballe, Prestant, 16'.

TIERCE EN TAILLE, Grand Orgue: the Flutte, Bourdon 4' and the Montre. Positif: Tierce, Nasard, Cromorne, Doublette, Prestant. On the Pédalle the Flutte, Bourdon.

The Art of Organ Building
by Dom François Bedos de Celles (1766–70)

PART 3, CHAPTER IV

The principal, ordinary combinations of organ stops.* Read, examined, corrected, and approved by the most competent and celebrated organists of Paris, such as Messiers Calviere,† Fouquet, Couperin, Balbâtre, and others.

1. For a Plein-Jeu

On the Grand Orgue and the Positif as well, draw all the Montres, all the open 8', the Bourdons, Prestants, Doublettes, Fournitures and Cymbales, and couple the keyboards. If there is a pedal part, use the Trompette and Clairon. In the event of several Trompettes and Clairons in the Pedal, use them all. Never in the Pedal should flutes be combined with Trompettes and Clairons. Sometimes in the Plein-Jeu, pedal flutes can be used in place of the Trompette and Clairon, especially if there is a 16'.

The Grand Plein-Jeu must be treated seriously and majestically; it should be played in large harmonic sweeps, interwoven with syncopation, dissonant chords, suspensions, and striking harmonic surprises; and may all that, however, form a regular, measured, rhythmical flow. The Plein-

---

* Toward the beginning of this century, an organist named M. LeBègue published some organ pieces. Appended to his collection were the stop combinations suitable to the way in which organs were then built and to the quality of sound they produced. Tastes have changed since that time. Because of different uses of stops and ways of treating them, certain alterations in those earlier combinations have been necessitated. Given here are those at least generally in use by the large majority of the best organists today.

† Although M. Calviere is dead, it should be pointed out that he was the first to have the kindness to correct and examine these stop combinations, they having been written before his death. I have actually seen his corrections, made in his own hand.

Jeu de Positif should be played more lightly; in sparkling style, with rolled chords [roulades], etc., the whole thing being directed toward a consistent musical effect.

2. For a Grand Jeu

On the Grand Orgue use the Grand Cornet, Prestant, and all the Trompettes and Clairons, if there are several. Likewise on the Positif, draw the Cornet, Prestant, Trompette, Clairon, and Cromorne (if the Grand Orgue has but one Trompette and Clairon, this last stop would be omitted). Couple the keyboards; the Pedal would be just as in the Plein-Jeu. If the Récit is needed, use the Cornet, in the manner of an Echo.

Many organists almost never touch the Grand Jeu without putting on the Tremblant-fort. It is noteworthy that this is never done by the ablest and most tasteful players, who feel very correctly that the resulting modification of the wind soils and damages a beautiful effect. The stops cannot speak so well, nor so cleanly, for the tremulant robs them of all the tenderness, the velvety quality of their sound. They lose the fullness and virility of tone which a good builder, expert in his art, has paid such a painful price to produce. The Cromorne is the most frequently abused. The Tremulant disfigures all that there is agreeable in its character, causing it to nasalize. One will do well therefore never to use it on the Grand Jeu, following the example of the greatest organists, who naturally should be the model for others.

3. For a Duo

Several different combinations can conveniently be used for a Duo, depending upon the manner of treatment.

   a. On the Grand Orgue, use all the foundation stops, even the 32', if there is one, as for the Plein Jeu. Add to this the two Nasards, two Tierces and Quarte, without Doublette, unless there is no Quarte. This is called the Grand Jeu de Tierce.

   On the Positif use the open 8', Bourdon 8', Prestant, Nasard, Quarte, and Tierce. If there is no Quarte, use the Doublette. This combination is called the Jeu de Tierce du Positif. The manuals are not coupled.

   The upper part is played on the Positif, and the lower on the Grand Orgue.

   It should be stated that to play rapidly in the bass will have no effect. The motion should be at most in quavers [eighths] of moderate beat, and the bass part should rise no higher than G re sol [or, G above middle C], the upper register in this combination being disagreeable.

b. Play the upper part on the Cornet of the Récit, and the bass on the Positif Prestant and Cromorne. If there is no Récit Cornet, the Grand Cornet alone may be used, or even the Petit Jeu de Tierce du Grand Orgue, which comprises only the open 8', and the Petit Bourdon (otherwise called the Bourdon 8' or 4'), Prestant, Petit Nasard, Quarte, and Tierce.

The two preceding combinations for the Duo are the most useful, and most appropriate to the characteristic Duo type: the first for a serious and dignified piece, and the second for a more brilliant one.

c. The upper part is played on the Récit Cornet, and the bass on the Positif Trompette alone.

d. Play the upper part on the Récit Trompette, and the bass on the complete Jeu de Tierce du Positif.

e. Play the upper part on the Positif Cromorne and Prestant, and the bass on the full Grand Jeu de Tierce of the Grand Orgue, taking care not to play too fast in the bass.

This combination is still more useful in a Trio, with the two upper parts on the Positif and the bass on the Grand Orgue.

f. Play both Duo parts in the tenor range, using the Trompettes and Clairons with the Prestant, on the Grand Orgue.

This registration is less suitable for a regular Duo than for an irregular Caprice, in which two parts might participate, or even three or four, according to the imagination of the performer.

g. Play the top part on the Positif, using both 8' stops, Flute 4', and Nasard, or better still the Cromorne alone with the Prestant, and the bass on both 16' stops and the Clairon of the Grand Orgue.

As the registration on the Grand Orgue is irregular, a reed stop being combined with foundations, it should not be played lower than F ut fa [F below middle C] at the most. It is most beautiful around the third octave. Arpeggios, scales, etc. can be played on this combination, but altogether legato. The combination is encountered more frequently in Trios than in Duos.

h. Play the upper part on the Récit Cornet, and the bass on all the Grand Orgue foundations, coupled to the Positif Cromorne and Prestant. Rapid passages in the bass should be avoided, lest the effect of the Grand Orgue foundations be spoiled.

4. For a Fugue Grave

On the Grand Orgue, use the Prestant, and all the Trompettes and Clairons, and on the Positif the Trompette, Clairon and Cromorne (this last stop is always used in this combination, though there may be only one

Trompette and Clairon on the Grand Orgue). The keyboards coupled. If the pedals are used, they should be the same as for the Grand Jeu and the Plein-Jeu.

A number of organists add the Grand Cornet to this combination, without noticing that this stop deprives the upper part of the reed stops of all their edge and sweetness. This is about the only sort of piece in which they can show in all their brilliance and beauty, and these fine qualities would be eliminated by the sudden brightness of the Cornet, which absorbs and muffles the reeds. Others even make it worse; they add the Tremblant-fort to all this. More tasteful organists are more attentive to drawing out all the beauty of which their instrument is capable; they do not, moreover, lapse into such inappropriate practices, which lack discernment.

A Fugue Grave may sometimes be played on the following combination, which is very beautiful: the foundations of the Grand Orgue, and the Cromorne and Prestant only on the Positif, the keyboards coupled.

This is a good combination for playing a caprice full of chords in the bass, in moderately detached style, if desired, and for making the upper parts sing, either as one or two voices.

5. For a Fugue de Mouvement

Ordinarily this is played on the Grand Jeu, but it can also be executed on the Grand Jeu de Tierce, coupled to that of the Positif. Some organists add the Clairon of the Grand Orgue; others the Cromorne on the Positif; but this combination is thus compromised, as a reed stop cannot speak in its true beauty and blending power in combination with the whole Jeu de Tierce.

6. For a Tierce en Taille

For the accompaniment use the Grand Orgue, both 8's, or three if there are that many. On the Positif, both 8's, Prestant (or better yet the Flute 4', if there is one, in place of the Prestant), the Nasard, Quarte (or, in the absence of a Quarte, the Doublette), the Tierce, and Larigot. For the bass in the pedal, use all the foundation stops, including 16', if there is one, as well as the 8's and 4's.

Many organists play the accompaniment too close in range to the Récit en Taille. It then has no effect, because it becomes confused with the Récit. The accompaniment must always be played as high as possible, for example, in the fourth octave, where it will sound good. Thus spaced, it will adorn the Récit very well, and it will also be more brilliant and imitative of the German flute.

The Récit, played in the tenor part in this type of piece, must be very songlike and ornamented with great taste. Some organists just trill from one end of the keyboard to the other, much too fast, full of passage work and cadences, all this being without lyrical effect. This does not result in a true Récit, for the melody must be made to sing.

7. For a Cromorne en Taille

The accompaniment is played on the Grand Orgue, with the same stops as in Article 6, above. On the Positif, the Cromorne with the Prestant, and the Pedal foundations. If there is a Tierce in the Pedal, it would be still better to use it for the bass, and the effect will be beautiful.

See the remarks in Article 6 above on the subject of accompaniment. It should be said that the Récit must lie more low than high, as far as is possible, that is to say that the melody must predominate in the second octave, where it is always more pleasing.

8. For a Trompette en Taille

For the accompaniment, use both 8's on the Grand Orgue, or three if there are that many. On the Positif, the Trompette alone, if it is beautiful. If it is not perfect, add the Prestant. In the Pedal, use foundations, or still better the Jeu de Tierce, if there is one. The Récit should be played on the second and third octaves of the Trompette.

9. For a Trio on Three Claviers

There are several suitable combinations:

a. The upper part is played on the Cornet of the Récit, the second part on the Positif Cromorne and Prestant, and the bass on the Pedal foundations, or still better the Jeu de Tierce, if there is one in the pedal.

A number of organists play all kinds of trios with too wide a spacing between the bass and the upper parts. When the voices are so widely spaced, often as much as a three-octave interval, there is no blend between bass and upper parts.

b. Play the top part on the Positif Jeu de Tierce without Larigot, and the second part on the Récit Trompette, or if there is none on the Récit, on the Grand Orgue Trompette with the Prestant. The bass will be played on the pedal Flutes, or the Jeu de Tierce.

c. The top part on the Récit Cornet, the second on the Positif Jeu de Tierce, and the bass on Pedal flutes or Jeu de Tierce.

Though the two upper parts in this combination are of a like character to one another, they are nevertheless in good taste. They all take the liberty of running over the keyboard with a certain scope; and one is not as cramped as he would be if both hands were working on the same keyboard, in the event that he wishes the two upper parts to be of the same timbre.

d. The top part on all the 8's, on both the Grand Orgue and the Positif, the keyboards coupled; the second part on the Récit Trompette, or the Cornet, if there is no Trompette; the bass on the Pedal flutes or Jeu de Tierce.

e. The top part on all the 8's of the Grand Orgue, even if there are three; the second part on the Cromorne and Prestant of the Positif; and the bass on Pedal flutes or the Jeu de Tierce.

f. One part on the Grand Orgue, using both 8's and the Petit Nasard; the Flute 4' may be added if there is one. The other part on the Positif Cromorne and Prestant, and the bass on Pedal flutes or the Jeu de Tierce.

g. One part on the Récit Trompette, and the other on both 8's, Flute and Nasard of the Positif. If there is no Trompette on the Récit, that of the Grand Orgue can be used. The bass on the Pedal Flutes or the Jeu de Tierce.

h. One part on the Jeu de Tierce of the Positif, and the other part on all the 8's of the Grand Orgue; the bass on the Pedal flutes or the Jeu de Tierce.

i. The top part on the Récit Cornet, or on the [Positif] two 8's alone, or on both 8's, Nasard, and Flute [4'], if there is one. The second part on the Voix-humaine, the Petit Bourdon [8'], and the Flute 4'. If there is no Flute, use the Prestant. The bass on the Pedal Flutes. The Tremblant-doux is used in this combination.

j. Both upper parts on all the 8' stops of the Grand Orgue and the Positif, with the keyboards coupled. The bass on Pedal Flutes.

10. For a Quatuor on Four Keyboards

a. Play the top part on the Trompette of the Récit, or on the two 8's (if there are two separate 8's); the second part on the Petit Jeu de Tierce of the Grand Orgue; the third part on the Cromorne and Prestant of the Positif; and the bass on the Pedal Flutes or Jeu de Tierce. Or better,

b. Play the top part on the Récit Cornet, the second on the Grand Orgue Trompette and Prestant, the third part on the Positif Jeu de Tierce, and the bass on the Pedal Flutes.

This way of doing the Quatuor for four keyboards is difficult to execute. The two upper parts can scarcely be made to sing because they must be played on two different manuals by the right hand. Likewise, according to the second way, the two middle parts must be played by the left hand on two different manuals. Therefore, here are two more possibilities for playing the Quatuor more easily, these being executed on three keyboards only.

11. For a Quatuor on Three Keyboards

Play the first and second parts on the Récit Cornet, the third on the Cromorne and Prestant of the Positif, and the bass on the Pedal Flutes or the Jeu de Tierce.

Or the same combination might be distributed with the top part on the Récit Cornet, the two middle parts on the tenors of the Cromorne, and the bass on the Pedal Flutes or Jeu de Tierce. This latter method is more brilliant and beautiful, without being more difficult in execution.

12. For a Fond d'Orgue

On the Grand Orgue and the Positif, draw all the Montres, Bourdons, open 8's, Flutes 4' and Prestants, with the keyboards coupled, and the Pedal foundations. The Tremblant-doux should never be employed in this combination, as certain distasteful organists have been known to do.

13. For a Basse de Trompette

    a. On the Grand Orgue, use the Prestant, the Trompettes and the Clairons, if there are several; on the Positif, the two 8's, Doublette, and Larigot. In the case of a Dialogue between soprano and bass use the Récit Cornet for the top part. Very poor organists might add the Tremblant-fort to this, but this is never done by musical connoisseurs, because the tremulant ruins the beauty of the reed stops. It disfigures and alters their sound.

    For this manner of playing the Basse de Trompette, the preceding combination is customary. The following combination is still more effective, but it demands tasteful treatment.

    b. On the Grand Orgue, use the same stops as above, and on the Positif both 8's, the Prestant, and the Cromorne, providing that the two 8's do not slow down the speech of the Cromorne.

    A Dialogue is played like a Duo, imitating the Basson on the tenor of the Cromorne, and the Cor de chasse [bugle] and a trumpet melody or song of triumph on the Trompette.

14. For a Basse de Cromorne

All the Grand Orgue 8's are used for the accompaniment, and the Positif Cromorne and Prestant for the melody.

The Cromorne should be played in imitation of the bassoon or the bass-viol.

15. For simple Récits de dessus

Récits de dessus are always accompanied with two 8's, in order to produce full bass notes. For a dessus de Cromorne, use the Prestant with the Cromorne and accompany on both Grand Orgue 8's, or even three.

For a Trompette de Récit, draw the Trompette alone and accompany as above. For a Cornet [melody], use the Récit Cornet; or if there is none on the Récit, use the Grand Cornet, and accompany likewise. If the Jeu de Tierce du Positif is specified, use it complete and accompany likewise. When two Trompettes are used together to make a more biting and brilliant melody, add the Prestant and accompany as above. If the Positif Trompette and Cromorne are used together, use the Prestant, with the same accompaniment.

Each of these types of Récit must be treated tastefully. The Positif Tierce or the Cornet should be played with rapidity, while others—such as Trumpets imitating fanfares—should be played more moderately. Each one should be handled according to its tonal character.

16. For a Voix-humaine

On the Grand Orgue, where this stop is supposedly situated, draw the Bourdon, Flute 4′, and the Voix-humaine. Failing the petite Flute [4′], use the Prestant in its place. On the Positif, use both 8′s with the accompaniment. The Tremblant-doux is used. For a Trio type, see Article IX above.

It must be mentioned that this is the only case where organists with fine taste use the Tremblant-doux, even when it is good, which is indeed rare enough. Necessarily the wind is enfeebled, and consequently the beauty and blend of organ tone are altered and deteriorated. Some great organists have called the Tremblant-doux "le perturbateur des jeux de l'Orgue." However, it must be accepted when it is needed in order to modify the sound of the Voix-humaine, which without the tremulant does not truly imitate the human voice. Still, I know of only two Voix-humaines which have achieved that quality. (Footnote: I believe the perfect success of these two Voix-humaines must be attributed principally to the quality of the Tremblant-doux, which having been well regulated effects the stops to the correct degree.)

The best way of playing on this stop is to make a simple Dialogue between soprano and bass, and then to play the parts together, always in imitation of a natural and simple manner of singing. This stop is charming when it imitates the human voice well, but it must not be played lower than the first F ut fa [second F below middle C], not higher than the fourth G re sol [second G above middle C], because natural voices do not ordinarily pass these limits.

Since it is rare to find an excellent Tremblant-doux, some good organists play the Voix-humaine with the Tremblant-fort, adding the Nasard with the Bourdon and Prestant. Though this combination draws away from the natural timbre of the Voix-humaine, it is a better alternative in the absence of a good Tremblant-doux. Nevertheless, this combination is a very imperfect imitation of the true human voice, for one does not sing so harshly.

17. For a Dialogue de Cornet, de Cromorne et d'Echo

Use the Récit Cornet, or alternatively the Grand Cornet. On the Positif use the Cromorne with the Prestant, and on the Echo the Cornet, with the accompaniment on the two 8's of the Grand Orgue. If the Grand Cornet must be used, the bass should be played on the Bourdon and Prestant of the Grand Orgue, which would be added to the Grand Cornet.

18. For playing Plain chant

For playing Plain chant in a slow tempo, use the Trompette and Clairon in the Pedal, and accompany on the complete Plein-Jeu of the Grand Orgue and the Positif, with the coupler.

If it were played in the manuals only, and straightforwardly, as in a prose hymn, etc., use the Grand Orgue Trompettes, Clairons, and Prestant. Accompany on the Positif Plein-Jeu. In order to fill it out more, the keyboards might be coupled.

19. To imitate the Flûte Allemande (German Flute)

Draw all the 8's on the Grand Orgue and Positif, the manuals coupled. Never should the Prestant or Flute 4' be combined with these, nor any 16'. If there is only a Bourdon on the Positif, without an open 8', then it must be used alone.

On this combination one must always play as high as possible, in imitation of flute-like melodies.

20. To imitate Petites Flûtes, or Flûtes à bec

Draw the Grand Orgue Prestant and that of the Positif; if there are Flutes 4', add them. Keyboards coupled.

21. For a Musette

If there is a Musette stop on the organ, use it with the 8' Bourdon, and accompany on two 8's. Ordinarily, a lead weight is placed on the tonic and fifth for the Musette and the two melodic parts are played on the same combination, though the top may be played on the two 8's. On the Pedal, the tonic note is held on Flutes.

If there is no Musette stop, then use the Cromorne without Prestant, and do all the rest as directed.

22. To imitate a Fife

On the Grand Orgue, use the Petit Bourdon with the Quarte de Nasard and Doublette. On the Positif, the two 8's, Prestant and Larigot. Airs de

Fifre and de Tabourin [fife and drum music] are played on the Grand Orgue, and the keyboard of the Positif is beaten, to imitate a drum.

23. To imitate a Flageolet

On the Grand Orgue use the Quarte and Doublette, and accompany on two 8's.

24. To imitate little birds

Couple the Grand Orgue Petit Nasard to that of the Positif, and play a fourth higher or a fifth lower, the bass being very high.

The chirping of little birds is imitated with scales, runs, and arpeggios, interwoven with trills and cadences. The bass should be done in somewhat the same manner.

25. To accompany voices

The accompaniment of voices must be proportional to their volume and brilliance. For a full choir and a whole singing congregation, the whole Plein-Jeu should be used, with the bass on Pedal Trompettes and Clairons. Aside from this circumstance, voices should be accompanied with well-balanced foundations. If several strong voices are singing in parts, they could be accompanied with three or four 8's; or, if they are of medium volume, the two Positif 8's would be enough. The same could be used for a single strong voice. If it is a feeble voice, use only the Petit Bourdon. The singing voice must always dominate, for the accompaniment is merely for adornment and sustenance.

26. The use of Bombardes

A Bombarde is never played alone. If used in the Pedal, it must be combined with the Trompettes and Clairons. It is used ordinarily for playing Plain chant; it can be used in the Plein-Jeu, if it is full enough; in the Grand Jeu it has a wonderful effect when it is properly played and when the character of the piece demands it. For this, taste and discernment are necessary.

If there is a manual Bombarde, it appears usually on the third manual, which is used in combination with the other two. It is then employed in the Grand Jeu, for slow-moving preludes, for certain grand harmonic effects to which one wishes to give stronger utterance through suspensions or certain harmonies, for organ points, for finales, and even for other circumstances where the particular character or expression of a piece demands it. If one wants to play a Fugue grave on the Plein-Jeu, the Bombarde can be added to it, if it is full enough; this combination is very effective, but it can be used only when the Bombarde plays from its own wind channels; otherwise, it will be effected by the Plein Jeu; thus this stop should have its channels independent of others, when it is played on a separate keyboard, which is the third. The Bombarde is even used to play the Plain chant manually, by combining it with the Grand Orgue Trompette and Clairon, keyboards coupled. In a word, an organist must have taste and acumen to use Bombardes properly.

1293. These are the stop combinations most frequently encountered and in use by the most accomplished organists. These players can certainly invent others in order to express with more energy and expressiveness the ideas which their genius furnishes to them. As fine organ players have a sense of good music and know the properties and nature of the stops on their organs, they do not make new combinations which are not reasonable or pleasing. They are intent upon playing each combination in the taste which suits its character. Much discernment is needed for that. Thus it does not befit everyone to invent new combinations, because the necessary character is not easy to obtain. An organist who has not yet attained a great degree of perfection must study in imitation of those who have more talent, and endeavor to conform to their taste and their combinations. As it is not easy to memorize them all, I judged it wiser to present them here in writing. It is however convenient to make some changes in certain circumstances, because all organs do not make equal effects. Here are some general rules, of which one can make use upon occasion; for in all that I have said above on the subject of registration, I have always supposed that the stops of the organ are well-placed and proportioned in their quality and force.

a. If the reed stops are short and consequently have a thin sound, rough, dry, and glaring, it will be expedient to take off the edge a bit. Toward this end, more foundation could be added, as a Petit Bourdon, and if this does not suffice to temper their sharpness, even add an open 8', and a Petit Nasard to the Grand Jeu. I presuppose that these foundations would not make the reeds slow in speech.

But if on the contrary the reed stops are too long, and they sound individually too heavy and sweet, play them without foundations; even the Prestant might be eliminated.

b. In the event that the reed stops have an unpleasant sound and do not blend, the Tremblant-fort may be used. The modification of the wind will confuse the music, and perhaps disguise some of the defects in the sound, if not augment them. But in organs which are good and come out well, the tremulant should be avoided, in the example of the most tasteful organists, as I have already stated. There are however occasions when it can be used, in order to give singular expression to some caprice that the organist wants to perform; these occasions are quite rare.

c. If the two 8's (by which is always understood the 8' open and the 4' stopped) are so feeble that they lose their effectiveness for accompaniment, the Flute 4' may be added, or, failing the Flute 4', the Prestant; never add 16' in this combination. On the other hand, the two 8's should never dominate in this kind of piece. If there is no 8' open in the Positif, add the Flute 4' to the Bourdon, or the Prestant if there is no Flute 4'; this is true only for accompaniments.

d. Tierces, Nasards, and Quartes must never be drawn in the Plein-Jeu combination; they muffle its sharpness, finesse, and brilliance. The stops are incompatible.

e. No Tierce, Quarte, or Nasard should ever be used in the Grand Jeu, even in the case of b above. All the beauty of the Grand Jeu being derived from the reeds, these stops would cause the combination to lose all its merit and graciousness; they would make the reeds heavy and slow of speech. They are especially ineffective in playing chords, as is often the practice on the Grand Jeu.

f. From what has been stated above, it will have been noted that the addition of the Prestant to the 8' must, as far as possible, be avoided in the accompaniment of the various Récits, be they in the tenor or in the higher parts. There results a clash which is not pleasant. It may be used only in the case of c above, and the Flute 4' is always preferable for that function.

g. If the Pedal includes one or two flutes of 16' pitch, along with the 8's and 4's, these stops (and even the 32' if there is one) must be employed in all kinds of pieces where pedal flutes are specified.

h. If the pedal has a Jeu de Tierce, that is to say Nasards, Quartes, and Tierces along with all the foundation stops, it may be used for the Quatuor, the Trio on three keyboards, and in other instances where it is judged effective; that depends upon the taste and skill of the organist.

i. There are those who almost invariably use the Nasard with the Cromorne. Now if the Cromorne were short, or were not full enough, that is to say were it not to blend as it should, this combination might do well enough; but when the Cromorne has a distinctly good quality of sound, it should never be combined with the Nasard.

j. An organist must devote himself to becoming well acquainted with the instrument he is playing, so that he can make the best possible use of it. How often have we heard the same organ played by two reputable organists, the one causing it to sound much better than the other. The reason for this is that the one has more taste in choosing stop combinations than the other, and stays better within the limits of the organ's tonal capacities and structure. Each combination has its particular character; there are some which are more brilliant in certain ranges of the keyboard than in others. For example, all the 8's together imitate a true Flute more adequately in the treble register than in the bass; Cornets sound better in a high range than a low; the contrary is true of the reed stops, where the high-pitched pipes taper off in brilliance and become a bit feeble. The Plein-Jeu is not so full-bodied nor so beautiful in the high parts; nor does the Grand Jeu de Tierce sound well in the treble. Indeed there are many fine organists who never play in the treble on these combinations, because they feel the 16′ dominates too strongly. Certain accompaniments must be played very low, others medium, and still others very high in range. There are some combinations that require rapid execution, others a more moderate motion, as for instance those where the foundations are used, and especially the Grand Orgue foundations, which would make no effect at all when played rapidly. It is up to an organist who has good taste and knows it at least to the point of being the master of his own music, to choose not only the stops to play upon, but also the ranges most favorable for these combinations. This is what I have tried to intimate in many of the registrations just given, as when I have stated on what stops or what manuals the first or second parts of a Trio (or Duo, according to the combination in question) should be played. The better an organist makes the organ sound, the more he is pleased, and the better he himself will play. I have seen one who was so meticulous in his attention to these matters that if he heard a pipe which was shockingly discordant to the ear, he would avoid that particular key for the whole Mass. To do this, one must really be the master of his own music-making.

Glossary

In assembling a Glossary to help the reader understand the more unfamiliar terms used in this study, it was unavoidable that the ultimately arbitrary selection would include some terms that a reader may know very well and omit some that another reader may find difficult to translate. In addition, some terms are found in the documents and text in slightly different forms, but in most cases only one version has been listed in the Glossary unless the difference in forms is so great that they might be mistaken for different terms. It is hoped that, in spite of its imperfections, the Glossary will prove to be a useful tool for readers.

Abrégé (m.), roller board

Accorder, to tune

Accouplement (m.), manual coupler

Agréments (m.), ornaments

Anche (f.), reed stop, or shallot

Anémomètre (m.), anemometer

Appel (m.), device operated by foot, admitting wind to a chest or part of a chest

Atelier (m.), workshop

Bague (f.), sealing ring of lead set a short distance above the block (noyau) of a reed pipe, for the purpose of strengthening and shutting off the top of the boot

Barrage (f.), frame (for wind channels)

Bascule (f.), swell pedal

Bémol (m.), flat

Bicinium, a two part verse or passage in music

Biseau (m.), languid

Blockwerk (Blokwerk), stopless chest, or division of Gothic or Renaissance organs

Bois (m.), wood

Boîte (f.) expressive à jalousies, swell box

Bordunen (Trompes), long bass pipes of Gothic or Renaissance organs, in separate cases

Borstlade, chest for the Borstwerk (Brustwerk)

Bouché, stopped

Bouche (f.), mouth

Bouchon (m.), stopper for metal pipe (uncommon)

Boursette (f.), bushing around the wire connecting the tracker to the valve, at the bottom of the wind chest

Bouton (m.) de combinaison, combination piston

Bouton de registre, jeu or stop

Boutons accessoires, accessories operated by hand

Buffet (m.), front of the organ case

Buffet séparé, case of Positif-à-dos (Rückpositiv)

Calotte (f.), metal cap for Bourdon or reed pipe, as in *Voix Humaine avec calotte*

Canard (m.), registration imitating the sound of a duck

Chamade (Trompettes en chamade) (f.), horizontal trumpets

Champignons (m.), toe studs

Chape (f.), top board (above table)

Cheminée (f.), chimney

Cheyère (f.), Positif-à-dos

Clair-voirs (m.), sculptured supports for tops of front pipes

Clairon (Cleron) (m.), trumpet reed at 4' pitch

Clavier (m.), keyboard

Coin (m.), wedge for reed pipe

Conique, (of pipes) flared toward the top; colloquially *conique* means flared both upward and downward

Console (f.), console

Copula, coupler

Cornet (m.), five rank compound stop of flute ranks, a half stop in the treble pitched at 8', 4', 2$\frac{2}{3}$', and 1$\frac{3}{5}$'; also, in northern Europe, the Cornet (Kornett) is a pedal reed stop 2'

Cornet séparé, Cornet de Récit, so called because it is played from its own keyboard, drawing wind from a chest separate from that of the Grand Orgue, or tubed from the Grand Orgue chest

Corniche (f.), cornice

Corps (m.), body, or resonator

Coupé(s), divided, as for certain registers on small organs, which provide for pulling the bass and treble individually, giving flexibility for melodic registrations on a single manual; always jeu(x) coupé(s)

Cuir (m.), leather

Cuivre (m.), copper

Cymbale (cimbal, simballes) (f.), high-pitched mixture, or a combination of stops

Dédoublement (m.), unification

Dents (f.), nicks

Dessus (m.), soprano part, or upper part

Diapason (m.), 1. scale, or proportion between a pipe's length and its diameter; 2. principal stop; 3. standard of pitch; 4. tuning fork

Dièse (m.), sharp

Dominos (m.) en fronton, tilting stop tablets

Dos (m.), back

Echalote (f.), shallot (archaic)

Echelle (f.), mechanism for supporting all squares for a keyboard, especially the pedal; not a roller board

Embouchure (f.), toe hole

Emprunt (m.), run (between wind channels)

Enchappage (f.), leather lining between the table and the top board

Enregistreur (m.), setter button

Entaille (f.), roll tuner

Equerre (f.), square used in tracker action

Etain (m.), tin

Etendue (f.), compass

Etoffe (f.), alloy of tin (35–40 percent) and lead, "common metal"

Etoile (f.), star, probably a revolving star (Zimbelstern)

Etroit, narrow

Evasé, flared at top, as in *flûte conique evasée au sommet* (conical flute tapered downward toward mouth)

Expression (f.), beard (especially for string stops)

Faux-registre (m.), guide for slider

Faux-sommiers (m.), racks for pipes

Feintes (f.), accidentals; sharps on the keyboard

Fenêtre (f.), opening in the main case for keyboards, music rack, and stops; commonly referred to as *console en fenêtre*, recessed in early instruments and often equipped with doors

Flageolet (flauioles) (m.), flute stop at 1' pitch, or combination using that stop

Flautat, Principal, or possibly a flute stop, or combination of such registers, in Spanish organs

Flûte (flutte, fleute, flautes, fleustes d'alemans) (f.), flute stop

Fonds, jeux de (m.), flue ranks (principals and flutes), especially those sounding 32', 16', 8', and 4'

Fourniture (furniture, fornitures) (f.), stopless chest or division in Gothic or Renaissance organ (Blockwerk), a Plein Jeu; Fourniture also indicated the registration usually called Plein Jeu

Frein (m.), beard

Frise (f.), frieze

Fuseau (m.), cone (of pipes)

Gemshorn, rank of pipes with tapered resonators

Glissière (f.), wooden slide tuner for open wood pipes

Gosier (m.), pneumatic pouch used in Barker lever (nineteenth century); also, flexible section of the wind trunk just above the reservoir (seventeenth century)

Gouvernail (m.), spring

Grand Orgue (grant jeu, grand jeu, gros corps de boucque) (m.), main division of a French organ played in classical instruments from the second manual keyboard

Gravure (f.), wind channel

Grille (f.), the structure of the wind chest before the top boards are placed

Hautbois (hautz bois) (m.), oboe; reed stop; reedy registration

Haute-contre (f.), alto part

Hauteur (f.), height

Jeu (jeulx, jeus, joc, jeuz) (m.), 1. rank of pipes; 2. registration; 3. stop knob

Jeux à bouche ⎤ synonymous, meaning
Jeux de fonds ⎬ flue stops of the funda-
Jeux d'octave ⎦ mental pitches

Jeux discordés and Jeux à battements, synonymous, meaning celestes

Lames (f.) de bois, panels of wood, used for swell shades

Languette (f.), tongue of a reed pipe

Larigot (m.), flute stop pitched at the nineteenth

Laye (f.), wind chest

Levier (m.), lever

Lèvre (f.) inférieure, lower lip

Lèvre supérieure, upper lip

Lumière (f.), flue, or windway of a flue pipe, at the mouth between the languid and the lower lip

Lunette (f.), square valve inside the wind conduit, which is the moving part of the *Tremblant à vent clos (Tremblant doux)*

Machine (f.) Barker, pneumatic aid to key action (nineteenth century)

Marche (f.), key (pedal); especially natural key

Marche pieds (archaic), pedal coupler, in ancient organs always from the Grand Orgue

Mécanique (f.), key and stop action (mechanical)

Mélange (m.), combination of stops, registration

Menuiserie (f.), carpentry

Montre (monstre) (f.), front or show pipes, customarily the diapason ranks of lowest pitch on the Grand Orgue and Positif

Musette (f.), reed stop imitative of the instrument

Mutation (jeux de) (f.), single stops sounding "quints" or thirds, or compound stops (Fourniture, Cymballe, Cornet)

Nachtigal, nightingale stop (Rossignol), speaking from two or three small pipes inverted in a pan of water, sounding like the chirping of birds

Nazard (m.), flute stop usually pitched

at the twelfth or nineteenth, or a registration using that stop

Noyau (m.), block (reed pipe)

Octavier, to sound the octave (as in harmonic pipes)

Oreilles (f.), ears (flue pipes)

Oter, to take off

Ouvert, open

Papegay (m.), popinjay or parrot; a registration of the early sixteenth century

Pavillon (m.), overlength of slotted pipes

Peau (m.), leather

Pédale (f.) d'expression, swell pedal

Pédale d'orage, pedal that caused the entire lower octave of all the pedal stops to sound at once, for use in imitating storms

Pédale empruntée, borrowed pedal

Pédales du combinaison, accessories operated by foot

Pédalier (m.), pedal keyboard

Pied (m.), foot (of pipe)

Pilote (m.), sticker

Pilote tournant, roller

Plate-face (f.), space between towers of organ case for flat arrangements of pipes

Plein Jeu (Plain Jeu) (m.), diapason chorus, organo pleno

Plomb (m.), lead

Portevent (m.), wind conduit

Posaune, trombone, reed stop in the trumpet family

Positif-à-dos (m.), Rückpositiv, or Chair Organ, in a small case situated on the gallery rail

Postages (m.), tubing for pipes not standing on chest

Posté (m.), stop equipped with postages

Poster, to set off long pipes with tube connections to chest

Pouce (m.), inch

Poulie (f.), pulley

Pression (f.), pressure (of wind)

Principal (m.), open diapason rank, or Blockwerk (staand principal, principau)

Quarte (f.), fourth

Quint (m.), stop sounding one of the fifth-sounding partials

Rainure (f.), groove (in chest)

Rang (m.), rank (of pipes)

Rasette (f.), tuning spring for reed pipes

Ravalement (m.), extension of lower pitches for pedal reeds (sometimes to FF); can also mean extension on manuals upward (Dom Bedos)

Récit (m.), 1. melody; 2. half keyboard controlling the Cornet Séparé (seventeenth century); 3. swell division (nineteenth century)

Regal (m.), short-length reed stop, or a reedy registration

Registre (m.), 1. slider; 2. stop knob

Répétition (f.), repeat, or break in a mixture stop

Reprise (f.), repetition or mixture break

Résonateur (m.), body of pipe

Ressort (m.), any sort of spring

Rétréci, tapered, as in *flûte conique rétrécie au sommet* (conical flute tapered in toward the top)

Ripieno, in classical Italian instruments, the plenum, or Plein Jeu

Rossignol (m.), nightingale (for explanation, see Nachtigal)

Rouleau (m.), 1. beard made of wood; 2. roller crescendo (Ger. *Rollschweller*, or Fr. *rouleau de crescendo*); 3. single roller on a roller board

Sacqueboutte (f.), sackbut, or reed stop imitating the sackbut

Schalmei, reed stop imitating the Schalmei

Scharf, sharp mixture in organs of northern Europe

Sesquialtera, two- or three-rank stop of narrow scale, sounding the twelfth, seventeenth, and nineteenth

Sommier (m.), chest

Sommier à coulisse, slider chest

Sommier à doubles laies, divided chest

Sommier à gravure, slider chest

Sommier à registre, slider chest

Sommier à soupapes, valve chest

Sommier à tirettes, Blocklade

Soufflerie (f.), blower

Soufflet (m.), bellows

Soufflet à éclisses, splint bellows

Soufflet à lanterne, lantern bellows

Soupape (f.), pallet

Taille (f.), 1. tenor; 2. scale; *grosse taille*, wide scale; *menue taille*, narrow scale; *taille moyenne*, medium scale

Tambour (m.) (or tabourin), drum; in Renaissance organs, this may have been pipes tuned off

Tampon (m.), stopper for wooden pipes

Tierçain (Tertian, Terzian) (m.), two rank stop of narrow scale sounding the seventeenth and nineteenth

Tierce (f.), flute stop sounding the third (seventeenth above the fundamental), or a registration built around the Tierce

Tiercette (f.), small Tierce (4/5'), an octave higher than the Tierce

Tige (f.) de bois, shank of draw knob

Tirage (m.), action (of stops)

Tirant (m.), draw knob

Tirasse (f.), pedal coupler

Tirer, to draw

Touche (f.), key

Traction (f.), key action

Tremblant (m.), wind-disturbing device placed in the wind conduit in order to cause the wind to vibrate

Trompes (f.), long bass pipes of Gothic or Renaissance organs, in separate cases

Trou (m.), hole, at foot of pipe

Tube (m.), extension of hollow shallot through the block (reed pipe)

Tuyau (tuelz, tuelx) (m.), pipe

Tuyau à anche, reed pipe

Tuyau à bouche, flue pipe

Tuyau à fuseau, tapered pipe

Untersatz, principal rank in pedal

Vent (m.), wind

Ventil (m.), device to shut off wind supply from all or part of chest

Ventilateur (m.), blower

Vergette (f.), tracker (tige)

Voix humaine (f.), reed stop of combination imitating the human voice

Zimbelstern, revolving star (étoile) activating small bells of random pitch

Bibliography

Adlung, Jacob, *Musica mechanica organoedi*, Berlin, 1768; facsimile, Kassel, 1931.

Andersen, Poul-Gerhardt, *Orgelbogen*, Copenhagen, 1956.

André, Ferdinand, "Notice sur les orgues de la Cathédrale de Mende," *Bulletin de la Société d'Agriculture de la Lozère* (Mende, 1871), Pt. II: Histoire et archéologie, pp. 15–26.

Anglade, J., "Contribution à l'histoire de l'art méridional," *Annales du Midi, 1917–18*, Toulouse, pp. 245–57.

Anglès, H., *Musica organici Iohannis Cabanilles* (Barcelona, 1927), Preface.

Antegnati, Costanzo, *L'arte organica* (1608), Neudruck, Mainz, 1958.

Apel, Willi, "Du Nouveau sur la musique française pour orgue au XVIᵉ siècle," *La Revue Musicale*, 18 (1937), 1, 96–108.

Arbois de Jubainville, H. d', "Notice sur la construction des orgues de la Cathédrale de Troyes," *Revue des Sociétés Savantes*, Ser. 5, *3*, 1872.

Arbus, M.—R. A., *Une Merveille d'art provençal*, Aix-en-Provence, 1955.

Baldello, F., "Organos y organeros en Barcelona," *Anuario Musical, 1* (1946), 225–27.

Bedos de Celles, Dom François, *L'Art du facteur d'orgues*, 4 vols. Paris, 1766–70; facsimile reprint by Bärenreiter, Kassel, 1934.

Bender, Antoine, *Les Orgues de Silbermann de Soultz (Haut-Rhin)*, Strasbourg, 1960.

———, *Les Orgues Silbermann de Marmoutier et Ebersmünster*, Strasbourg, 1960.

Bitterman, Helen R., "The Organ in the Early Middle Ages," *Speculum, 4* (1929), 390–97.

Blindow, Martin, "Die Trierer Orgelakten, ihre Bedeutung für die deutsche Registrierkunst des 16 Jahrhunderts," *Musik und Kirche, 31* (1961), 115–20.

Bormann, Karl, *Die gotische Orgel zu Halberstadt*, Berlin, 1966.

Bouman, A., *De Orgels in de groote of Martinikerk te Groningen*, Amsterdam, 1941.

———, *Orgels in Nederland*, Amsterdam, 1949.

Brunold, Paul, *François Couperin*, Monaco, 1949.

———, *Le Grand Orgue de Saint-Gervais de Paris*, Monaco, 1934.

Cellier, Alexandre, *Traité de la registration de l'orgue*, Paris, n.d.

————, and Henri Bachelin, *L'Orgue, ses éléments, son histoire, son esthétique*, Paris, 1933.

Chartraire (Abbé), *Les Orgues de la Cathédrale de Sens*, Sens, 1889.

Clutton, Cecil, and Austin Niland, *The British Organ*, London, 1963.

Collette (Abbé) and Bourdon, *Notice historique sur les orgues et les organistes de la Cathédrale de Rouen*, Rouen, 1894.

Dähnert, Ulrich, *Die Orgeln Gottfried Silbermanns in Mitteldeutschland*, Leipzig, 1953.

————, *Der Orgel-und Instrumentenbauer Zacharias Hildebrandt*, Leipzig, 1962.

Dehaisnes (Mgr.), *Documents et extraits divers concernant l'histoire de l'art dans la Flandre, l'Artois et le Hainaut avant le XVᵉ s.*, Lille, 1886.

Denis, Jean, *Traité de l'accord et l'espinette*, Paris, 1650.

Deschampes, L. de Pas, "L'Eglise Notre-Dame de Saint Omer," *Mémoires de la Société des Antiquaires de la Morinie*, 23 (1896), 82–104.

Despierres, G., "Les Orgues de Notre-Dame d'Alençon," *Bulletin de la Société Scientifique Flammarion Argentan*, 6 (1888), 165–72.

Diruta, Girolamo, *Il Transilvano*, Venice, 1597.

Dufourcq, Norbert, *Les Clicquot*, Paris, 1942.

————, "Les Différents Jeux de l'orgue français de la Renaissance," *La Revue Musicale*, 14 (1935), 175–93.

————, *Documents inédits relatifs à l'orgue français*, 2 vols. Paris, 1934–35.

————, *Esquisse d'une histoire de l'orgue en France du XIIIᵉ au XVIIIᵉ siècle*, Paris, 1935.

————, *Le Grand Orgue de la chapelle du Prytanée Militaire de la Flèche*, Paris, 1964.

————, *Le Grand Orgue de la Collégiale Saint Jean de Pézenas*, Paris, 1932.

————, *Le Grand Orgue et les organistes de Saint-Merri de Paris*, Paris, 1947.

————, *Jean de Joyeuse*, Paris, 1958.

————, *La Musique d'orgue français de Jehan Titelouze à Jehan Alain*, Paris, 1949.

————, *Nicolas LeBègue*, Paris, 1954.

————, *L'Orgue*, Paris, 1948.

————, *Orgues comtadines et provençales*, Paris, 1955.

————, "Recent Researches into French Organ Building from the Fifteenth to the Seventeenth Century," *The Galpin Society Journal*, 10, (1957), 66–81.

————, "Remarques sur le clavier dans la première moitié du XVIIᵉ siècle," in Jean Jacquot, ed., *La Musique instrumentale de la Renaissance*, Paris, 1955.

Durand, Georges, *Les Orgues de la Cathédrale d'Amiens*, Paris, 1903.

Eberstaller, Oskar, *Orgeln und Orgelbauer in Österreich*, Graz, 1955.

Fallou, Robert, and Norbert Dufourcq, *Bibliographie de l'histoire de l'orgue en France*, Paris, 1929.

Farcy, M. L. de, *Notices archéologiques sur les orgues de la Cathédrale d'Angers*, Angers, 1873.

Fedke, T., "Der niederländische Orgelbau im 16 Jahrhunderts und seine Bedeutung für Sweelincks Instrumentalmusik," *Musik und Kirche*, *26* (1956), 60–67.

Fellerer, K. G., "Orgeln und Organisten an St. Niklaus zu Freiburg in der Schweiz im 15–19 Jahrhundert," *Kirchenmusikalisches Jahrbuch*, *42*, (1958), 112–13.

Fellot, Jean, *L'Orgue classique français*, Sèvres, 1962.

———, and Michel Chapuis, "La Registration," in *Musique de tous les temps*, *18* (Sèvres), n.d.

Flade, Ernst, "Hermann Raphael Rottenstein-Pock, ein niederländischer Orgelbauer des 16 Jahrhundert in Zwickau i. S.," *Zeitschrift für Musikwissenschaft*, *15* (1932), 1–24.

———, "Literarische Zeugnisse sur Empfindung der Farbe und Farbigkeit bei der Orgel und beim Orgelspiel in Deutschland ca. 1500–1620," *Acta Musicologica*, *28* (1956), 176–208.

———, *Der Orgelbauer Gottfried Silbermann*, Leipzig, 1926.

Fleury, P. de, *Les Anciennes Orgues de la Cathédrale d'Angoulême*, Angoulême, 1890.

———, *Les Anciens Orgues de St.-Hilaire-le-grand de Poitiers*, Paris, 1922.

———, *Notice historique sur les orgues de la Cathédrale de Nantes*, Angoulême, 1890.

Forestie, Ed, "Les Vieilles Orgues de Montauban," *Bulletin Archéologique de Tarn-et-Garonne*, Montauban, 1886.

Froidebise, Pierre, "Sur Quelques Editions de musique d'orgue ancienne," in Jean Jacquot, ed., *La Musique instrumentale de la Renaissance*, Paris, 1955.

Frotscher, Gotthold, *Geschichte des Orgelspiels und der Orgelkomposition*, 2 vols. Berlin, 1935.

Gardien, Jacques, *L'Orgue et les organistes en Bourgogne et en Franche-Comté au 18ᵉ siècle*, Paris, 1943.

Garros, Madeleine, "Notes biographiques sur Guillaume Nivers (1632–1714)," *Revue de Musicologie*, *22* (1950), 73–74.

Gastoué, A., *La Musique de l'église*, Lyon, 1911.

———, *L'Orgue en France de l'antiquité au début de la période classique*, Paris, 1921.

———, "Three Centuries of Organ Music," *Musical Quarterly*, *3* (1917), 173–88.

Gauthier, J., "Marché conclu le 18 janvier 1499 par le chapitre métro-politain de Besançon, pour la réparation des orgues de la cathédrale," *Bulletin du Comité des Travaux Historiques et Scientifiques*, 1883.

Gay, C. (O.S.B.), "Notes pour servir à la registration de la musique d'orgue française des XVIIᵉ et XVIIIᵉ siècles," *L'Organo*, 2 (1961), 169–99.

Geer, E. Harold, *Organ Registration in Theory and Practice*, Glen Rock, N.J., 1957.

Got, Roger, "Orgues et organistes de Thuir sous l'ancien régime," *Centre d'Etudes et de Recherches Catalanes des Archives des Pyrénées-Orientales*, 20, 1963.

deGraaf, G. A. C., *Literatuur over het orgel*, Amsterdam, 1957.

Gravet, Nicole, "L'Orgue et l'art de la registration en France, du XVIᵉ au début du XIXᵉ siècle," *L'Orgue*, No. 100 (1961), pp. 202–57.

Grignon, Louis, *Vieux Orgues, vieux organistes*, Châlons-sur-Marne, 1879.

Guillaume (Abbé), "Les Orgues de Notre-Dame d'Embrun," *Réunion des Sociétés des Beaux-Arts des Départements*, *10* (1886), 249–71.

Hardouin, Pierre, "La Composition des orgues qui pouvaient toucher les musiciens parisiens aux alentours de 1600," in Jean Jacquot, ed., *La Musique instrumentale de la Renaissance*, Paris, 1955.

———, "De L'Orgue de Pépin à l'orgue médiéval," *Revue de Musicologie*, *52*, No. 1 (1966), 21–54.

———, "Le Doyen des buffets d'orgues parisiens," *L'Orgue*, No. 110 (1964), pp. 52–59.

———, "Essai d'une sémantique des jeux de l'orgue," *Acta Musicologica*, *34* (1962), 29–64.

———, *Le Grand Orgue de Saint-Gervais à Paris*, Paris, 1949.

———, "Jeux d'orgues au XVIᵉ siècle," *Revue de Musicologie*, *52*, No. 2 (1966), 163–84.

Hess, Joachim, *Dispositien der merkwaardigste kerk-orgelen*, 1774; facsimile reprint by Wagenaar, Utrecht, 1945.

———, *Luister van het orgel*, Gouda, 1772; facsimile reprint by Wagenaar, Utrecht, 1945.

Hill, Arthur G., *The Organ Cases and Organs of the Middle Ages and Renaissance*, 2 vols. London, 1883.

Howell, Almonte C. "The French Organ Mass in the Sixteenth and Seventeenth Centuries," doctoral dissertation, University of North Carolina, 1953; available from University of Rochester microcard series.

Huré, Jean, *L'Esthétique de l'orgue*, Paris, 1923.

Kastner, Santiago, "Rapports entre Schlick et Cabezon," in Jean Jacquot, ed., *La Musique instrumentale de la Renaissance*, Paris, 1955.

———, "Relations entre la musique instrumentale française et espagnole au XVIᵉ siècle," *Anuario Musical, 10* (1955), 84–108.

Klotz, Hans, "Niederländischer Orgelbaumeister am Trier Dom," *Die Musikforschung, 2* (1949), 36–49.

———, "Sweelinck spielt Sweelinck," *Beiträge zur rheinischen Musikgeschichte, 36* (1960), 37–49.

———, *Über die Orgelkunst der Gotik, der Renaissance, und des Barock*, Kassel, 1934.

Kobel, Heinz, "Die Orgel des Johann Andreas Silbermann von 1761 im Dom zu Arlesheim," *Katholische Kirchenmusik, 2* (1962), 1–10.

Kruijs, M. H. van't, *Verzameling van disposities der verschillende orgels in Nederland*, 1843; facsimile reprint by Knuf, Amsterdam, 1962.

Lasceux, Guillaume, *Essai de théorique et pratique sur l'art de l'orgue*, 1809.

Lunelli, Renato, *L'Arte organaria del rinascimento in Roma*, Florence, 1958.

———, *Der Orgelbau in Italien in seinen Meisterwerken vom 14 J. bis zur Gegenwart*, Mainz, 1956.

Mahrenholz, Christhard, *Die Orgelregister*, Kassel, 1930.

———, "Samuel Scheidt und die Orgel," *Musik und Kirche, 25* (1955), 38–50.

Martinot, E., *Orgues et organistes des églises du diocèse de Troyes*, Troyes, 1941.

Mazerolle, F., "Marchés passés pour la construction des orgues d'Ivry et de Sarcelles," *Correspondance historique et archéologique* (Ivry-sur-Seine, 1895), vol. 2.

Merklin, Albert, *Aus spaniens altem Orgelbau*, Mainz, 1939.

Merlet, Lucien, "Documents inédits relatifs aux orgues de la Cathédrale de Chartres," *Bulletin Archéologique* (1885), 247–52.

Mersenne, F. Marin, *Harmonie universelle*, 1636; Roger E. Chapman, trans., The Books on Instruments, The Hague, 1957. (Translations in this volume are my own.)

Métais, Charles (Abbé), "Les Orgues de la Cathédrale de Chartres," *Archives Historiques du Diocèse de Chartres, 21*, 1918.

Meyer-Siat, P., *Les Orgues Callinet de Masevaux*, Mulhouse, 1962.

Nederlandse orgelpracht, Haarlem, 1961.

Nivers, Guillaumme Gabriel, *Dissertation sur le chant grégorien*, Paris, 1683.

Oldham, Guy, "Louis Couperin, a New Source of French Keyboard Music of the Mid-Seventeenth Century," *Recherches* (1960), 51–59.

Pirro, André, "L'Art des organistes," *Encyclopédie de la musique et dictionnaire du Conservatoire*, Pt. II, 2 (1926), 1181–1374.

———, "Nicolas de Grigny," *Travaux de l'Académie de Reims, 110*.

———, "Un Organiste du XVIIᵉ siècle, Nicolas Gigault," *Revue Musicale, 3* (1903), 7–10.

Planté, J., "La Facture d'orgues au XVIᵉ siècle," *Bulletin de la comm.*

historique et archéologique de la Mayenne, Ser. 2, *1* (1888–89), 214–58.

Praetorius, Michael, *Syntagma musicum* (Wolfenbüttel, 1619; facsimile reprint by Bärenreiter, Kassel, 1929, Pt. II: *De organographia*.

Quoika, Rudolf, *Die altösterreichische Orgel*, Kassel, 1953.

———, *Vom Blockwerk zur Registerorgel*, Kassel, 1966.

Randier, F., "Les Orgues et les organistes de l'église primatiale Saint-André de Bordeaux du XVᵉ siècle a nos jours," *Revue Historique de Bordeaux et de la Gironde, 14*, 1921.

Raugel, Félix, *Les Anciens Buffets d'orgues du département de la Marne*, Paris, 1931.

———, *Les Grandes Orgues de la Basilique de Saint-Nicolas-de-Port*, Paris, 1949.

———, *Les Grandes Orgues des églises de Paris et du département de la Seine*, Paris, 1927.

———, *Les Organistes*, Paris, 1962.

———, *Les Orgues de l'Abbaye de Saint-Mihiel*, Paris, 1919.

———, *Recherches sur quelques maîtres de l'ancienne facture d'orgues français*, Paris, n.d.

Raymond, P., "Marché pour la construction des orgues de la Cathédrale de Bayonne," *Revue des Sociétés Savantes*, Ser. 5, *6* (1873 [2]), 315–18.

Reuter, Rudolf, *Orgeln in Westfalen*, Kassel, 1965.

Reyher, Paul "Les Orgues de Saint-André au XVIᵉ siècle," *La Revue Historique de Bordeaux et du Département de la Gironde*, 1909.

Rokseth, Yvonne, *Deux Livres d'orgues parus chez Pierre Attaingnant en 1531*, Paris, 1925.

———, *La Musique d'orgue au XVᵉ siècle et au début du XVIᵉ*, Paris, 1930.

Rudolz, Rudolf, *Die Registrierkunst des Orgelspiels in ihren Grundlegenden Formen*, Leipzig, 1913.

Sauver, Joseph, *Application des sons harmoniques à la composition des jeux d'orgue*, Paris, 1704.

Schaefer, Marc, *Les Orgues Stiehr-Mockers de Riquewihr*, n.d.

Schlick, Arnold, *Spiegel der Orgelmacher und Organisten*, Heidelberg, 1511; facsimile reprint, Mainz, 1937.

Servières, M. G., *La Décoration artistique des buffets d'orgue*, Paris, 1928.

———, *Documents inédits sur les organistes français des XVIIᵉ et XVIIIᵉ siècles*, Paris, 1923.

Sicard, P., *Les Orgues du diocèse de Bayonne, Lescar, Oloron*, Lyon, 1964.

Sonnet, Martin, *Ceremoniale parisienne*, 1662.

Stellfeld, J.A., *Bronnen tot de geschiedenis der Antwerpsche clavecimbelen orgelbouwers in de XVIᵉ en XVIIᵉ eeuwen*, Antwerp, 1942.

Sumner, W. L., *The Organ*, London, 1952.

Tessier, André, "François Couperin à l'orgue de St. Gervais," *Revue de Musicologie*, 7 (1923), 56–59.

————, "Les Messes d'orgue de Couperin," *La Revue Musicale*, 6 (Nov. 1924), 37–48.

————, *Les Musiciens célèbres—Couperin*, Paris, 1929.

————, "Un Exemplaire original des pièces d'orgue de Couperin," *Revue de Musicologie*, 10 (1929), 109–17.

Trichet, Pierre, *Traité des instruments de musique*, c. 1640, Neuilly-sur-Seine, 1957.

Tusler, Robert L., *The Organ Music of Jan Pieterszoon Sweelinck*, Bilthoven, 1958.

Vanmackelberg, Dom. M., *Les Orgues d'Arras*, Arras, 1963.

————, "Les Orgues de Saint-Martin à St.-Valery-sur-Somme," *Recherches*, 7 (1967), 5–23.

Vente, Maarten A., *Bouwstoffen tot de geschiedenis van het nederlandse orgel in de 16e eeuw*, Amsterdam, 1942.

————, *Die brabanter Orgel, zur Geschichte der Orgelkunst in Belgien und Holland im Zeitalter der Gotik und der Renaissance*, Amsterdam, 1958.

————, "Een Lierse orgelmaker in de 16e eeuw: Jan Verrijt alias Liere," *Driemaandelijks Cultureel Liers Tijdschrift*, 1960.

————, "Iets over Deventer orgels . . . ," *Verslagen en mededeelingen van de vereeniging tot beoefening van overijsselsch tegt en geschiedenis*, 5 and 6, 1950.

————, "Influence des Flamands sur les Français en matière de construction d'orgues," *L'Orgue*, Nos. 48 and 49 (1948), 78–83, 110–15.

————, "Mitteilungen über iberische Registrierkunst unter besonderer Berücksichtigung der Orgelkompositionen des Juan Cabanilles," *Anuario Musical*, 17 (1962), 41.

————, "Schets der geschiedenis van het orgel in de Nederlanden," *Handboek voor de kerkorganist*, Goes, 1948.

————, "Slider Chest or Spring Chest?" *Bulletin of International Society of Organ Builders*, 2, Nos. 1 and 2 (1962), 7–11.

Villard, Jean-Albert, "Qui était François-Henri Clicquot?" *Bulletin Association Fr.-H. Clicquot*, 1 and 2 (1962–63), 13–32.

Werkmeister, Andreas, *Orgelprobe*, 1698; facsimile reprint by Bärenreiter, Kassel, 1927.

Williams, Peter, *The European Organ, 1450–1850*, London, 1966.

Woersching, Joseph, *Der Orgelbauer Karl Riepp*, Mainz, 1940.

Young, William, "Keyboard Music to 1600," *Musica disciplina*, 16 (1962), 115; 17 (1963), 163–95.

Zachariassen, Sybrand, "Aktuelle Orgelbaufragen und Möglichkeiten zu ihrer praktischen Lösung," *Musik und Gottesdienst*, 1952.

Index

Douglass

Language of the classical
French organ